Murder in Miami

Chubbie Miller & Bill Lancaster
1932

Mark John Maguire

Lightfast Publishing

ISBN 978-1-8384858-1-8

Lightfast Publishing

For my mother, Margaret Maguire:

For all her help over the years

Words are insufficient to thank her.

ACKNOWLEDGEMENTS

I am fortunate to be surrounded by many clever people, and my work is better for it. I cannot possibly thank all those who have helped and advised me along the way, but I hope they will regard it as implicit in these words. However, I must thank my family who have been such a support to me during my work on this project: first, I would like to thank Margaret Maguire, Karen Maguire, and Melanie Maguire, my proof-readers-in-chief, for identifying my errors; those which escape them are mine alone. I would like also to thank Kathy Young and John Maguire for their support, and Lucy Maguire for convincing me the book should be written in the first place. Thanks are also due to Jack (John) Maguire and Kara Harvey-Maguire for good counsel.

And finally, to the many people on Youtube and elsewhere, too numerous to mention, who have encouraged me these past three years on my channel 'They Got Away With Murder.' I often say I have the best and most erudite subscribers on YouTube, and their comments on my video essays are the proof of this.

Here I present the case for the murder of Haden Clarke, without fear or favour, and hopefully for the truth. Nothing less will do. The case is now made: read, retire and consider your verdict.

Mark John Maguire 2022

CONTENTS

1. A Shot in the Night

It was 2.45 a.m. on 21st April 1932, when Charles Ditsler, ambulance driver for the Philbrick Funeral Home, arrived at a bungalow at Coral Gables, South Florida. He was met at the door by an Englishman called Bill Lancaster, who took him upstairs to a large room with four beds in it. Here he found a young man lying in bed with a gunshot wound to the head and a revolver lying beside him. A famous Australian aviatrix called Chubbie Miller was also there; she was excitable and in some distress. Lancaster was, by comparison, calm but anxious. He told Ditsler that the young man had shot himself:

'Do you think he'll talk again?' he inquired of the ambulance driver.

Ditsler looked at the injured man, whose name was Haden Clarke, and said he doubted it. In fact, as the Philbrick Funeral Home had the dual function of providing both ambulance services and funeral services to the community, he probably felt all bases were covered.

Chubbie Miller told Ditsler they were awaiting the young man's physician, Dr Carleton Deederer, who had been called to the house a little earlier. It placed Ditsler in a predicament – the injured man,

Haden Clarke, needed to be taken to hospital immediately, but the woman did not want him moved before the doctor had arrived. Ditsler called his supervisor, Olon Charles Yeargin, the Assistant Manager of Philbrick's, who set off directly on learning he had a customer of one sort or another. Dr Deederer, meanwhile, was taking his time getting to the bungalow – apparently he had difficulty finding it and had to return home to look up the address.

At about 3.15 a.m. an attorney called Ernest Huston arrived. Apparently, he had been called earlier by Chubbie Miller, who had told him of the shooting. He it was who had notified the ambulance. Ernest Huston found Chubbie Miller and ambulance driver Charles Ditsler in the living room. He went upstairs and saw the injured man, Haden Clarke, and was told by Lancaster he had been awoken in the night by a loud bang, to find his friend, with whom he shared a bedroom, lying in his bed with a gunshot wound to his head and a revolver lying by his side. Bill Lancaster said he had tried to talk to Haden Clarke, but that he was incapable of replying. He showed Ernest Huston two typewritten notes he said he had found on a table in the room, next to a typewriter – one was addressed to himself; it read:

'Bill,
I can't make the grade. Tell Chubbie of our talk. My advice is never leave her again.
H'

The other letter was addressed to the woman:

'Chubbie,

The economic situation is such I can't go through with it. Comfort mother in her sorrow. You have Bill, he is the whitest man I know.
Haden' (*Miami Herald*, 21st April 1932)

Although both notes were typewritten, the signatures were written in pencil.

Bill Lancaster was anxious to destroy both letters, but the attorney Ernest Huston advised against this – he told him they must be preserved. Nevertheless, Chubbie placed the notes in the telephone table drawer and asked Huston, and the ambulance driver Ditsler, not to mention them to anyone.

Still they waited for Dr Deederer.

'I wish Haden would talk, so he could tell us why he did it,' Lancaster told Huston.

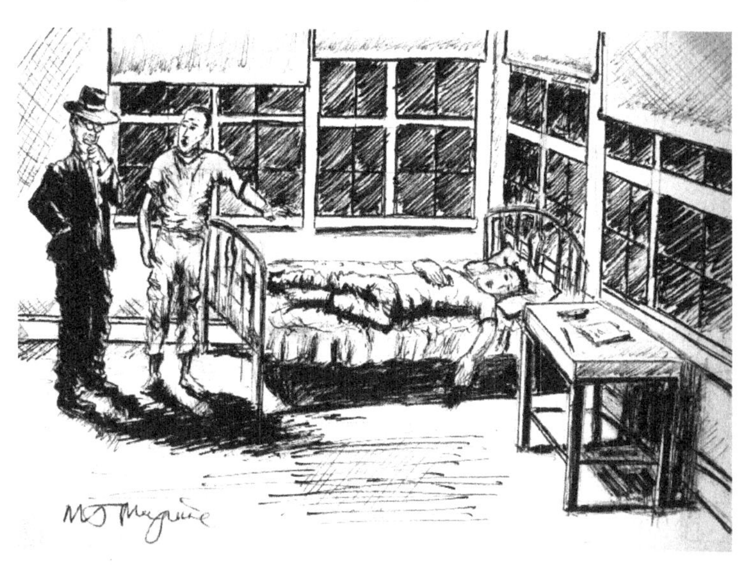

The Assistant Manager of Philbrick's Funeral Home, Olon Yeargin, arrived, and in spite of further protestations from Bill Lancaster and Chubbie

Miller that they should await Dr Deederer's arrival, he directed the men from Philbrick's to carry the injured Haden Clarke down the stairs to the ambulance. Bill Lancaster and Chubbie Miller both decided to travel with the ambulance to the hospital. Before he left, Lancaster turned to Huston:

'If it should become necessary, will you represent us?' he asked.

Huston agreed he would do so.

The ambulance departed for hospital with the injured man, along with Chubbie Miller and Bill Lancaster. Dr Deederer arrived at the bungalow soon afterwards. He was told briefly of the matter by Huston, who remained at the bungalow, and he set off for the hospital immediately.

On arrival at the Jackson Memorial Hospital in Miami, Haden Clarke was admitted to the emergency room, where he was examined, and his wound dressed. Dr Deederer arrived and also examined Clarke's injuries. He found that a bullet had entered the right temple and exited higher up and to the rear on the left of his head. There was little could be done for him. Lancaster and Miller found two emergency policemen, Fitzhugh Lee and Earl Hudson, awaiting them. The latter apparently knew the injured man, and the two officers drove Chubbie Miller and Bill Lancaster back to the Coral Gables address, where the attorney Ernest Huston awaited them.

On the journey in the car, Lancaster inquired of Emergency Police Officer Earl Hudson whether Clarke would ever be able to talk again. It seemed to Hudson he was rather insistent on this point. At the bungalow, Fitzhugh Lee and Earl Hudson examined the scene and Hudson, finding the revolver on Clarke's bed, picked it up with a handkerchief to secure it as evidence, placing it in his pocket. He declared it to be a .32 pistol, but Lancaster corrected him:

'It is a .38,' he informed him.

The detectives made a cursory examination of the scene, and took some notes regarding the circumstances, but they could not locate the bullet, as the bedclothes and pillow were a mass of heavily congealed blood. Officer Earl Hudson had been informed at the hospital that Haden Clarke had left suicide notes and he requested these - Chubbie Miller fetched the one addressed to Bill Lancaster and gave it to him. But Hudson, in spite of Chubbie's injunction to attorney Huston and Charles Ditsler, had been informed by the latter that there were two notes:

'There were two notes, weren't there?' he said quickly. 'Where's the other one?'

Chubbie now fetched the second note from the telephone table drawer and handed it to officer Hudson.

Hudson examined the notes, and the policemen finished their inspection of the premises and left. It seemed to them to be a case of attempted suicide.

When the police had gone, attorney Ernest Huston asked Lancaster about the gun – he had apparently loaned one to Lancaster several weeks before, and he inquired now whether this one was his?

Lancaster said it was not Huston's gun, it was one he had bought, but –

'Is it alright if I say it belongs to you?'

Huston said it was not.

Huston then drove Chubbie Miller and Bill Lancaster to the Everglades Hotel in Miami to inform Haden Clarke's mother, who resided there, of her son's condition. When they arrived, Dr Deederer, who had travelled in his own car to the hotel, informed Mrs Clarke of her son's injuries and of his grave condition. She asked him if Haden would live, and he told her, candidly, that he would not. She was distressed and said in that case she would not go to the hospital.

After this, Huston took Bill and Chubbie from the Everglades Hotel back to the hospital: here they found two more detectives awaiting them, who informed them they would have to accompany them to Dade County Courthouse to give statements on the matter. They were then taken directly to the high rise building on Flagler Street, which served as courthouse and also fulfilled numerous other civic functions, including that of county jail, and there the couple were held separately as material witnesses to await formal questioning by the State attorney, Nathaniel Vernon Hawthorne (1890-1957).

The sun rose just before 7 that morning. Miami awoke to the shocking news of a young man's attempted suicide, and the lurid details attending it spread like a miasma across the city and beyond. Two famous flyers were involved: Captain Bill Lancaster and Mrs Keith Miller, the latter known as 'Chubbie' to her friends. The third man, who lay seriously injured in the Jackson Memorial Hospital, was a young writer, who had been staying with them. It also became known that the young man was engaged to Chubbie Miller... The day was hot, the sun rose above the city and the temperatures climbed steadily into the mid-70s Fahrenheit (mid-20s Celsius). The bougainvillea grew splendid against the white walls of the terracotta roofed villas in Coral Gables, which was conceived along the lines of a Spanish town. It would be another fine day.

Later that morning, at 20 minutes past 11 o'clock, Haden Clarke died of his injuries.

The bungalow at Coral Gables, scene of the tragedy. *(Daily News)*

Charles Haden Clarke. (*Miami Herald*)

Captain William Lancaster
(*Miami Daily News*)

Jessie 'Chubbie' Miller.
(*Miami Daily News*)

Police Emergency Officer
Earl Hudson (*Miami Herald*)

A young Haden Clarke.
(*Daily News*)

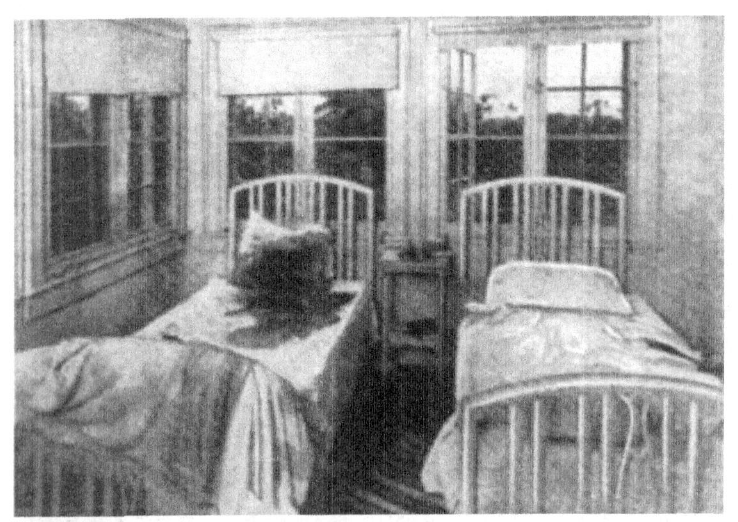

The 'sleeping porch' was where Lancaster and Clarke slept on the night of the tragedy. Haden's blood-soaked pillow is clearly visible. The gun was said to have been left on the table between the two beds. (*Daily News*)

The Everglades Hotel in Coral Gables c.1930. Mrs Clarke lived here and ran, inter alia, the Miami Chess Club from here.

Mrs Ida Clarke was a well-known writer, a campaigner on women's issues, and public speaker. (*Daily News*)

2. An Investigation Begins

Haden Clarke was just 26 years old at the time of his death. An occasional journalist and aspiring writer, he had been born Charles Haden Clarke in Tennessee in 1905, to Thomas Clarke (1859-1911) and Ida Clyde Clarke (1878-1956). The family were well regarded; Haden Clarke's grandfather had been Congressman Beverly Leonidas Clarke of Kentucky (1809-1860), and his father, editor of the *Nashville Banner* in Tennessee. Haden's mother had been star reporter on the newspaper, known for her anti-corruption campaigning. His father died in 1911 when Haden was six years old, and thereafter he lived with his mother and elder brother, also named Beverly Clarke (1900-1981). Haden was a very bright boy, with a gift for writing. He went to university but dropped out before completing his degree; thereafter he had a series of short-lived jobs, including as an editor for a publisher, and worked for a time as a journalist on the *New Orleans Times*, which his father had helped found.

Haden had lived at the bungalow at 2321 SW, 21st Terrace, in Coral Gables where the tragedy occurred, for a little over two months, occupying the bedroom above the porch, which he apparently shared with the other man in the house, Bill Lancaster. He had few possessions – some clothes and a few books, writing materials, and a typewriter too, which sat listless on a table in the bedroom; it was rarely in danger of employment. Clarke was a tall, handsome, intelligent and charming man, who had an eye for women and a certain way with them. His mother was currently a teacher of Journalism and Creative Writing at the Miami University, which had been established only 7 years earlier in 1925, sprawling across a 240-acre estate in the city. She and her son Haden had a difficult relationship, but there is little doubting her devotion to him – nor her faith in his writing talents. She did all she could to encourage him in his endeavours, and to help him find positions of employment using her many connections, but Haden was easily distracted – usually by women, or cards, or drinking, his preferred occupations. He had married Kathryn Farnham Korn (b.1908) in 1926 but it hadn't lasted; she had taken action in San Francisco Superior Court against her errant husband for desertion, and since then he had had a stream of new partners. Although the news of his death was devastating for Mrs Clarke, she said she had expected it. Haden had visited her on the afternoon preceding his death in company with Mrs Chubbie Miller, and she had had a sense of foreboding since that time, she said.

Meanwhile, early that same morning of 21st April 1932, Vernon Hawthorne, the Florida State Attorney, had been informed of the tragedy, and took charge of the investigation. He knew the case would attract widespread coverage because the man and woman involved, who shared the house with Haden Clarke, were well-known aviators. He had heard of them, of course; Chubbie Miller in particular was a famous flyer in an age when aviation was a thrilling new frontier of adventure, and her escapades and record-breaking attempts were frequently covered in the news.

Hawthorne questioned Lancaster and Miller separately about the circumstances of Clarke's death. Bill Lancaster told Hawthorne that he had been asleep in the room above the porch, which he shared with Haden Clarke, and had been awoken by the sound of a gunshot – at first he thought it was a window banging shut – he jumped out of bed and found Haden Clarke with a bullet wound to his head and a gun by his side. He discovered two typewritten letters addressed to himself and Mrs Miller – suicide notes – and woke Mrs Chubbie Miller, whose bedroom was across the hallway. It was clear to him that Haden Clarke had taken his own life. They did what they could for Haden and called a doctor, and he was removed to the hospital. Chubbie Miller told much the same story. She said Haden Clarke had been staying at the bungalow with herself and Lancaster for the past few weeks in order to help her write her memoirs – she and Clarke had fallen in love and were intending to marry the following month.

Hawthorne initially believed Lancaster – and although both he and Chubbie Miller continued to be detained at Miami County Jail as material witnesses, it was by way of being a cautionary measure. It seemed straightforward enough: a man had been discovered dying with a gunshot wound to his head; beneath him lay a pistol, and two suicide letters had been written by him to the man and woman who shared the house with him, clearly indicating what he had done and that he alone was responsible for his actions. Nevertheless, Hawthorne, in company with investigators and attorneys, interviewed both Miller and Lancaster several times that day to try to get the facts straight. Hawthorne compared the accounts of the two aviators and discussed them with investigators. He was considering the matter carefully. He believed Chubbie Miller's account for the most part, but there were aspects of Lancaster's account which he found puzzling. It made him thoughtful.

Later in the morning, following the death of Haden Clarke, Vernon Hawthorne, along with Constable Dick Meschendorf, State Investigator John B Rowland, and other law enforcement officers, visited the bungalow at Coral Gables to conduct a thorough search of the property and secure any possible evidence. Here they found the missing bullet embedded in the feathers of Clarke's pillow. They also found letters belonging to Bill Lancaster, Chubbie Miller and Haden Clarke, and collected pages of Clarke's typing, and other materials belonging to him. Other items were retrieved from Bill Lancaster's aeroplane, which was parked at Miami Viking Airport. Of particular interest were three diaries belonging to Bill Lancaster, whose entries in recent weeks provided a curious narrative concerning the relationship between the three friends; and together with letters found at the bungalow, these offered a suggestive line of inquiry. In fact, they proved to be a game-changer in the investigation.

Vernon Hawthorne was, by degrees, becoming increasingly suspicious. To begin with, the circumstances of the three were unusual. It was clear from their letters, from Lancaster's diary and their own depositions made in the Attorney's office, that Bill Lancaster and Chubbie Miller had been in a relationship of several years' standing; both had been married, and although Mrs Miller had recently become divorced, Bill Lancaster was still married to a woman in England with whom he had two children. Of particular interest, though, was the fact that Mrs Miller had recently been working on her memoirs with the young man, Haden Clarke, whom she had engaged for this purpose. The three had grown close, and as they were in dire financial straits - partly owing to the depression, and partly due to the fact that none of the three had a wage-paying job - Bill Lancaster had gone west in early March in the hopes of finding employment in a venture called Latin American Airlines, which was seeking pilots and planes for what turned out to be a dubious enterprise. In his absence, the evident closeness between Mrs Miller and Haden Clarke had become a passionate affair. The errant lovers were, in fact, so smitten with each other that they had decided to marry, but feeling somewhat guilty about this occurring in Bill's absence, they wrote to inform him of their plans. He took it rather well. He promptly telegraphed his congratulations to them – but he asked them to wait until his return so he could attend the wedding and act as best man. It was thoroughly sporting of him. But from the entries in Lancaster's diary during this period, and from his letters and telegrams, it was gleaned that Lancaster was deeply in love with Chubbie Miller and wracked with suspicion and jealousy that she had deceived him with the man whom he had trusted and regarded as a friend. That man was now dead.

Bill had duly arrived to offer his hearty congratulations to the couple just the previous day, on the evening of Wednesday, 20th April: a few hours later, his friend and rival, Haden Clarke, was dead, apparently having committed suicide. It seemed to be a tragedy, albeit one which had a certain fortuitousness for Bill Lancaster. It also turned out that the gun supposed to have been used by Clarke and found on his bed, was Bill Lancaster's .38 colt revolver, one which he had bought along with ammunition just two days previously. He had borrowed $100 that same day, for this purpose. The purchase of a gun seemed to be an extravagance given the parlous state of the finances of the three friends. On inspection, the gun was declared by a fingerprint expert to have been wiped clean – although there were smudged fingerprints detected on the barrel end, which were incapable of being identified. In addition, the trajectory and location of the bullet wound suggested that Clarke could not have fired the gun himself without great difficulty: everything pointed to its having been fired by a third person.

Mrs Miller, in her statement to authorities, said:

'Lancaster and I had been making the bungalow our headquarters. The depression hit us and we found difficulty even in finding money to pay light and water bills. A Latin American Airline venture was suggested, and Captain Lancaster went out west to investigate possibilities. During his absence young Clarke and I started to work on my biography. Suddenly we found ourselves in love. We were sort of conscience-stricken and surprised; so we wrote to Captain Lancaster telling him we intended to marry. He sent a wire wishing us luck, and offering to be best man if we would defer the wedding till after his return from St Louis. He said he did not want to be a dog-in-the-manger.

'That wire arrived last Sunday. Captain Lancaster returned to the bungalow on Wednesday and about midnight I retired. About 2 o'clock Captain Lancaster was awakened by a shot and found Clarke lying on the floor of the porch with a gun under his leg.' (*News Chronicle*, 25th April 1932)

Lancaster had come to her room, she said, and banged on the door, calling out: 'Come quick! Haden has shot himself!'

She went quickly to Haden's room and found him covered in blood:

'I thought it was a haemorrhage, as I could not see any gun,' she said. 'I yelled to Bill to get a doctor, then I got a sponge and started to wash the blood off Haden. Meanwhile Bill was phoning for a doctor.

'Then I looked and saw the barrel of a gun sticking from under his leg. I pulled it out about an inch by the barrel. Bill was still phoning, and I ran downstairs to see if the doctor had gotten there. The doctor was not in sight so I phoned Mr Huston, a lawyer, to come over and bring a doctor. I called Dr Deederer again and he said he had gotten lost and had to go back home again, but that he would be right over. The ambulance took Haden to the hospital. Dr Deederer and Bill and myself went to the hospital and met police.' (*Miami Daily News*, 21st April 1932)

Lancaster's statement was consistent with that of Mrs Miller, but it provided a little more detail:

'Haden and I said goodnight to Chubbie and went into the sun porch where we sleep. This was about 12.45 a.m. We talked for about an hour of home troubles and several other things. We were in a cheerful mood and laughing. I soon went to sleep as I was dog-tired because I had been flying for 12 hours during the day.

'I was awakened by a report and called "What's that?" The room was in darkness and Haden did not answer me. I looked toward him and he was making a funny noise. I got out of bed and looked closer and saw there was something wrong with him. I shook him and he did not make any statement so I turned on the light.

'His face was covered with blood and he was lying on his side. I ran to Chubbie's door and shouted "Get up!" Together we went back into the room and could see him lying there, his face covered with blood.

'At first we could not see the gun, but later saw it by his side. I ran down to call a doctor and an ambulance. The ambulance came and carried Haden to hospital. *I then phoned Mr Huston*. A doctor arrived and Mrs Keith Miller and myself went to the hospital.' (*Miami Daily News*, 21st April 1932)

It seemed to State Attorney Hawthorne that Mrs Miller's account was essentially truthful; her grief for Haden Clarke seemed genuine, and she appeared to be in the dark about his death. On the evening of 21st April she was permitted to attend the funeral service for Haden at Miami Beach Community Church, at which she was seen to be greatly distressed. [1]

'I am alone in the world. I have nothing to eat and nowhere to go!' Chubbie Miller sobbed at Haden Clarke's funeral on entering the church, where she was comforted by Haden's mother, Ida Clarke. (*Daily Herald*, 22nd April 1932)

Mrs Clarke seemed sure that her son had committed suicide. She told news reporters she had seen him in company with Chubbie on the afternoon before his death:

'He spent two hours with me and seemed depressed over finances. He was worried because he couldn't be more help to me and indicated that he might get some help through Captain Lancaster, who had recently returned from a business trip north.[2]

---

[1] A superficial autopsy was conducted by the County Medical Examiner, which established that Haden Clarke had died from a gunshot wound to the head. A full autopsy might have been indicated, especially given the circumstances, but was not undertaken. The reason for this omission was never elicited but probably indicates a belief on the part of the Attorney's office at this stage, that the matter was suicide.

[2] Mrs Clarke was mistaken here as Captain Lancaster would not arrive for several more hours at the time of this visit.

'He had been working at high speed on the book and articles, and was very much wrought up. I can't help but feel that he attempted to take his own life.

'The note to Mrs Keith Miller was shown to me, and I was uncertain as to the signature.' (*Miami Daily News*, 21st April 1932)

Hawthorne found himself sympathetic towards Lancaster. Lancaster was frank, open, and in spite of the circumstances and some nagging doubts, Hawthorne was persuaded that the case was probably one of suicide. Lancaster also told Hawthorne of a malady from which Haden Clarke was suffering – probably syphilis – which he thought might have prompted his suicide. He requested of Hawthorne that the nature of Haden Clarke's disease should not be made public, to spare his mother – a request Hawthorne acquiesced to.[3] Hawthorne remained equivocal in the matter – he had certain misgivings but no real evidence, and after all, Lancaster seemed to have an excellent character. He expressed this equivocation publicly to the press indicating that it was 'murder or suicide,' but he firmly exonerated Chubbie Miller of any involvement:

'I am convinced that Mrs Miller was not connected with Clarke's death, but she is being detained for further questioning to determine

[3] The nature of Haden's 'malady' was never explicitly defined in court. It was made clear that it was a sexually transmitted disease, which he had contracted some time before, and received several treatments for. It is usually assumed that the disease was syphilis, but it could have been gonorrhoea – both diseases were difficult to treat before the use of penicillin became widespread in 1943.

whether the man committed suicide or was slain.' (*Daily News*, 23rd April 1932)

Of course, it begged the question:

'While there are many things would substantiate a theory of suicide, there are a number of facts which, taken either separately or together, hinder the final acceptance of that theory.' (*The Chattanooga News*, 22nd April 1932)

By the following day Hawthorne seemed to have made up his mind in Lancaster's favour:[4] both Miller and Lancaster were released without charge on 23rd April, and went directly to see Mrs Clarke at the Everglades Hotel to assure her of Lancaster's innocence. She believed Lancaster – so much so that she recommended her own attorney, James H Lathero, to represent him. Chubbie and Bill then returned to the Coral Gables bungalow to find it had been thoroughly turned over by police. It was a depressing spectacle. They were exhausted as they set about trying to right the place.

A coroner's inquest was scheduled for Monday 25th April but was postponed until the completion of investigations.

Perhaps with a view to railroading Hawthorne in his deliberations, Lancaster issued a statement via his attorney James H Lathero:

'It is gratifying that I have been cleared of all suspicion in connection with the death of Haden

[4] He had in any case nearly held Lancaster for the maximum 72 hours permitted under State law.

Clarke. He was my friend – one of the most admirable characters, one of the most charming personalities I have ever known.

'I wish to express my appreciation of the thoroughness and the fairness with which the State Attorney and his assistants conducted the investigation, and their courteous treatment of me...

'I feel very deeply Mrs Clarke's attitude toward me during my visit to her immediately following my release...' (*Miami Daily News*, 24th April 1932)

It was certainly a bold bluff to try to force the issue to a favourable conclusion – but it was premature. Investigations by police continued in an attempt to ascertain precisely what had occurred. A timeline of events was established which was far from clear or satisfactory:

12.45 a.m. Chubbie Miller, Clarke and Lancaster retire to bed.

Chubbie reads until 1.45 a.m; Clarke and Lancaster talk until 1.45 a.m.

Before 2.00 a.m. Haden Clarke is shot.

2.00 a.m. or after, Ernest Huston is called.

2.30 a.m. Ernest Huston calls an ambulance and doctor via the Physicians' Emergency service.

2.45 a.m. An ambulance arrives at the bungalow.

3.00 a.m. Earl Hudson and Fitzhugh Lee arrive at hospital to await the ambulance and Haden Clarke.

3.15 a.m. Attorney Huston arrives at the bungalow.

3.30 a.m. Ambulance departs bungalow for hospital.

3.40 a.m. Dr Deederer arrives at bungalow.

3.40 a.m. Ambulance arrives at Jackson Memorial Hospital with Haden Clarke, Miller and Lancaster.

11.20 a.m. Haden Clarke dies.[5]

When was Haden Clarke shot? Clearly it was some time 'before 2 a.m.' because both Lancaster's and Miller's statements confirm this. Huston claims he received the call from Chubbie at 2.00 a.m. What did he do for the remaining 75 minutes? Why was the ambulance detained for 45 minutes while a seriously wounded man was in want of urgent medical attention?

These questions and others began to unsettle Hawthorne's conviction in the matter. If he was uncertain himself, he was also under considerable pressure from the press, the public and some influential people to act against Lancaster. There was a widespread belief that Lancaster had killed his love rival.

Photographs of the scene of the shooting, taken by a police photographer, showed that Lancaster's bed was undisturbed and his pillow unruffled when examined – had he slept in the bed that night at

---

[5] These times are open to doubt; in particular, it should be noted that the times given by Miller and Lancaster prior to 2 a.m. are dependant entirely on their accounts of the evening and early hours of 20th and 21st April. Huston's being called at 2 a.m. is also open to doubt: as there is no surviving transcript of the court proceedings, we are dependent on newspaper accounts of events, and these vary widely. The time of the call received by Huston is sometimes given as 3 a.m. – as this is impossible, it must be assumed that it has been mis-transcribed or given in error.

all? When questioned specifically on this, Lancaster said he had offered the pillow to the ambulance driver Ditsler for Haden's stretcher, but he had rejected this and so he had replaced it on his bed. That seemed a reasonable explanation for the smooth appearance of the pillow – but when questioned Ditsler denied this had happened.

A bloodied pencil found on the table could not have been placed there by Haden Clarke, because it had his blood on it, but Lancaster explained this by stating he had found it on the floor near to Clarke's bed and picked it up and placed it on the table in that condition.

There were many reasonable explanations... The recently bought gun with money Lancaster had borrowed seemed a distinctly odd circumstance; Lancaster told Hawthorne he had purchased the gun to replace one his attorney Ernest Huston had loaned him. Attorney Huston confirmed he had loaned a gun to Lancaster – but it was subsequently discovered that Lancaster had given his reason for wanting to buy a gun, to the sheriff in St Louis, as his needing it for 'international travel.' It was another minor discrepancy. Above all, the menage in which the trois were caught was particularly suspicious - and Bill's state of mind as evidenced by his diaries, his letters, and other anecdotal evidence, all weighed against him to nurture a growing suspicion. In addition, Dr Deederer reported that when he examined Haden Clarke no powder burns were evident in the vicinity of Haden Clarke's head wound, which suggested to him the bullet had been fired from a distance; he alluded to bruises he and the undertaker had found on Clarke's head and right shoulder, which might suggest a fight of some sort had occurred before death...

Mrs Ida Clarke was also having doubts: in fact, in the space of 24 hours she had changed her mind completely. It was reported, that –

'Mrs Ida Clarke no longer accepts without reservation the theory that her son, Haden Clarke, 26, took his own life at the home of Mrs Keith Miller, famed Australian aviatrix, yesterday morning as he lay in a bed in the same room with Captain WN Lancaster, the long-time companion of Mrs Keith Miller in many aviation enterprises.' (*Miami Daily News*, 22nd April 1932)

The reasons for her change of heart were given as:

1. Since boyhood Haden had had an aversion to firearms, that 'amounted to a complex.'
2. She was told by Dr Carleton Deederer that there was no trace of powder marks to indicate a shot had been fired from close range. She said he had told her that he had shaved Haden's hair to look for powder and found none.
3. The undertaker told her of a large bruise on Clarke's right shoulder. What was its cause?
4. When Lancaster was broke in El Paso, he had phoned to say he was trying to pawn his pistol to get some money. Haden told his mother: 'I hope he does. I hope he doesn't bring that damned thing back here.'
5. 'A short time ago when she and Haden visited friends in Sanford, Haden refused to even view a collection of old and modern firearms which one of the men they were

> visiting had collected.' (*Miami Daily News*, 22nd April 1932)

Mrs Clarke also said, that on his visit to her in company with Chubbie at 4.30 on the afternoon prior to his death, she had a premonition.[6] She cancelled her appointment with a student because she felt in some way disturbed. All night, she said, she had a feeling of impending disaster. She talked with a friend until 1.30 a.m. (this would have been close to the time when Haden was shot) and continued to lie prostrate on the couch. When the phone rang at 4 a.m. she answered with 'full knowledge that something had happened to Haden,' she said.

She also said Haden was an 'expert typist' and her cursory inspection of the notes was that they had not been typed by a proficient typist. The margins were wrong – the typing was crowded at the top of the page, not centralised. She had come to doubt Haden had written them at all.

If such reports were creating misgivings in State Attorney Hawthorne's mind, he still had no doubts concerning Mrs Miller. But the more he learned of Bill Lancaster, the more uncertain he became of his innocence: he studied the diary written by Lancaster, and especially the entries written while Lancaster had been away out west: it was clear from these that he had been anxious over the closeness exhibited between Mrs Miller and Clarke. Furthermore, references in the diary to letters sent to Mr Jack F Russell, an associate in the Latin American venture, spoke of the relationship going on between Chubbie and Haden in Lancaster's absence. It was clear from the diary

[6] They called on her on their way to the airport to collect Lancaster.

that Russell had shown these letters to Lancaster while they were together in Los Angeles. Lancaster's diary confirmed his jealousy and turmoil of mind at the growing suspicions of a relationship he detected between the pair.

One diary entry read:

'Russell shows me two letters – one [from his wife] says "Chubbie and Clarke were round tonight all ginned up. I really think now that Clarke has gained Chubbie's affections, and Bill has lost them." My mental agony is hell.'

When subsequently questioned, the man, Jack Russell, told the Attorney's Office that Lancaster had told him he would 'get rid of Clarke.' Another associate who had been out west with Lancaster, Mark Tancrel, told of Lancaster's stating he had 'seen many dead men during the war – one more won't make any difference.' (*Daily Herald*, 8th August 1932)

The evidence against Lancaster was mounting. It was by no means complete, though: although the letter from Clarke, which had awaited Lancaster and been read by him on his arrival in St Louis, was found – another by him and two Mrs Miller had sent Lancaster informing him of the affair and the impending marriage, could not be found... Neither Lancaster, nor Mrs Miller could offer an explanation for this. It seemed to Hawthorne these must have been destroyed by one of them. Why?

To complicate matters further, on 23rd April a young woman named Peggy Brown walked into Hawthorne's office and informed him that she was Haden Clarke's fiancé, not Chubbie Miller. She had stayed at the Coral Gables bungalow with Haden many times, she said. The character of Haden Clarke was not at all straightforward: many letters taken from the bungalow were found to be from different women – one was from a New York widow Virginia Van Wert, to whom he had been engaged; another from a divorcee named Eleanor Griffin, also from New York, and to whom he had also been engaged. He was a much-engaged man.

Chubbie was questioned about the claims made by Peggy Brown that she was Haden's fiancé, and told a *Miami News* reporter:

'I met Peggy Brown several times when she was here at parties. I do not think she was ever more than a friend to Haden. The last time I saw her was six weeks ago. She drove up one night with a message for Haden and I have not seen her since that time,' (*Miami Daily News*, 26th April 1932)

Mrs Miller was not being truthful in this, as she knew very well that Peggy had stayed with Haden many times and had been staying at the bungalow up until 6th March with him, when she had travelled with Haden and Chubbie herself to Viking Airport at dawn to see Lancaster off on his trip west. Presumably she believed that Haden had subsequently broken off this engagement.

And then came a bombshell: the two suicide letters written by Haden Clarke, which had apparently been found by Lancaster on the typewriter table some three feet from the foot of Clarke's bed, were examined by detectives: something was amiss.

The signatures on both letters had been written in pencil – the name 'Haden' written at the foot of the letter to Chubbie had apparently been done with such meticulous care, that the hand of the writer had left the page a number of times... It looked as though someone had forged the signatures, copying them carefully – too carefully.

Furthermore, the typing was also determined to be heavier than that which characterised Haden's usual quick, light, expert typing, and the verb 'advise' had been misspelled as 'advice' in the note addressed to Bill, something which Clarke was thought unlikely to do. His sentences also had no space between them after a full stop - but on comparison with notes Bill Lancaster had typed on the same typewriter, they showed certain unmistakable similarities: the two suicide notes were suspected of being fakes. Questioned on these by John B Rowland, chief investigator, Lancaster expressed astonishment. When similarities between his own typing and those of the suicide notes were pointed out to him, he exclaimed 'What a coincidence!' and suggested helpfully that handwriting experts should be consulted – even offering to help locate one in New York. Hawthorne, the State Attorney, ordered this to be done. Lancaster meanwhile returned home from this interview. He was thinking furiously on this new development. He had read of Mrs Clarke's doubts too - and as a result of this, later that day he returned to make a new statement at the courthouse: he now admitted he had typed the suicide notes himself and signed them.

'When I switched on the light and found Haden Clarke had shot himself, I suppose I was a little panicky. I had been awakened out of a deep sleep and may have been befuddled. I spoke to Haden, I shook him, and the only noise that came from him was a sort of gurgling noise. His body was twitching violently, and his legs moved. When the full seriousness of the situation sank in, my first thought was: Chubbie will think I am responsible. I did not know how seriously Haden was injured. I thought he might be dying. I sat down at the typewriter and typed two notes. I typed them as I honestly thought Haden would type such notes. I used expressions he had used to me that night in a talk we had earlier in the evening. I picked up a pencil which was by the side of the typewriter, and I went back to the bed where Haden Clarke was lying. I spoke to him. I begged him to sign the two notes I had written.'

Of course, Haden was not able to oblige him, so Lancaster said he 'scribbled' *Haden* and *H* in pencil at the foot of the two notes he had typed addressed to himself and Chubbie. He said:

'It is the only thing I have done that is not strictly honourable in connection with the death of Haden Clarke. I did not kill him. In no way have I willingly been a reason for his death.'

Hawthorne, nevertheless, submitted the two 'suicide' notes to a leading expert in the field, J V Haring, and asked him to produce a detailed analysis and report on them. Haring's report was unequivocal: the two notes were forgeries and had almost certainly been typed by Captain Lancaster.

As a direct result of this, Hawthorne decided to act. On 2nd May 1932, Bill Lancaster was arrested and charged with the first-degree murder of Haden Clarke. On the following day, the matter was placed before a Grand Jury, which subsequently indicted him to stand his trial on the charge. The date for the trial was fixed for 5th July 1932. If found guilty, Bill Lancaster would face the electric chair.

High Flyers: Chubbie Miller and Bill Lancaster maintained a public fiction that they were merely flying partners. The revelations of the investigation blew this myth apart. (*Miami Herald*)

Nathaniel Vernon Hawthorne, the State Attorney, became convinced Lancaster was guilty of murder.

Peggy Brown was Haden's girlfriend, and believed she was his fiancé...So did other women. (*Daily News*)

The most familiar photo of a youthful Haden Clarke c1925. This is usually shown reversed. As Haden was right-handed and wore his hair-parting on the left-hand side, the photo here is correct. The fold in his tie also indicates this

Attorney Ernest Huston. His evidence was important in Lancaster's case. (*Miami Daily News*)

Dr Carleton Deederer was a man of many interests, Deederer claimed to have carried out the first organ transplant in 1918, was a cosmetic surgeon, a sculptor, and an early opponent of the use of DDT. (*Miami Daily Herald*)

3. A Chance Meeting

The press coverage Bill Lancaster received was in stark contrast to that which he and Chubbie Miller had received just five years earlier in 1927. Then he had been riding high, a well-known aviator, enjoying the benefits of fame. He believed his future was a bright one; the best was yet to come. Now he was being held in Dade County Jail, charged with murder, the subject of prurient public fascination; his personal affairs and life were pored over by a public which was eager to learn of them, and a press as eager to supply them. Although nothing had been proved against him, his fall from grace had been sudden and spectacular.

Bill Lancaster was born William Newton Lancaster on 14th February 1898 at King's Norton, a town in Worcestershire, England, which later that same year became part of the urban sprawl of Birmingham. He was the son of a successful civil engineer, Edward William Lancaster (1859-1952) and his rather eccentric spiritualist wife, Maud Lucas (1870-1950). His father, Edward, had three children from a previous marriage, and after his first wife's death in 1892, a further three followed from his marriage to Maud Lucas. Bill was the eldest.[7] William, who was known as Bill to most and affectionately as 'Billee' to his mother, went to Ardingly College private school in Sussex.

[7] His full siblings were Jack Kelvin Lancaster, (1899-1946), and Grace 'Betty' Lancaster, (1907-2000).

Although a bright boy, he wasn't an outstanding student, nor academically inclined, but he had imagination and a restlessness for adventure, and in 1914 he went to Australia where he lived with an uncle. His brother Jack joined him there a little later.

When the Great War of 1914-18 broke out, Bill was too young for active service and worked as a rancher and did a variety of other odd jobs in Australia until he reached the age of 17, when he joined the mounted unit of the Australian Expeditionary Forces. After a brief spell of basic training, he was despatched to Britain with the Field Engineers. That was in October 1916. It was here that Lancaster saw aeroplanes being prepared for action and read of their exploits above the trenches on the Western Front. It was the first time aircraft had been deployed on this scale in war.[8] The esprit de corps, the camaraderie of the pilots, became legendary and captured the public imagination. They were knights of the sky, riding high above the mud and gore of trench warfare, engaging in airborne duels and adhering to an unwritten code of honour. Lancaster was seduced by the romance of it, and he succeeded in transferring to the Australian Flying Corps as an air mechanic in June 1917. He wanted to be a pilot, and fortunately for him there was a voracious demand for new pilots, owing to the high mortality rate of the role – which, of course, perversely, increased the glamour of it. In 1916 and 1917

---

[8] The first use of aeroplanes in conflict was in the Italo-Turkish war of 1911, when, on 23rd October that year, Carlo Piazza flew his Bleriot XI 25 hp aeroplane on a reconnaissance mission above enemy lines. A week later Lieutenant Guido Gavotti dropped four grenades manually from a Taube monoplane over Turkish lines.

when demand was at its greatest, civilian flying schools were commandeered and cadet flyers were given just a few hours training before being turned out as fully fledged pilots. This inevitably led to even more deaths – it has been estimated that more pilots died during training in this period than died in actual combat. By the 'Spring of 1917 the life expectancy of a new pilot could be measured in weeks.' (RAF Museum – *First World War Flying Training*).

It was into such a world of glamour, intensified by the high risks of death, that Lancaster was accepted as a cadet pilot in the Royal Flying Corps (RFC), receiving his flying certificate on 1st November 1917. He was commissioned as a Second Lieutenant, assigned to 80 Squadron and was employed in transporting newly manufactured planes from England to France. For the most part these would be flown from Lympne in Kent, to one of the ports on England's south coast and then shipped across the channel, to be flown on to the squadron of assignment.

It was an exciting new world. Flying was very much in its infancy: just 11 years before, Orville and Wilbur Wright had succeeded in flying a 605lb (274kg) aluminium framed glider with a 12hp motor attached, for a wayward 105 ft (33m) for just 3.5 seconds at Kitty Hawk, North Carolina. That was in December 1903: since then, aeroplanes had made astonishing progress – and spurred on by the demands of war, their development was accelerating rapidly. The planes were highly dangerous to fly – and the occupation of pilot was made even more hazardous under fire from ground gunners, and from that of opposing fighter planes.[9]

Lancaster succumbed to such an accident himself in March 1918 as a result of flying in a snowstorm, and he was hospitalised for a period, which put paid to his dreams of glory as a flying ace on the Western Front; he was deemed medically unfit for service and invalided out; and soon after, in November 1918, the war ended.

In April 1919 Lancaster married Annie Maud Besant (1896-1953), known as 'Kiki' to her friends, who was from Kildare in Ireland. She was a war widow, whose husband, Mervyn William Colomb, an Irish classical singer, had been severely wounded by shrapnel at Ypres, and subsequently died in hospital in England on 11th May 1915. She and Lancaster had 2 daughters - Patricia Anne Lancaster (1922-1980), and Nina Ann Lancaster (b1927).

The newly married and recently demobbed Lancaster commenced studying dentistry at the Royal Dental Hospital in London in 1919, but it was short-lived – for whatever reason – and he left his studies and re-joined the RAF in 1920 as a Flying Officer, presumably now being deemed fit for service by this time.[10] He was demobilized just a year later and returned again to his dentistry studies, this time managing a full year, before once again re-joining the RAF in April 1921. Whatever the cause of these sudden changes of career, Lancaster's lack of staying power in anything he

---

[9] The quintessential British fighter plane, the Sopwith Camel, had such a reputation amongst pilots, that it was humorously characterised as guaranteeing either 'a wooden cross, the Red Cross, or a Victoria Cross'! (*Fighter: Technology, Facts, History*, Ralf Leinburger, Parragon, 2008)

[10] The RFC became the RAF in April 1918 when it ceased to be a division of the British army and became a separate service.

undertook certainly characterised most of his endeavours in life. He saw service in the RAF with 25 Squadron at Folkestone and then in India with 31 Squadron at Peshawar. His stay in India was short-lived, too – reasons for this are speculative, but he seems not to have been well-regarded there as a flyer and in 1923 he was posted to administrative duties at RAF Halton, UK. There were tales of his sporting endeavours – of boxing and parachuting, even of rodeo escapades – which speak to his love of adventure and also to his attention seeking nature at that time. There was a certain fearlessness in his nature, too, which earned him a grudging admiration amongst his detractors. The general verdict was that he was inept at these undertakings, though cheerful and good-natured by disposition – and quite fearless. Lancaster's RAF career finally ended in 1926, and he established himself as a car salesman for a short time, running a garage he set up with the help of his father.

Lancaster was not really cut out for civilian life – he had a restless nature, a love of adventure and especially of flying. Those who knew him at this time described him as a show-off, an exhibitionist even. He certainly had an impetuous and reckless daring about him. He had a lack of direction in his life too. By the spring of 1927 he was essentially unemployed and living alone in Kensington, his wife Kiki seemingly growing tired of his inability to hold down a job or provide for his family. She had recently given birth to their second child, Nina, and they were financially reliant on Bill's parents at this time.

Then in May 1927, Charles Lindbergh (1902-1974), an unknown US Air Mail pilot, took off from an airstrip in New York's Long Island in his high-wing Ryan monoplane the *Spirit of St Louis*, loaded with 450 gallons of fuel. He touched down in Paris some 33 ½ hours later, having flown an incredible 3,600 miles across the Atlantic Ocean alone. It was a seminal moment in the history of aviation, a prodigious achievement of mental strength, physical endurance, courage and determination: and it inspired the world. His achievement was headline news wherever there were headlines, and Lindbergh became one of the most famous men in the world. He was feted wherever he went; he became a wealthy man too. It inspired many young pilots, and it gave a new impetus to the somewhat aimless Bill Lancaster, who at that time was a man looking for a cause. He conceived of the idea of flying from England to Australia – a 13,000-mile journey, following the route of the Imperial Airways, largely relying on outposts of the British Empire as stopping points. This had never been done in a light airplane at this time, and although it was not quite the equal of Lindbergh's achievement, it was a huge enterprise for a man to undertake.

Bill was not a great pilot, and not a great organiser either; and the idea would very probably have remained a daydream had it not been for a chance meeting in London's Baker Street just a month after Lindbergh's transatlantic triumph. Everyone was talking of Lindbergh's achievement; it was a natural subject of conversation for any young flyer. It was probably all bluster on Lancaster's part; he had no money and no real idea of how to go about his venture. Although his father was reasonably well-off, and his mother had her own income too, there were a great many costs associated with the flight – and other difficulties.

Bill was a freemason, and he could use this to leverage some support and favours - but his idea was essentially a dream. It was at this point, at a party at 15 Baker Street, London (seven doors, numerically, from the legendary fictional home of Sherlock Holmes), that he met Jessie 'Chubbie' Miller. It was to be a life-changing meeting for them both.

Chubbie Miller was then 25 years old, having been born Jessie Maude Beveridge in Southern Cross, in south-west Australia, on 13th September 1901. She was the daughter of a bank manager, Charles Beveridge and his wife Maude, who were of strong religious heritage and belief, and they imbued in their children a keen sense of religious devotion. Jessie was brought up in Perth, Australia, and in Timaru in New Zealand. A small, petite, but lively and athletic girl with an extravert nature, she was known by her nickname of 'Chubbie' to her close friends throughout her life. She married a journalist for the *Herald* and *Weekly Times* of Melbourne, George Keith Miller (1896 - c1943) on 3rd December 1919, when she was 18 years old. It didn't last – she is said to have had three miscarriages, and the marriage foundered somewhat. It was a time of personal tragedy and upheaval for her: her father died in 1924 and her younger brother Thomas died at the age of 20, in 1926, of cerebral meningitis. It seems to have been a concatenation of these events which led her to decide to travel. In 1927, in company with a female friend, Margaret Starr, she sailed for Britain, her husband Keith Miller providing her with £3 a week allowance for what was intended to be a six-month trip. She was seeking to fill a void, and it was here she met another person with a void to fill, Bill Lancaster, at a party in the flat above hers.

She was obviously taken with him – he was an aviator in an age when there was really nothing more glamorous, and to an adventurous girl, this offered something of an escape and an opportunity. Bill Lancaster always knew how to play up the role of the dashing RAF hero; he did so now. He told her of his plans to fly from England to Australia, though it was little more than a pipedream at the time. She was thrilled. It fired her enthusiasm and brought the dream into focus: he backed off a little; a natural reaction to her excitable enthusiasm. It would require a lot of money – he would need to raise the necessary funds…

Chubbie was a woman of unbridled energy and enthusiasm: she seized the moment and offered to help him raise the money if he would allow her to be his passenger. Until now, Lancaster's idea had been a daydream; he had no means of giving it employment. He demurred; he had not cast his idea in concrete terms; he had no means of carrying it through. It was one thing to boast of his plans to an attractive young Australian woman at a party, obviously impressed by his flying credentials just 4 weeks after Lindbergh's achievement, and quite another to put those plans into action. But Chubbie Miller was impetuous by nature, a bundle of enthusiasm; if she was not thrilled, she was depressed; perhaps today she would be said to have been somewhere on the bipolar spectrum. She was now on an upswing fuelled by alcohol and the thrill of new horizons - and she pushed him to the recklessness of a decision: she wanted to be his passenger, and would help him raise the funds for the flight. The two met for lunch the following day at the Author's Club in Whitehall.[11] Lancaster was out to impress. If he intended to parlay his dreams into a pleasant afternoon's idle self-delusion, she did not. Chubbie pressed him to a decision in her forthright way. In fact, she brushed aside his objections and hesitations, and the result was that he accepted her offer. No sooner the word than the blow with Chubbie, they went to the map makers Stanford's at 12-14 Long Acre, Covent Garden, where they examined charts and plotted a journey to Australia, Chubbie apparently paying for a set of the folding travellers maps plotting their course.[12]

Chubbie later claimed she raised 50% of the cost of the trip as her end of the deal – a claim vigorously challenged by Lancaster's parents, who paid £700 (£50,000 in 2022) for the plane alone.[13] But if Chubbie was prone to seeking the limelight and appropriating the credit to herself on occasion, there is no doubting that the momentum for the enterprise was hers - something of a force of nature inhabited her - and there is no doubt either,

---

[11] Oscar Wilde denounced the censorship of his play Salome at a dinner here, HG Wells was a member, so was author Graham Greene - and the other third man, British spy Kim Philby, was a member too.

[12] Chubbie's accounts in respect of this vary – in one version she claims the visit to the mapmakers was immediate, following their lunch at the Author's Club; in another she describes it as occurring 'days later.'

[13] It was a source of great and lasting annoyance to Lancaster's parents that Chubbie made this claim: 'People said at the time it was Mrs Keith Miller who found the money. People said it was her flight. The whole thing was an act of love on the part of Lancaster's mother, who, [bought] the Red Rose, the aeroplane, and bore all the expenses,' wrote Hannen Swaffer in the *Daily Herald*, 11th August 1932.

she was the means of turning an idle dream into concrete plans. And her £3 per week allowance (£200 in 2022) from her husband Keith Miller, would ultimately prove invaluable during hard times.

Things had moved with astonishing rapidity in the time of their brief acquaintance; the two were caught up in the excitement and thrill of their enterprise, fuelled by the prospect of adventure – and the mutual attraction it fostered. Both were married, though not very securely, at the time. According to Chubbie, Bill told her he was separated from his wife Kiki at this time. Physically this may have been true, as Lancaster appears to have been living in Kensington, and his wife, who had recently given birth (March 1927) was living in Bournemouth, preoccupied with their daughters, and involved in an anti-vivisection cause.[14] In any case, Chubbie met Kiki, who generously approved of the scheme of her husband and his exuberant female companion. Apparently Kiki's chief concern was that Bill should relieve her financial pressure and bring in some money for the family.

Lancaster's parents were less taken with Chubbie Miller, nor were they enthusiastic at the notion that their son should abandon his wife and daughters and embark on a trip halfway around the world with a married woman. According to Chubbie, Lancaster's mother, Maud, took her to her medium to see if the spirits would guide her as to whether or not she was the right person to

---

[14] Chubbie was certainly aware of Bill's wife and children, and it is possible that her subsequent recollections are calibrated to spare herself – and others – the candid nature of their relationship and its implications.

accompany her son to Australia, and was assured by them that she was. If it is true, Maud may later have had good reason to think the spirits had done a rather poor job of this. Nevertheless, Bill's parents footed the bill for the plane in return for Bill agreeing to distribute Maud's leaflets containing a poem she had written for her religious organisation, *The Mission of Flowers*. In this order she was known as 'Sister Red Rose' – suggested by her surname of Lancaster, the red rose being the heraldic symbol of the Royal House of Lancaster since the 14th Century. The poem, fashioned as an answer to Kipling's poem 'Mother o' Mine,' was dedicated to 'My Son Little Billee'. It ran:

'Thou son o' mine into the mist hast gone,
Oh, son o' mine, with the light seek morn,
And in the pathway will blossom red,
A little flow'r from God.
'Tis but a Red Rose symbolical of Love,
Look to the light dear, and God above
Will send down Grace and Justice true,
In love Divine for me and you.'

And –

'A Red Rose
'My symbol is "Red Rose" noble and grand,
For kindness and Brotherly Love it should stand.
God grant that my deeds every hour of my life,
May be such as to show love to keep down strife
Worthy to carry the emblem I wear,
To look to His Light and then all crosses bear.'
(*Daily Herald*, 11th August 1932)]

It is not known if Mrs Lancaster's poetry was inflicted on the world, by those entrusted with its delivery, but the couple took reams of these pamphlets on their journey.

The purchase of the aeroplane by Mrs Lancaster solved the main financial obstacle to the enterprise, but there were many other costs to be met. They believed they would be able to recoup the costs, as Lindbergh had, following his transatlantic flight, by means of the publicity which would naturally follow: the success of their flight would translate into financial terms. Chubbie planned to make a full account of their journey and it is clear even at this stage, there was an intention to write a book about their adventure. She also arranged to cable a regular account of their progress to the *Daily Express* newspaper in London. It was obvious to them that money would only be a temporary obstacle. Nevertheless, the upfront costs involved a serious financial commitment: at least 1,000 gallons of fuel would be required for their 13,000-mile journey, possibly 1,500 gallons. It was a substantial financial outlay. They succeeded in gaining sponsorship from Shell and BP to provide the necessary fuel, in return for the publicity, and they planned to use RAF staging posts along their journey for the purpose of refuelling. Other businessmen, some Australians, were persuaded to pitch in to defray out of pocket expenses - and Chubbie still had the financial support of her husband Keith. In one way or another, they scraped together the financial means for their journey. From its conception in June, it took them just three months to secure the means and in September 1927, Avro Aviation in Cheshire, provided a brand-new discounted Avian III biplane, which, in honour of his mother and her support, Lancaster named 'Red Rose.'

The 549 Avro Avian III was the first model of its kind produced, and Bill took the train to Manchester on 10th October to collect it. He test flew the aeroplane at Woodford Aerodrome, and from here he flew the plane to Croydon Airport in Surrey. The plane had dual controls fitted so that Chubbie, who would occupy the front cockpit, could take over from Lancaster during the flight. For this purpose she had received some flying lessons in Croydon, later claiming to have soloed on her second lesson when Bill was late, apparently taking off and landing several times. This claim should be treated with extreme scepticism: she was permitted neither to land the plane, nor to take off by Lancaster during their journey. The control of the plane and its operational surfaces once airborne, being a quite different matter, she would fly under Lancaster's direction. They had no intercom on board, of course, and so their only means of communication, once airborne, was by means of passing notes to each other between the fore and aft cockpits via a serving hatch.

They loaded up with fuel and stowed a minimal quantity of clothing, toiletries and rations in the plane – although Chubbie took an evening gown and a light pair of shoes with her, apparently being advised to do so.

It was clear from the outset that although Chubbie was simply a passenger in the *Red Rose*, she was the chief attraction for the media:

'Mrs Keith Miller is not only making a bid for the world's longest flight by a woman, but wants to show her friends in Australia that it is possible to travel over the world for next to nothing.

'Mrs Miller will take with her a baby cinematograph camera, and will not only take photos through the trapdoor at the bottom of the machine, but has practised lying on the wings and "shooting" her films like a machine gunner.' (*Dundee Evening Telegraph*, 12th October 1927)

There was clearly a good deal of fantasy or self-publicity in all of this! Nor was Bill Lancaster above some self-publicity either:

'Captain Lancaster, in addition to being a daring airman, is a well-known athlete. He was captain of the boxing team which won the boxing championship of the RAF in 1925, and won the Empire Broncho contest at Wembley in 1924, and was christened by his Air Force friends "Bronco Bill Lancaster."' (*Newcastle Journal*, 15th October 1927)

The flight was scheduled for 12th October and Chubbie had succeeded in persuading the High Commissioner for Australia, Sir Granville Ryrie, and Director of Civil Aviation Air Vice-Marshall Sir Sefton Brancker, to see them off; Lady Ryrie agreed to 'christen' the plane before departure.

They were delayed until 14th October by insurance matters and as a result Sir Granville was unable to attend - in his place Lady Ryrie did the honours, Colonel Ivo Edwards standing in for AVM Brancker. On the 14th October 1927 Kiki and the two girls, Pat and Nina (the latter just six months old), members of the press, and Lancaster's parents, assembled at Croydon Aerodrome. Chubbie declared:

'I am an Australian and have always wanted to be the first woman to fly from London to Australia.' (*Newcastle Journal*, 15th October 1927)

They told the reporter from the *Daily Mirror* their flight to Port Darwin in Australia would take them five to six weeks. They would follow the Imperial Airways Route to India and then south-east via Burma and Siam.[15]

Five-year-old Patricia, held aloft by her mother, scrawled on the fuselage for luck and at 2.35 p.m., as the autumn mist cleared, the Avro Avian III rose in the grey October sky; southwards it went, for Lympne and then the coast.

It would be five years before they would see Britain again.

---

15 Now Myanmar and Thailand.

Captain William Newton Lancaster (*Miami Daily News*)

Maud Lancaster, Bill's mother. (*The People*)

Bill gets his wings, November 1917. (*National Archives)*

Chubbie and Bill (*Sunday People*)

Kiki holds 5-year-old Pat up to the fuselage to scrawl a good luck message (*Daily Herald*).

Kiki, kisses Bill farewell before take-off at Croydon. Chubbie Miller watches. (*Daily Mail*)

4. The Flight to Australia

There was bound to be an added frisson attending a trip halfway around the world involving a man and a woman. Not that it was especially rare at that time – that same year a number of women had engaged in long haul flying adventures as passengers. The male pilots were hardly noticed. It seemed sufficiently novel to the press and public, for a woman to partake in so dangerous an occupation as flying, even as a passenger. And so it was with the Miller-Lancaster flight: the attraction was Chubbie – 'Mrs Keith Miller' as she was widely referred to in the press. Lancaster hardly minded this; he seems to have been sufficiently taken with Chubbie Miller to quash any feelings of envy he might have had over her garnering all the attention. In any case, a great deal of useful additional publicity was gained for their trip. They were a somewhat attractive couple, both personable and married – although not to each other – but publicity of this kind doesn't necessarily hurt such a venture.

It was an age in which taboos were being broken. Women's dresses had shortened, due to the need for economies with fabric during WW1, and also due to the practical necessities afforded to women entering the male-depleted workforce during this period. Women were finding their way into many positions which had hitherto been the province of men only, and breaching the traditional male citadels of the professions as doctors, lawyers and politicians.[16] The advent of female flyers seemed to be a natural extension of this: the fact that they adopted traditional male clothing, of trousers and jackets, added to the novelty. It didn't detract from their glamour, either: the advent of female pilots fascinated the public: just the day before the Miller and Lancaster flight, Fraulein Lilli Dillenz (1896-1964), a glamourous Austrian actress, took off from Lisbon to fly the southern Atlantic via the Azores; and 25-year-old Ruth Elder (1902-1977) was rescued by a Dutch oil tanker during her Atlantic crossing attempt, also that day. The skies were alive with aviatrixes!

The attempt to be the first to fly a light aircraft from England to Australia was, Lancaster and Miller insisted, a serious venture on their part. And yet it started off unpropitiously enough, and in dilatory fashion. For all their haste to be off – the plane had been flown for the first time only 4 days previously by Lancaster – their haste was not matched by speed. The necessity of ensuring a good press send-off, and a suitable attendance of dignitaries, parents, et al, at the start of their flight from Croydon, was in part responsible for the lateness of their take-off – 2.35 p.m. They had barely 3 hours flying time remaining to them in the contracting daylight hours of mid-October. The first

[16] Since 1918 women over thirty had been allowed to vote; in 1919 women had been admitted to the legal profession; and that same year Nancy Astor became the first female Member of Parliament when she was elected for Plymouth Sutton.

leg of their flight, therefore, was a mere 80 miles hop across the Channel, taking little more than an hour. Their arrival was inauspicious too – unable to find the airport north of Abbeville in the failing light, Lancaster put the plane down in a field near the River Somme. Inquiries of locals elicited the location of the airport, and - unable to gain sufficient roll for a take-off with the *Red Rose*'s heavily laden fuel tanks, and Chubbie and their luggage on board - Lancaster took off alone, flying the short distance to Abbeville airport. Chubbie, and the luggage, were escorted there on foot by locals.

If their first day had shown scant progress, then after a night spent at Abbeville, their second was no more impressive. They flew a further 80 miles due south to Paris in the morning, arriving at Le Bourget Aerodrome, where they topped up their fuel and then dined out in Paris - and ate and drank more than was advisable for would-be record breakers. Two days had passed, and the sum total of their progress was 160 miles. On the third day they fared a little better, flying some 400 miles to Marseilles, stopping off at Dijon and Lyon en route, an advantage which they then squandered by passing a leisurely time sight-seeing and socialising with flying enthusiasts and other aviators in the port.

From here they headed a further 250 miles east, along the coast, and across the Ligurian Sea spanning Nice to Pisa, landing at San Giusto aerodrome.[17] From here they flew to Rome, 150

---

[17] Most of the navigation was by Visual Flight Rules (VFR) and

miles south-east, where they spent two days being feted generously by their Italian hosts and took in the ancient splendours of the Colosseum and the ruins of Rome. Leaving Rome, they settled into a determined flight first to Sicily, via a brief stop at Naples, and then on to Malta on Saturday 22nd October, where they were hosted by the British contingent of the RAF station there, before crossing the Mediterranean a further 250 miles south to Tripoli. Here there was further hospitality from the Italian colonial administrators - Chubbie got to wear her evening dress for an afternoon dance, and they had dinner that evening at the British Consulate. From here they made a series of crow hops along the coast of North Africa, via Sirte, where a sandstorm delayed them, and Benghazi; Sallum in Egypt followed, and they arrived at Heliopolis, Cairo, on 29th October.

Here they visited the Great Pyramid at Giza, the fragments of ancient Egypt, the Nile delta and crossed the Suez Canal headed north-east for Baghdad, following in the wake of a helpful RAF Vickers Vernon troop-carrier plane. They flew east of the Dead Sea, marvelling at the sites of the ancient civilisations beneath them; re-fuelling at Ziza on 1st November they crossed the great western desert of Iraq, landing at Rutbah Wells, again to refuel.

---

involved following geographical features and landmarks. All of the flying would be done by daylight.

A generator had burnt out and this, together with a rainstorm and high winds, delayed them for two days. They arrived at RAF Hinaidi, Baghdad, on 8th November, where they spent four more days, before making south-east for Basra on the Persian Gulf. They were a week here hosted by the RAF, and spent their time sightseeing, dealing with magneto problems – and then were quarantined due to a cholera outbreak. They were six weeks into their journey; it should have been over by now. They were a long way off their schedule and didn't care: if they had lost focus, then it was because they were enjoying themselves. Time seemed unimportant to them. According to Chubbie's account, it was here, beneath the stars of an Arabian night in late November, they made love for the first time.

If it had taken this long for their romance to blossom into a physical realm, then it was only because they had not hitherto had the opportunity for it. Their natures, the closeness, their constant proximity to each other, their interdependence, and shared experiences all conspired to make this inevitable. The intimacy of their journey, and the sanitary considerations such flights required of flyers, made such an outcome all but certain.

Their journey progressed, haltingly, as they continued across the Persian Gulf to Karachi. Further delays, both of their own choosing and necessitated by poor weather conditions, meant it was to be 19th December before they reached Calcutta. Their intimacy had grown; they were in love. They didn't heed time. It didn't matter. They had a careless, profligacy of time which only lovers can afford. They were now more than halfway through their odyssey, closer to their destination, yet their journey was, by any standards, a pedestrian one. A series of hops along the east coast of the Bay of Bengal to Rangoon in Burma, where they spent Christmas, followed. A broken piston caused further delay; they spent New Year in Rangoon, attending a fancy-dress dinner given in their honour. They were enjoying the plaudits of success precipitately, and certainly before it was merited - and in doing so were jeopardising the purpose of their flight. As they took off from the racecourse where the plane had been laid up, Chubbie reported by telegram that she had to kill a snake – a deadly krait – which had found its way into the cockpit and showed itself only when they were airborne. She beat it to death with her detachable flying stick, according to her account!

They were greeted enthusiastically on their arrival at Kuala Lumpur, where they delayed further; they played tennis and swam – enjoyed dinner and even played bridge. There is a sense that the purpose of their flight, if not quite forgotten, had been supplanted by a certain indulgence. They indulged a great deal and time passed unnoticed.

They arrived at Singapore on 6th January 1928. By now the reports and wires Chubbie was relaying of their progress were attracting attention in the press; they were also ensuring that the couple were treated as celebrities at each stop. Their trip was at last gaining traction in the media. Chubbie's cables to the press infuriated Bill's parents:

'Mrs Miller raised the necessary finance by sheer pluck and persistence and never lost her sense of humour. The flying people at Croydon, where they made their meagre preparations, treated their scheme as a joke and refused to believe they would get much further than France. But in spite of all they have made good,' wrote CG Grey (1879-1953), editor of *The Aeroplane*.

Such claims did not endear Chubbie to the Lancasters. But the couple were too preoccupied to worry about such things. They enjoyed the media coverage, and their increasing celebrity: their faith in the benefits of their record attempt was well-founded, it seemed. In Singapore they dined at the Raffles Hotel and stayed at the Flying Club. On their departure from Singapore, they circled the port in the *Red Rose*, to acknowledge the well-wishing crowds gathered there. Further south, at Sumatra, they crossed the equator, Chubbie Miller becoming the first woman to accomplish this in a north-south direction in an aeroplane. They were greeted with great enthusiasm and hospitality by the Dutch settlers and inhabitants on Bangka Island, east of Sumatra

– their fame having extended to such small outposts of Western civilisation even. It was intoxicating. They were famous and in love. Money would surely follow. A welcome fit for heroes awaited them at Port Darwin, Australia in a few days' time. They had now reached their penultimate stop before the last leg of their journey across the Timor Sea for Darwin, Australia. They had almost reached their journey's end - victory was within their grasp. But the gods are jealous creatures; jealous of lovers, of happiness, and of those who fly too close to their domain, and they punish hubris.

They were soon to be brought down to earth with a bump – figuratively and literally. As they took off from Bangka at 7 a.m. on 10th January 1928, the engine failed as they climbed to 150-200 feet, and they crash-landed badly, tearing off a wing and flipping the plane onto its back. Both were injured, Lancaster requiring stitches to his lip and Chubbie injuring her nose. The plane was wrecked. When they inspected it the following day at the crash site, it was in poor shape. There was nothing for it but to return to Singapore, which they did next day by steamer. A Dutch cargo boat helpfully transported their damaged plane back to the British colony.

It was a double misfortune as it turned out. Seeing their failure, a far more determined and experienced aviator - a man of steely record-breaking stuff - Australian Bert Hinkler, who was residing in England at this time, decided to take on the record himself. He did. Departing from Croydon on 7th February and flying from dawn till dusk, covering vast distances, flying above adverse conditions when he could, and through them when he could not, Bert Hinkler overtook Lancaster and Miller at Singapore, where he stopped overnight, before heading out on the final leg of his journey. He reached Australia in just 15 days. It was an astonishing achievement. What was even more remarkable – and somewhat embarrassing for Lancaster and Miller – he did it in an Avro Avian III plane: the exact model they had used, but with the forward cockpit sealed off. Of course, he had the advantage of less weight because he flew solo, and was able to carry more fuel and thus increase his range – but nevertheless it was a humiliating turn of events for the lovers.[18] Hinckler met the couple in Singapore where he stayed briefly overnight. They saw him off with a certain wistfulness the following day, 20th February, and would learn two days later, that Hinkler had landed at Port Darwin on 22nd February, to a hero's welcome. The welcome they had anticipated for themselves was his.

It was a bitter blow – the record they had been pursuing for over four months had been snatched from under their noses by a man who flew the same model of plane and did it in just over two weeks. In 15 days, Bill and Chubbie had barely managed to cross the Mediterranean.[19] In many

---

[18] Bert Hinkler (1892-1933), the 'Australian Lone Eagle' was a remarkable man – awarded the Distinguished Service Medal during his WW1 service, he had many strings to his bow: he was a mathematician, an inventor, he designed aviation instruments, and in 1931 he crossed the South Atlantic single handed. His daring was legendary and perhaps because of this character, he crashed and died in the Tuscan mountains, while attempting to fly from London to Australia in less than 8 days.

ways they had only themselves to blame. Lancaster was publicly supportive of Hinkler – in truth, he could hardly complain at this usurpation - but their thunder had been well and truly stolen. Bill was generous by nature, and he defended Hinkler's right to try for the record. Jessie was somewhat resentful of Hinkler.[20] She later claimed the reason for the accident was Bill's fault: he had omitted to open the fuel valve before take-off, with the result that the engine, starved of fuel, quickly failed.

Grounded in Singapore for two months while the *Red Rose* was fixed – a generous rubber broker paid for the repairs and RAF engineers did much of the structural repair work to the spruce truss frame, and also extensive work to the broken wing – they must have rued the time lost. They had lost it in their overnight stays, their dinners, their celebrations in Rome, an afternoon tea-dance in Tripoli, their sight-seeing in Egypt – none of this time could now be recovered. Their sense of adventure, their love for each other, their thrilling to the adulation that gathered about them as their odyssey progressed, had seduced them from their purpose. The first flush of love, and the intoxicating effects of celebrity, had proved a heady mix. It gave them a soft landing from their disappointment, at least. On 12th March they took off from Singapore, thoughtful, muted; the record,

---

[19] It is interesting to note that six years later in 1934, CWA Scott and Tony Campbell Black were to cover the journey from England to Port Darwin in just 2 days 4 hours and 33 minutes – a record which stands today for a piston engined aeroplane.

[20] 'Hinkler butted in before us – which, of course, he could not have done but for the crash,' she told the Australian press.

their chief purpose, was now gone. Again Sumatra, again they crossed the equator, arriving at Timor on 17th March – their final stop-off – but now with no reason for urgency. They had neglected it woefully when it was needed and now had no need of it. They crossed the Timor Sea, some 400 miles distance, a prodigious journey in tough conditions. At some point in their journey the engine faltered; the plane was barely staying in the air: all seemed lost. The uncertain crosswind rocked the plane and they thought it was the end: Lancaster scribbled a note and passed this to Chubbie:

'I don't think we're going to make it...Still, we did our best.'

But somehow they got through, and some 8 hours later they landed at a deserted, rainswept airfield in Darwin on 19th March 1928. Their journey was done.

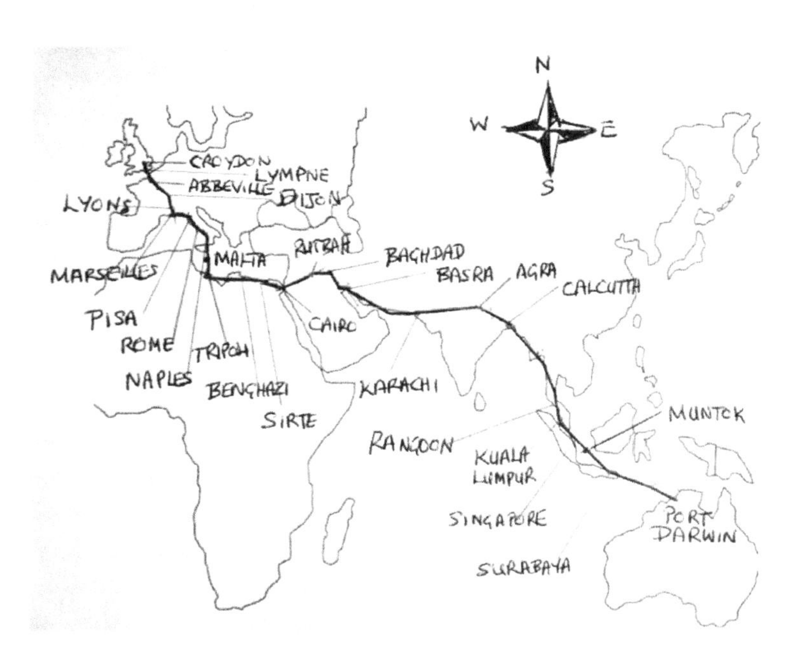

The flight of Lancaster and Miller from Croydon to Port Darwin, 1927-28.

The *Red Rose* in flight... (*Miami Herald*)

Bill and Chubbie refueling en route. It was necessary to strain the fuel through chamois leather to ensure no impurities reached the carburettor.

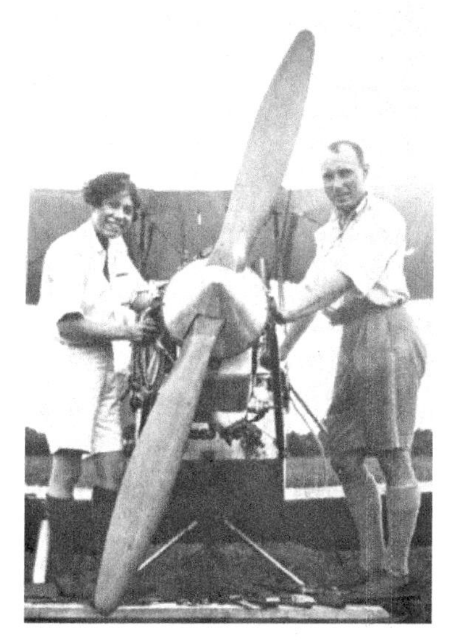

Bill and Chubbie pose with the *Red Rose.* (*Daily Mirror*)

Partners and lovers: a conspiratorial moment on arrival in Australia.

5. A Hard Landing

It was a crestfallen couple who touched down at Port Darwin in a terrible rainstorm. No crowds were there to greet or cheer their journey's end. It was a difficult landing due to the heavy surface water accumulated at the aerodrome. The crowds which had greeted Bert Hinkler's arrival a month earlier were absent – deterred by the rain and the fact that this had been done before. Chubbie was returned to her homeland, but it was a bitter-sweet return. Their adventure had been incomparable, the footprint of their experience unrivalled; an illicit romance, a secret shared by them alone, a conspiracy of two; they had enjoyed the highs of celebrity and the lows of failure, of defeat. The grinding poverty of Calcutta slums, the bodies of the dead floating in the Ganges River below, the vast desert wastes East of Eden - and the majestic panoply of half the globe; of civilisations and their histories, which had risen and fallen, and crumbled to dust - all glided beneath their feet. They had fulfilled their dream. And yet all that now remained to them was the comparatively light-weight achievements of Chubbie's north-south first equator crossing in a light aeroplane, and her becoming the first woman to fly from Britain to Australia in a light aeroplane. *The Evening Telegraph* report of 19th March 1928 said it all:

'Another Croydon-Australia flight has been accomplished, Captain Lancaster and Mrs Keith Miller having arrived at Port Darwin. The flight is the longest yet undertaken by a woman.

'In contrast to Bert Hinkler, who did the journey in 15 ½ days, Captain Lancaster and Mrs Miller have taken over five months.' (*Evening Telegraph*,19th March 1928)

The unintended bathos in the report is unmistakable.

CG Grey in *The Aeroplane*, made the best he could of it, declaring it was 'the longest flight ever made by a woman.' And from these qualified pickings, it was indeed Chubbie, who could take most comfort. From this moment their relationship would change – they would not realize it yet, but the dynamics had altered: Chubbie was the record-beater and celebrity, an Australian in her own land; the local girl who had made good. Lancaster was her pilot, her facilitator; but the journey of triumph and disaster was now over. The intimacy that had been theirs, cloying and exclusive for six months, was lessened. It would not regain the heights it had known.

Chubbie was re-united with her husband Keith in Australia; he appears in many of the press photographs of events which Lancaster and she attended - the dinners given in her honour or to which she was invited. He knew nothing of his wife's affair with Lancaster and was keen to return to normal married life, but any attempt made seems to have been short-lived: Chubbie, at least, had moved on.

Although Lancaster and Miller's record attempt had failed and they were beaten to the punch by another pilot in an identical plane, upon their arrival in Australia they would be much feted once the press had rallied to their cause. The flight, however much devalued since Hinckler's triumph, was still remarkable. Being Australian and a woman, Chubbie was greeted with especial enthusiasm: she became famous – even though it was to be a further 14 months before she actually gained her pilot's licence! She was hooked, more on fame and flying than on Bill Lancaster, and she quickly eclipsed him. Not that he resented it – or minded at all: he was in love. He was always supportive. His father, Edward, sailed for Australia in anticipation of their arrival, and met his son there – he also had a serious purpose: he urged upon Bill the necessity of breaking with Chubbie and returning to his wife and children. But Lancaster could not.

Chubbie was able to make good money in Australia by undertaking speaking engagements and a paid tour of Australia in the weeks that followed; and Lancaster had a series of ad hoc flying jobs which brought in some cash. But it was all too short-lived - the opportunities, and the money, dried up. Charles Kingsford-Smith's arrival with his Fokker F. VII *Southern Cross* monoplane on 8th June 1928, having crossed the Pacific Ocean from the US, drew a vast crowd of people to greet him at Sydney. Bill and Chubbie were still highly regarded for their achievement, but it was distinctly yesterday's news. And of course, it was dwarfed by the enormity of Kingsford-Smith's Pacific crossing achievement. Lancaster sold the *Red Rose*, Avian III in Sydney – there would be no return journey, and they needed the money. A film project in Hollywood was suggested to them by

Harry Lyon (1885-1963), Charles Kingsford-Smith's navigator. He and the Southern Cross's crew had received a $75,000 offer to help make a Hollywood aviation film. Kingsford-Smith was not interested. He was intent on staying down-under for a while. Lyon and Kingsford-Smith's radio operator, James Warner (1891-1970), extended the tentative offer to Lancaster and Miller – and they jumped at the chance. In a state of high enthusiasm at this prospect, the four friends sailed from Sydney Harbour to the US on board the *Sonoma*.

On arrival in San Francisco on 23rd June, they were greeted enthusiastically, on account of Lyon and Warner's achievement as part of the Pacific crossing crew led by Kingsford-Smith. Lancaster and Miller basked in the slipstream of their success. They attended dinners, social and celebratory events, drank far too much, in spite of Prohibition laws - but no film project materialized. There was a proposal for a transatlantic flight of some kind, but nothing came of it. Other proposals came and went the same way.

One project did materialize: Lancaster, Harry Lyon and the publisher George Palmer Putnam (a publisher and promoter who was to marry Amelia Earhart in 1931) left Long Island at 1.30 p.m. 27th October 1928, to fly to Bermuda. It was only 800 miles away, but the challenge for a pilot lay in finding the island, which might easily be missed in the Atlantic. It had never been done before – nor was it on this occasion. Engine trouble forced them down soon after take-off in a muddy field in New Jersey. Further problems led to the project being cancelled.

Lancaster and Chubbie stayed at Lyons' parents' house in Maine and spent time in New York. It was the roaring twenties. A great deal of drinking was done, and a hedonistic lifestyle was de rigeur. The prohibition of liquor had spawned a new tax-free industry, and raised such an illicit lifestyle to an artform. *Let's Misbehave*, wrote Cole Porter. It was an anthem for youth, for an emancipation from the strictures of hardship and war for a certain stratum of society who were rich enough to enjoy it. Scott Fitzgerald found both sides of paradise here and defined the Jazz Age. Proposals, ideas and dreams of one sort and another ran through the couple's fingers, and so did money.

Meanwhile, Lancaster's wife, Kiki, who had been living at Bournemouth on the south coast of England and working for her beloved anti-vivisection cause, had returned to London. She was now living in Fulham, her mother looking after Pat and Nina while she worked. Lancaster sent Kiki money from time to time, but it didn't last – the employment he and Chubbie found first in Australia, and then in the States, was erratic and unpredictable at best: Kiki had to rely on her own resources and those of her family - and Bill's parents helped out too. She had been in receipt of a widow's war pension following her first husband's death in World War 1, but she forfeited this when she married Bill. Her predicament was unenviable – she had lost one husband and faced hardship, and her second showed not the least inclination for returning to England and supporting his family. She was keenly aware of this.

Throughout 1928 Kiki was begging Lancaster for money to support his children. He did his best and Chubbie helped, but it was an unreliable source of income. Kiki visited him in December that year, hoping to persuade him to return to his family. It was reported that she had brought out a compass for Bill, but it was held up at US Customs because it contained four ounces of alcohol! The Customs officials wished to drain the alcohol from the instrument, but Lancaster managed to persuade them not to, as it would upset the calibration of the compass. Alcohol in the US was a serious business for both proponents and opponents of Prohibition – the same day it was reported in *The Graphic* that Mrs Maude Wilson of Kansas City had attacked a 'so called soft drinks bar with an axe because it had sold liquor to her husband.' It was one of many 'speakeasies' – a 'speakeasy', explained the *Graphic*, 'is a disguised restaurant or bar where, if you ask the attendant nicely, he will give you a real drink.'

Kiki spent Christmas of 1928 with Bill in New York, while Chubbie was in Los Angeles. Lancaster's interest in his children was seemingly insufficient to draw him back to Britain: his obsession with Chubbie was running deep and she occupied all his thoughts. Kiki tried her best to indulge her husband's lifestyle – flying from New York to Miami with Lady Mary Heath (1896-1939) in her Gypsy Moth in January 1929. 150 planes attended the Miami fly-in for the All-American Races there. It was a major event in the aviation calendar. It was also good to escape the biting chill of the New York winter (there were seven snowfalls there that January) and enjoy the Florida sunshine, with its 23C temperatures. But after a flurry of indulgence and excitement, Kiki sailed for England alone, in quiet reflection, returning to her job and caring for their two girls.

Lancaster got a job as a test pilot for Avro Avian in the US, promoting the merits of the Cirrus engine, and embarked on a tour of the West Indies for this purpose. He was planning a flight from Bermuda to New York as part of this – a distance of 675 miles - to top off the tour. But he crashed while taking off from Port of Spain, Trinidad, for a flight to Maracay, Venezuela on 7th April 1929, and spent ten days in hospital at Trinidad as a result. It was the worst possible sort of publicity for American Cirrus engines Inc, and this, added to his prolonged incapacitation, lost him his job with them.

Chubbie got her flying licence in New York in May 1929 – she had done a great many more hours at the stick than most pilots on securing her pilot's wings and she had a vast knowledge of aircraft mechanics and maintenance which she had picked up from Bill and the trip to Australia. Now there were opportunities opening to her. She proved to be a rather good pilot and took part in the *Women's Air Derby* from Santa Monica, California, to Cleveland, Ohio, that year - the *Powder Puff Derby*, as it was dubbed. It was to be the high point of her career in the US. She flew a Fleet biplane along with 19 other female flyers, coming third in her class and winning $325 (approx. $5,000 in 2022). It was an excellent outcome: she had proved herself as an aviator. She took part in other events at the *National Air Races*, and she won a further $500 (approx.

$8,000 in 2022). This was a triumph. Her star was in the ascendant, and she was making some money at last. She placed in two other races, had established herself as a solo pilot and was receiving offers to pilot aircraft, make paid appearances, and to enter invitation-only contests.

Things had moved on for women since 1927; it was no longer enough for them to travel to distant places, cross oceans and traverse deserts as passengers in the pursuit of fame, they had to pilot the aeroplane. Amelia Earhart, Ruth Elder, and many others had graduated from passengers to pilots in the late 1920s, and were keen to demonstrate their prowess. It was the age of the female aviator; it was in perfect sync with the spirit of the age, of emancipation; of all things women. The suffragettes may have blazed a sober trail in the Edwardian period, opening up the dusty male corridors of power to women, but it was the hedonistic lifestyle of the roaring twenties that set them free. Nothing epitomized such freedom as the aviatrix: fearless, dressed like a man, taking the same risks, extending the frontiers of human experience, which had previously been the exclusive province of men. Chubbie was in great demand, was earning good money and her celebrity seemed assured. Lancaster, who was still suffering the effects of his crash in Venezuela supported her; he acted as her manager; but his own career seemed to have stalled. He'd had one too many accidents. He was very much Chubbie's passenger now.

Both obtained commercial pilot's licenses in Canada with a view to obtaining employment with the Stork Corporation, demonstrating planes as part of a sales drive. At the medical examination for the licence, apparently, Chubbie was drunk after a liquid lunch, but passed her medical in spite of her condition. It was a sign of things to come.

Chubbie and Bill with Keith Miller in Australia. Keith was quite oblivious to the affair of the pair.

Arrival at San Francisco with high hopes for the future. (*Brooklyn News*)

Kiki in New York with the alcohol filled compass, that transgressed US Prohibition laws. She hoped to persuade Bill to return to his family. She was to be disappointed. (*Daily Graphic*)

Chubbie gets her wings... (*Daily News*)

Chubbie was in demand. She turned out to be a rather better pilot than Lancaster.

Chubbie goes solo...

6. The 1929 Wall Street Crash

America was a land of innovation and wealth in the 1920s, communications were its lifeblood. The motor car had transformed the lives of people across the vast country, becoming a symbol of freedom and individualism; the aeroplane was extending this; and radio and telephone had improved communications in a more immediate way: the drive for improved communications in the US was a drive for power and wealth, because the size of the US territory required it, and prosperity demanded it. The US financial system which underpinned its great success depended on these communications – and they were to play a major part in its collapse at the end of the decade. It was the greatest financial collapse the world has known: the Wall Street crash of 1929.

Before the burst, of course, there had to be a bubble: through the 1920s, the financial system expanded – fortunes were made, there was money for everything: for speculation, investment trusts abounded: America was brimming with confidence. In moving pictures, a new artform was created; in literature the Fitzgeralds and Hemingways brought a new confidence to the genre of the American novel. New dances, new music, new art forms, and a new journalism, were all driven by unbridled confidence. The Dow Jones Industrial Average, weathervane of the US economy, rose from 63.9 in the last week of August 1929 to a staggering 381.2

just a week later. The bubble was dangerously inflated, but only hindsight would know it. On Monday 28th October 1929 the Dow Jones Index fell suddenly by 12.8%. Investors began to sell; it created a sense of brooding anxiety in the market, which grew exponentially. The telephone and telegraph systems, which were the lifeline of the stock market, could not cope as people sought to sell: panic set in. The following day, Tuesday 29th October 1929, the stock market collapsed.

As it did so, all confidence in the system failed: the Wall Street Crash signalled a crisis of confidence in the system of money and trade, which supports modern industrial society. It infected every aspect of the financial system: from the prices of basic commodities like crops to the incomes by which the members of society are remunerated and governed. Growth and development, construction and trade all ground to a halt. The Great Depression followed: it affected most people and most of the world.

Bill Lancaster and Chubbie Miller fell on hard times. Various ventures fell through, a string of opportunities and attempts to carve out careers for themselves as charter pilots also came to nothing. A litany of failures dogged them. Jessie had proved to be a better pilot than Lancaster – he supported her, there was no envy in his make-up – although he was increasingly the junior partner in their relationship. But as the Depression bit deep, Chubbie's star waned too – the 20s barnstormers who had plied their trade touring the States with demonstrations of wing-walking, performing air acrobatics and offering rides in their planes for money, had had their day – there was a glut of flyers, ex-wartime pilots, or chancers, without employment, and there was little enthusiasm amongst hard-pressed businessmen to sink money into funding flying ventures. People were tightening their belts. It was a hard time for Lancaster and Miller too, and it got harder. Chubbie drowned her sorrows at being grounded and being without any reliable earnings, without the celebrity status she craved: she drank too much; it was a weakness; one she indulged when the highs had gone, the highs she lived for. And her relationship with Bill was going nowhere. She knew that now. He showed little inclination for divorcing his wife and he displayed a certain infuriating contentment with the status quo. When Lancaster was injured after the crash in Venezuela, convalescing first in Trinidad and then back in hospital in the US, Chubbie was elsewhere; she had commitments, certainly, but her life was moving on a different plane to that of Bill's. They were still close, but it was different. It was for her, anyway – for his part, Bill still possessed a certain dogged devotion to Chubbie which was not fully reciprocated.

By the summer of 1930 the couple were struggling to make ends meet or to find gainful employment. It was a frustrating business for them: opportunities presented themselves vaguely and failed to amount to anything: hopes were raised and then slowly dissipated. There were some triumphs amidst the gloom: Chubbie broke the US coast-to-coast record, beating Laura Ingalls' record – it was a sudden lift amidst the bleakness of the Depression – and it led to newspaper articles, for which she was paid decent money. Articles became the only means a flyer could make money.

It was a highly competitive business. Then in late November Chubbie flew an Alexander Bullet monoplane to Havana, Cuba and on the return journey, on 28th November, she went missing.

She was last seen flying low 25 minutes out from Havana. Her plane was known to have 6 hours fuel on board, according to the *Liverpool Echo*. Further:

'A premonition of death which she thrust aside for fear of being a coward haunted Mrs Miller before she took off from Cuba. "I don't know why it is, but something tells me I'm going down," she said just before she took off. Mrs Miller called her machine an unworthy crate, one which anybody but herself would refuse to fly.' (*Edinburgh Evening News*, 29th November 1930)

Ferries and shipping in the Gulf of Florida were alerted; four aeroplanes were sent in search of her, but nothing was discovered. On 30th November it was reported:

'The Havana air officials have abandoned virtually all hope for the safety of the woman flyer...who is thought to have fallen into the Gulf of Florida.' (*The People*, 30th November 1930)

Bill Lancaster didn't give up. He drummed up support in the press and mustered efforts to search for her. Then on 2nd December, when all hope seemed to be lost, Chubbie turned up in the Bahamas, safe and sound. Her mother received a telegram from Nassau:

'I am at Nassau. Safe. Chubbie.'

Apparently, she had been blown off course by strong cross winds soon after leaving Havana. She was aiming for the Florida Keys just 90 miles to the north, which can be seen on a clear day at 5,000 feet, but was so off-course and disoriented that she landed in the Bahamas, some 270 miles away to the west! She later wrote that she despaired during the flight and attempted suicide by diving the plane from 6,000 feet, but at 1,000 feet pulled out of the dive, her sanity returning. She landed at Andros Island in the Bahamas and received help from the Australian swimmer, Percy Cavill (1875-1940), who lived there. She had been believed to be lost for four days, during which Lancaster had made a great fuss, whipping up newspaper interest and pressing the US Navy to search for her. It drew much press attention, largely due to Bill's efforts – although some newspapers believed it to be a stunt. Chubbie claimed she had been unable to calculate her direction as her compass had failed... Her reappearance in Nassau with a plane which had sustained minimal damage fuelled further suspicions. It wasn't helped by the fact that the couple were asking $5,000 ($80,000 in 2022) for their story... Those who had believed it to be a publicity stunt nodded cynically. But it did draw sufficient interest to earn her $1,500 ($25,000 in 2022) for her story. It was a tidy sum. Other mishaps suffered by aviators were becoming widely regarded as ploys to drum up interest at this time.[21] There was an element of showmanship in

---

[21] Charles Kingsford-Smith was accused of this in 1929 when he and his crew made an emergency landing in a remote part of western Australia. A huge search was undertaken for the famous missing pilot, during the course of which two of the searchers died after a crash-landing in the Tanami Desert. The incident became known as the 'Coffee Royal Affair,' and accusations were made that it was

the business, of course, and as the competition between pilots for fewer opportunities became stiffer, pilots became more enterprising. The accusations of Chubbie Miller having faked her disappearance as a publicity stunt stung – she and Lancaster were furious in their denials, and at least one other pilot came to Chubbie's defence. Whether it was true or not, she earned $1,500 from her story. It kept the wolf from the door a little longer.

It was becoming increasingly obvious, though, that some form of reliable employment was required. Lancaster had little in the way of education and seems to have been constitutionally incapable of holding down any position for long. He had simply never shown any aptitude for it from his earliest days in Australia. His entire life thus far was characterised by a series of short-lived positions, none of which he had excelled in, or even shown any special competence for. He was not short of contacts and as a freemason was able to leverage many favours in the New World as in the old – but his benefactors were becoming fewer, and most of them were struggling financially in the Depression themselves. One benefit he received was a Lincoln car, given to him by way of a severance handshake by Jack Maddox, the President of Transcontinental Western Airways, for whom Lancaster had worked as an assistant for a short time in Los Angeles.

But the couple had reached a dead end, both as a couple and as a flying partnership. Chubbie was

---

merely a stunt by Kingsford-Smith to drum up publicity for himself. An inquiry was held which exonerated him, but his reputation was nevertheless tarnished in Australia afterwards.

divorced from Keith Miller in June 1931, but Bill's marriage to Kiki, such as it was, survived in name at least. This didn't seem to trouble him to any great extent – and in truth, Chubbie had already fallen out of love with Bill, although blithe as ever, he didn't seem to know it.

An aviator friend of Lancaster's, William Gentry Shelton,[22] suggested a scheme for a charter business in late 1931. It was a straw Lancaster was willing to grasp at. Shelton was an unreliable companion; but he had a Lockheed monoplane - it was in poor condition, apparently; Shelton also drank a great deal, and little came of his numerous ventures. He fitted in with the company of dreamers and wastrels who inhabited their world. It was a world Chubbie Miller was growing tired of.

On 1st January 1932 Chubbie rented 2321 SW, 21st Terrace, Coral Gables, Florida, in time for the All-American Air Races that year at Miami. They drove down from Los Angeles in their Lincoln car with their two dogs Bozo, a British Bulldog, and a Fox terrier called Mickey. The place in Coral Gables was a two-storey house in an acre of grounds, described as a bungalow, but more like a villa, with bougainvillea and trailing jasmine to its exterior, and a small grapefruit grove to the rear. There was a lawn, too, which surrounded the bungalow. The rent was $45 pcm ($700 in 2022). The strictures of prohibition were less strenuously enforced here. The Caribbean, as ever, proving an excellent route for smuggling liquor into the US,

---

[22] William Gentry Shelton (1895-1948) was a well-known pilot, whose great claim to fame was staying aloft for 5 days with a co-pilot.

there seemed to be a great deal of it here. The high points of law enforcement over liquor had, to an extent, passed; just two years earlier, in March 1929, Canada had sent a Note of Protest to President Hoover over the sinking of the schooner *I'm Alone*, 200 miles off the Louisiana coast. Subsequently, a suspected liquor steamer from Norway which claimed to be carrying bananas, was fired on and boarded by US Customs in Chesapeake Bay. It was found to be carrying...bananas. President Hoover issued a stern rebuke to prohibition agents concerning the violation of 'constitutional rights and international courtesies.' Since then, there had been acknowledged limits to the enforcement of Prohibition in many parts of the States.

The couple were delighted with the bungalow at Coral Gables; it was to become a squalid nirvana in the distinctive, sprawling 'Mediterranean Revival' style metropolis. They took in a lodger, a Major Jack C French, to help pay the bills, but he proved to be an ill-choice of companion too. Chubbie had some acquaintance with Jack French, and he had acted in a business capacity for her previously, but they squabbled. He objected to her temper, which he told Bill was discourteous. He was himself a drinker and impecunious, like so many of their acquaintances - another high liver without any highs. He probably wasn't a major, either, Lancaster concluded. There were three sleeping rooms in the bungalow. French occupied a ground floor bedroom which had its own bathroom facilities; Lancaster slept in an upstairs room called the 'sleeping porch' and Chubbie's room was across the landing, some 18 feet away. They were delighted to have what they hoped would provide a long-term base for them and a refuge from the harsh realities of winter and the Depression:

'Chubbie seems so happy over the house. She is her old sweet self again.' Lancaster recorded in his diary on Sunday 3rd January 1932.

A few days later, on 7th January, the annual Air Races kicked off in Miami – a number of people stayed with them during this event. The weather was fine, wall to wall sunshine, and temperatures were routinely in the mid-20s. There was a great deal of drinking ('They are here for a good time and get very tight. So too, does Chubbie,' Lancaster noted) and on one occasion Chubbie became very drunk. Lancaster was sober apparently, and yet for some reason not explained, he allowed Chubbie to drive some friends to the Columbus Hotel, while he himself was in the back seat. She had an accident driving the car, running into a Buick driven by a man named Leonard Brown; they quickly switched seats, Lancaster, with misplaced gallantry, taking the rap: he spent an hour in the city jail, received a $50 fine and had his driver's licence suspended for drunk driving. He recorded in his diary of this incident:

'American justice is all wet. As a matter of fact, I had not had a drink... I think this will be a lesson to Chubbie not to drive when she has been drinking.' It was good advice.

They were still lovers, perfunctory on her part. Lancaster was utterly devoted to Chubbie, but his constant schemes and their failure irritated her. She resented his inability to make a living – he was a drag on her. Her feelings for him had cooled, and her irritation with him showed. They were bound together chiefly by habit and a bond of mutual failure.

Money and pervasive pessimism were their chief preoccupations in January 1932:

'Chubbie raises hell about the lack of cash...' Lancaster wrote on 13th January. Her mood was black:

14th January: 'Chubbie raises hell about the agreement with the landlady,' and on 15th January, without cash or food,

'Jack French and I butcher a couple of white rabbits.'

Presumably, as white rabbits were then bred exclusively from albino rabbits, these were someone's pets...

There was swimming in the sea, though, and occasional dinner invitations at which a bottle of gin materialized. They even went to see *Frankenstein*[23] on 18th January, although they were disappointed in it.

Conscious of the need to make some money, both Chubbie and Bill tried their hand at writing some of their flying stories up and submitting them to magazines.

Then Gentry Shelton, who had not turned up as expected with a plane for the Miami Air Races earlier that month, came up with a new scheme in New York: another charter plane scheme.

Lancaster hoped to hitch a lift on a flight to New York to explore Gentry Shelton's scheme further,

---

[23] Frankenstein (1931) starred Colin Clive, Mae Clarke and Boris Karloff. In 1991 it was selected by the Library of Congress for preservation in the National Film Registry as being a work 'culturally, historically or aesthetically significant.'

but had no luck, and in the end he caught a slow bus from Jacksonville, which took him two long days. He had to pawn his watch for his fare. Gentry Shelton had now purchased a Curtiss Robin, high-wing monoplane with a 185 hp Curtiss Challenger radial engine powering it. More promises came from Shelton in New York, but these came to nothing: when he informed Chubbie of this, she was angry, petulant. She blamed Lancaster for his failures. He had exhausted his own funds and hers too, apparently. Things looked dire indeed. He borrowed a few dollars and won some money playing bridge at his club, the Army and Navy, at 30 East 44th Street. He couldn't pay his membership dues here, but the management didn't seem to mind – most of the members were broke these days, they told him. Lancaster seemed complacent; he had the gift of complacency in the direst of circumstances – as long as he had Chubbie he didn't care. But she did. Resentment of Lancaster was growing with Chubbie. He didn't see it – he simply thought of it as one of her many black moods. He had managed to send her $10 and she used this to renew her drinking. On 30th January Lancaster phoned her and recorded in his diary, 'She sounded as though she had one or two cocktails.' Her drinking was a constant worry to him.

Then a ray of hope appeared with the Florida sunshine in early February 1932: their friend and helpful attorney, Ernest Huston, deposited $200 in Lancaster's account. This was while he was still in New York, exhausting the last of Chubbie's money exploring the vain hope of the Shelton charter business scheme. When he returned to Miami

Airport, feeling comparatively – and gratifyingly - flush, he was met by a Captain Mark Tancrel (1888-1967) and a Mrs Russell: he now learned that they wished to enter into some form of charter business with him and Chubbie under the auspices of a company called Latin American Airways (LAA), of which Tancrel was president. The venture was vague, and perhaps because he had been disappointed too often, he was suspicious of those involved. The woman's husband Jack F Russell, in particular, struck Lancaster as untrustworthy. However, he was quite broke apart from the $200 they had forwarded to him, and with no other prospects on the horizon, he and Chubbie were willing to suspend their doubts for the moment. They signed a contract in attorney Huston's office the next day, which divided the profits of their proposed venture six ways, between the Russells, Tancrel, Shelton, and Chubbie and Lancaster themselves. Huston was to be Treasurer and Secretary.

Chubbie had some other news for Bill on his return: a New York publisher she had contacted expressed interest in a book on her flying experiences – she would need to write it, of course. It opened up a new possibility for her to make some money. Other female flyers had taken this route, earning good money in these lean days. During Lancaster's absence in New York Chubbie had met a professor of Journalism at Miami University, which is situated in Coral Gables, called Ida Clyde Clarke. Chubbie spoke to her of her need to find someone who could help her write her book – Ida Clarke suggested her son Haden for this... Chubbie met Haden and liked him – he was tall, handsome, intelligent and charming. When Lancaster returned from New York after his failed new venture and met Haden Clarke, he shared her enthusiasm for the affable young man. Clarke's curriculum vitae was excellent, too – he was 31 years old, had a degree from Columbia University, and had held various newspaper jobs - or so he said. The Depression had deprived him of paid work also. It was a familiar story at that time, one Chubbie and Bill could readily sympathise with. Haden told them he had a wife in California, but they were in the process of getting a divorce. Chubbie couldn't pay Clarke for the writing job, she told him, but they struck a 50:50 deal in which they would share the proceeds of its sales between them. She and Lancaster immediately invited Clarke to come and live with them at the Coral Gables bungalow, so that they could work on the book. In fact, Haden Clarke was 26 years old, born in Tennessee, his education did not extend to a degree from Columbia, nor was his employment record as extensive as he claimed. And although he had some talent as a writer, he was incorrigibly lazy.

He moved in the next day, along with his typewriter and a kitbag of a few possessions. He fitted in with their lifestyle rather too well: he and Chubbie drank most of the time; Clarke went fishing and flying with Lancaster. But no writing was done. He needed the muse to visit, he said. She didn't – but Gentry Shelton did, and Haden had found himself a new drinking partner: Haden, Shelton and Chubbie seem to have been seldom sober throughout that February 1932.

'Chub and Haden got cock-eyed, but not unpleasantly so,' Lancaster's diary tells us on 11th February – just one day after Haden had moved in. Lancaster alone did not share their weakness for drink. Its effect on him was different: while they became hyper, careless, uninhibited; he became morose, silent. He preferred to fish or fly when he wasn't in attendance on Chubbie. February came and went in this way. Visitors came and went; they had parties – slovenly drinking parties with plenty of illegal hooch, which they laughingly referred to as 'G and Ts.' They had bridge parties, too. Haden liked to play bridge – he was regarded as an 'expert' at it, and he often won money - and he was seldom sober; nor was Chubbie. Lancaster was concerned – Chubbie became highly unpredictable and erratic in temper when she drank; she lost all self-control. Major Jack French moved out; he was a dead weight and incapable of contributing to the bungalow's meagre finances in any way. On the plus side, there was no doubting Chubbie's mood had lifted since Haden's arrival. On 12th February 'Chubbie is running the house and doing most of the work', Lancaster writes. She is nesting. 14th February was Lancaster's 34th birthday and the three friends went to Miami Beach to do some fishing. Lancaster fished, but 'Chubbie and Haden drank instead,' we learn.

Money was still their greatest concern. The rent was due, and Haden pressed his considerable charm into service with the irate landlady. She was pacified for now. On 21st February Lancaster's diary informs us,

'Haden Clarke and I got 2 ducks and 2 rabbits.'

By the first week in March, a great deal of alcohol had been consumed; and many chickens, ducks and rabbits had gone missing from the neighbourhood, but no writing had been done. The electricity had been cut off; so had the phone, due to non-payment of bills; relations with their landlady had deteriorated – they narrowly avoided eviction by making a last-minute payment for rent, which secured the property through until June. They had no money for food and no means of cooking it – Lancaster and Haden Clarke continued to filch chickens, ducks and rabbits from their neighbours, and they cooked these over an open fire in the backyard. Surprisingly, Chubbie was uncharacteristically chipper:

'Chubbie quite fit, helping out no end. A bit jumpy sometimes...' he says on 27th February. And on 28th February, in spite of all the hardships, 'Chubbie quite sportful about everything... quite perfect.' Perhaps it should have told him something. Her mood which could turn quickly, was, in spite of all the difficulties, happy. Haden Clarke proved to be excellent company, and his girlfriend Peggy Brown was often staying at the bungalow – to which she brought much-prized flasks of hooch.

It was at this time, on 3rd March, that Russell's partner in the LAA venture, Mark Tancrel, arrived at Coral Gables, and asked Lancaster to go to Mexico to explore the LAA business – whatever that might be – with him. Lancaster and Shelton agreed to accompany him out west: they would fly there in the Robin aircraft which Lancaster had been working on to improve its airworthiness.

Concerned at the extent of Chubbie's drinking, the evening before he left, Lancaster confided in Haden Clarke of his love for Chubbie; he told him he had loved her for five years, and also intimated the trust and reliance he placed in Clarke. Although we have only Lancaster and Chubbie's account for much of what occurred in this period, there is no doubt that Lancaster did discuss the matter with Haden Clarke, because not only his own version and diary entries refer to it, but Haden's subsequent correspondence confirms it. In confiding such things to Haden Clarke, he was undoubtedly trying to set Clarke himself on the right path; and was genuinely concerned that the two would simply spend their time in his absence, drinking, with the many risks, legal and personal, that entailed. He may have feared a romantic liaison between them too – perhaps had observed something in embryo, something in Clarke's demeanour, a subtle alteration in Chubbie - but if he did it was subconscious, and his principal concern was for their sobriety. He may also have had other concerns about Clarke: he knew him to bring women back to the sleeping porch and spend the night with them – this was usually, but not exclusively, Peggy Brown (1909-1980). In any case, Clarke agreed to curb his drinking and that of Chubbie, and settle to writing her autobiography with her.

He gave Lancaster his word as a gentleman.

7. The Latin American Airways

Lancaster left Miami with Shelton and Tancrel for Nogales, Arizona on 6th March. Before he left, the attorney Ernest Huston (1895-1970) gave him his own .38 colt revolver to allay any risks he might encounter in what seemed to be a dubious venture. The three men stayed at St Petersburg for a night, and from here Lancaster sent Chubbie a cable begging her to stay sober, and to settle to writing her autobiography with Haden. Frustratingly, he could not speak to her by phone as the connection had not yet been restored following late payment of the bill. Although he had implored Haden Clarke to curb both his own and Chubbie's drinking, he knew Chubbie well enough to fear her abstinence would be short-lived – so he was writing now to reinforce this. Her first letter to him confirmed these fears:

'We have no booze in the house and I can't afford to buy any,' she wrote glumly.

'I adore her and want to see her happy,' Lancaster wrote in his diary. 'If only she did not drink while I was away I would feel ok. Gent [Shelton] says she has two personalities, Chubbie drunk and Chubbie sober. I love both personalities.' (*Miami Herald*, 5th August 1932)

It was an astute observation by Shelton.

The three men flew from St Petersburg at 6 a.m. next day, 7th March. They flew for a gruelling 13 ½ hours, Shelton and Lancaster piloting the plane in turn, and arriving in Beaumont, Texas by nightfall.

Lancaster sent Chubbie a $1 bill – it was all he had:

'Don't laugh at the dollar, but it will put five gallons of gas in the Lincoln,' he wrote. (*Miami Daily News*, 5th August 1932)

Chubbie wasn't laughing.

Problems with Shelton's Robin Challenger plane, which Lancaster was dissatisfied with, delayed them, and so did bad weather – snow in Texas, even, hampered their progress. On 8th March, he wrote to Chubbie:

'Don't leave my letters lying around, they are letters to you only.' He was referring to Latin American Airways (LAA) business here, but it may also indicate a measure of discomfort that his endearments and expressions of love to her might not be safeguarded. There may have been a niggle in his mind that Chubbie was sharing his intimacies with Haden. She was terribly indiscreet, especially when drunk.

Delayed further at Beaumont when a tail wind tipped the Robin Challenger plane up on its nose and broke its propellor, he wired Chubbie asking her to send him a spare prop she had. He also told her –

'As soon as I can beg, borrow or steal some cash will send it to you. In the meantime you will have put in some really constructive work on the book!' (*Miami Daily News*, 5th August 1932)

It provided a promise and another gentle reminder about drink.

While they were stranded in Beaumont, still concerned about Chubbie and her drinking, he wrote to Haden Clarke:

'Haden, old man, the knowledge that you are "standing by" the fort and looking after Chubbie, has meant more to me than you will ever know...' (14th March)

He was leaning on Haden's conscience, reminding him of his promise – and he had good reason to be concerned, not only about drink...

He wrote to Chubbie at this time:

'I love you and long for you, my sweetheart. I lay in bed at night and pray you are not suffering too great a hardship. I want to have you in my arms again, Chub. I love you more and more each moment of my life.' (*Miami Daily News*, 5th August 1932)

Her thoughts were elsewhere. She and Haden Clarke amused themselves in the evening, she said, playing Russian Bank (a competitive two-player game of patience). Haden was still acquiring liquor from his girlfriend, Peggy Brown, in spite of his promise to Lancaster.

The Robin Challenger fixed, the trio took off across the Guadeloupe mountains, Shelton being forced to make an emergency landing at the foot of El Capitan when the engine problems re-emerged. Lancaster and a mechanic, working in sub-zero temperatures and snowfalls, removed the engine from the plane and took it to El Paso. After some phone calls from Gentry Shelton, a new engine was purchased by Shelton's father and arranged to be sent to them direct from Curtiss Wright.

On 17th March Lancaster was disappointed that still no letter had been received from Chubbie, and on 18th March he wrote in his diary:

'I am plumb crazy, all because of no news of Chubbie... Chub, my darling, how are you? And what are you doing?'

Chubbie's reply was not what he had hoped for:

'You have messed things up as usual. I drove out to the field this morning (4 gallons of gas) and they told me you had checked it (the prop) in your name. I tried to convince them it was mine... Why the hell you didn't tell them it was mine and I would come for it I don't know... There is also not a drop of booze in the house and we can't afford to buy any.' (*Miami Daily News*, 5th August 1932)

Her teeth were playing up too, and she couldn't afford to pay the dentist and had a three-week milk bill to pay – and the battery on the Lincoln was dead.

She managed to get the prop off to him in the end, but he had already found another – she was very displeased. Lancaster phoned her now with the suggestion he send the prop back to her – she wrote to him next day:

'I have used every cent I have in the bank and am completely penniless. You said last night you would send the prop back. What a colossal waste of money... It is a great pity you didn't make sure you needed it before sending for it...'

And regarding some transgression by the LAA president, Mark Tancrel:

'What the hell does he mean by it? I wish to God you had been firm and business-like for once in your life...'

In the same letter – 'The mail has just come...a letter from the Aberdeen bank about a returned cheque. I'll enclose it. I simply cannot understand why you give cheques when you know they are no good. I think it is dishonest... The best thing to do is to burn your cheque book if you can't resist giving bum cheques.' (*Miami Daily News*, 6th August 1932)

When Chubbie was angry everyone knew it.

Short of cash, he was becoming increasingly convinced that the LAA scheme involved something illegal:

'I have not the slightest intention of doing anything dishonest or breaking the laws of the USA,' he wrote on 20th March. But Chubbie's lack of money and her constant complaints were deeply worrying for him, so in desperation Lancaster loaned the .38 revolver Huston had given him to a 'gangster friend of Russell's' for $5 ($100 in 2022). Unable to repay the man subsequently, he forfeited the gun. But at least he was able to send a few dollars to Chubbie. He was constantly on edge at her lack of communication, though:

'No letters – Chubbie you wretch!' his diary exclaims on 22nd March.

Meanwhile, his suspicions about Tancrel and Russell were confirmed: he learned the business of the LAA was indeed dubious: it involved smuggling people, drugs, or both from Mexico. He was momentarily and uncharacteristically tempted... Tancrel told him that they would get $1,000 ($20,000 in 2022) per person smuggled, and for a small suitcase of dope, they might get as much as $30,000 ($600,000 in 2022) in San Francisco. He was unhappy, away from home and quite broke, and here was the answer to all his problems. He wrote to Haden Clarke – again taking him into his confidence on 21st March – asking him to sound out Chubbie on the notion of making a single trip to

Mexico for the LAA, smuggling what he referred to as 'unmentionable cargo.' He asked Haden to test the water with her:

'This for only you,' he wrote. 'Haden, old man, I cannot sleep, so I decided to express the thoughts running through my mind...'

He put the idea to him. Lancaster was clearly tempted by easy money. But Haden was playing a two-handed game; his intimacy was either too advanced with Chubbie to undertake this in Bill's favour, or he had ambitions for it and used it as an opportunity to advance his own position – because he told Chubbie plainly of the plan, and of Bill's suggestion of making a single illicit trip. He had placed his confidence in Chubbie, not Bill. To add insult to injury, Bill received a united response from 'Haden and Chubbie' which rapped him on the knuckles severely, telling him to have nothing to do with such a plan or he would be in the 'doghouse.'

It was a sign which perhaps only Lancaster would have failed to see the significance of: the balance of power between the three was shifting. Haden had increased his standing with Chubbie at Bill's expense.

After the slap down he had received from Chubbie, and possibly from the joint response from Haden and her, he was more worried than ever. He was smarting from Haden's breach of confidence, too:

'I do not quite know how you know I was contemplating anything hazardous, but can only surmise Haden and you have been putting your heads together,' he wrote on 25th March.

'Alright my sweetheart, I will abide by your decision... I will not take any chance at all... As long as you stick by me, Chub, in this worrying time, I don't care a damn. You alone are the one thing that matters to me.' (*Miami Daily News*, 6th August 1932)

There was reassurance and a condition in this proposition – *as long as she stuck by him.*

And further, there was a warning:

'I felt I could trust him [Haden] more than anyone else I have met in a long time. I hope this has turned out to be so...' he wrote.

Perhaps this gave Haden and Chubbie some cause for disquiet, because a couple of days later, Haden wrote to Lancaster clarifying the message from himself and Chubbie, admirably:

'The risk involved is entirely out of proportion to the gain you can anticipate. The slightest slip would result in your being deported, the loss of all the prestige you have worked 16 years to gain, and an awfully tough road to the future for you. The amount of money you would make would furnish only temporary relief at best, and would in no wise help you to become permanently established...

'You are surrounded by people who are using every argument in their favour to convince you and put the matter in the best possible light... You promised Chubbie that you positively would not swerve from your original intentions, and I am convinced for you to do so would make her most unhappy regardless of the outcome. I appreciate that your one idea in the whole matter is her welfare and happiness, so since the move must defeat this purpose, what possible argument is there in its favor?' (*Miami Daily News*, 6th August 1932)

Haden also intimated in his letter to Lancaster that as long as the neighbours continued to raise chickens they wouldn't starve!

The letters from Chubbie are now few and far between – it is notable too, that when she does write, she is adopting Haden Clarke's brand of slang: she 'opened an envelope and ten fish fell out!' (dollars), 'Haden earned six fish!', she tells him; and she also informs him that the Lincoln battery is 'on the fritz' – all slang words Haden uses in his letters. She even uses Haden's favourite phrase, which defines his character so well: 'God will provide.'

On 28th March Lancaster records that Haden is more enlightening in his letters – 'Hope he is keeping his promise to me, feel sure he is. But Chubbie – Hell!!!'

Interestingly, in the margin of this particular entry, Lancaster wrote: 'Gent said Mrs R[ussell] writes to R[ussell] saying Chubbie is on a bender!!!'

She was.

The new engine now fixed and installed into the Robin they flew on to Nogales, Arizona. Bill's lack of insight was becoming wilfully obtuse:

'No news from Chubbie. Why does the child not write?' (30th March), and,

'No news from Chubbie. The little devil! I should not think of her so much. She does not deserve it. Hell!!!' (31st March)

Lancaster was, as ever, leaving a trail of debts in his wake as he traversed the southern states of the US. Shelton told him at Nogales that Chubbie and Clarke were having a great deal of fun in his absence. He seems to have been trying to wake

Lancaster from his slumber to the rumours that were reaching the party out west. Lancaster longed even for Chubbie's perfunctory replies.

There was a growing disparity in their letters to each other. Hers were quite unequal to his own in quantity and depth – Clarke's missives were soothing still... But by 31st March Chubbie's letter was seeking to delay his return – it was ominous.

On 1st April, thoroughly disillusioned with the LAA scheme, Lancaster flew to Los Angeles with Russell. Their scheme, now exposed, of drugs and people trafficking, was firmly rejected by Lancaster. Russell, probably with a view to lowering Lancaster's guard and persuading him to throw caution to the wind, showed him two letters he had received from his wife in Miami. In one, she said:

'Chubbie and Clarke came round tonight. They were all ginned up. I really think now that Clarke has gained Chubbie's affections, and Bill has lost them.'

Another said:

'Was round at Chubbie's tonight. She and Clarke got all ginned up together. Don't tell Bill but I believe she is well satisfied.' The underlining was Mrs Russell's. It seems clear that for some little time now, everyone in the LAA party knew of the affair except Bill...

'Mental agony!!! Hell!!!' he comments on these revelations in his diary, yet on 3rd April, his diary records: 'Wired Chubbie every cent I could raise. It leaves me flat broke, but God may provide. How to get out of the hotel is the problem!'[24] 'Why no wire

[24] Bill had no means of settling his hotel bill. Various establishments

from Chubbie?' he wonders, and, '4 a.m. been trying to telephone Chubbie. No reply. Why? Ill with nervous worry. Phone, Gent says – do anything!!!'

On 8th April, Gentry is clearly trying to intimate the truth to Lancaster:

'He [Gent] is anxious about Chubbie, too – says Russell was so sure.' [That Chubbie and Haden Clarke are having an affair]

Russell's attempt to swing Lancaster in behind his scheme and abandon Chubbie's injunction against his illegal venture failed. Lancaster was not interested in Russell's scheme – he had his orders, and his sole thoughts now were of Chubbie and Haden. But he wired Chubbie in a restrained manner, not letting on that he had any intimation of her betrayal and that of Haden:

'No news from you before leaving Nogales. Terribly anxious. Tell Haden stand by, I trust him...'

In spite of all, Lancaster continued to write impassioned letters, too:

'I miss you, Chub, terribly. Have wanted you more than I can describe.'

And –

'Oh, to give you a great big hug and feel you close to me once more.'

Her replies, infrequent at best, were cool by comparison. To an extent the development of her relationship with Clarke can be traced in these letters. Chubbie had expressed her irritation at Clarke initially, because of his failure to write anything or make progress of any kind on the

---

contacted the State Attorney's office after Bill's arrest inquiring how they might seek restitution for unsettled bills.

book, but this softened. Her irritation with Bill did not:

'I am sorry to have to write this, but I told you when you cleaned me out of the little reserve I had in the bank that I would be stranded in the end… I have used every cent I have in the bank and am completely penniless.' Her admonishments could hardly have been more severe, but Bill seemed wilfully blind to it. She continued to receive letters filled with endearments, when she wished they were filled with dollars. Not surprisingly, Lancaster's effusive replies of love and affection often met with stony silence. Her neglect of him is palpable. In the early days of Bill's absence, she was no warmer in her opinion of Clarke. She wrote to Lancaster in early March:

'He is without doubt the laziest, slowest writer I have ever seen.'

Under duress, it seems, Clarke had asked Chubbie to put down on paper for him a list of details so that he could write these up. She did so in a diligent fashion and gave it to him. Clarke then forced the muse, or perhaps, decided to work without her assistance, handing Chubbie a short piece of writing – the result of his labours. She was utterly dismayed: he had not troubled to read the details she had set down for him and turned out a wholly inadequate short piece of writing for her. The muse was, apparently, still absent. Chubbie seems now to have abandoned any hope that Haden would write the book for her and set about writing it herself, in the hope that he would then polish it for her.

This all occurred in those first days of Lancaster's absence. She was becoming impatient with Haden Clarke: he was another foolish man with dreams beyond his reach or capability. She was tired of such men; of dreamers and liars whose reach exceeded their grasp; men without means. Haden Clarke was not a fool though. He sensed it, and he certainly knew women - he changed tack. When Chubbie confronted him in the third week of March, he was sitting pensive and silent before his typewriter, devoid of inspiration; she knew he was not going to produce the book she had employed him to write. He knew it too. That night, before they went out to attend another boozy party, he forestalled the thoughts he read in her, flattered her on her choice of outfit – he expressed a preference for her wearing one he said was his particular favourite on her, one with a rose on it…

It was a decisive move. At a single blow he had told her of his attraction to her, and had given her the opportunity of signalling the reciprocity of hers by acquiescing to his preference. She did. She wore the preferred dress, and he understood this subtle engagement..

Captain Mark Tancrel (left) and Jack F Russell (right) with Bill Lancaster and Shelton's Robin Challenger monoplane. (*Miami Herald*)

Gentry Shelton (left) a St Louis socialite and competent pilot, went out west with Lancaster as part of the LAA venture, sharing piloting duties with him. (*Blackwell Tribune*)

Haden Clarke moved into the bungalow in February – he was a highly intelligent young man, but undeniably lazy. (*Daily Herald*)

Chubbie Miller's mood lifted with the appearance of Haden Clarke. (*Daily News*)

Sunday April 10th 1932

Awaken with misgivings — suffer the tortures of the damned! Ways & means have to be found today to get on East - that is where my life has everything I hold dear is there. If its gone from me I will end this life, I can't stand the strain much longer.

What a year 1932 is proving. I still have the courage to carry on. The uncertainty is hurting deep through.

Telephone Chubbie at Gentry's insistence - wish I had not. She did not make it easier for me. Am going to Miami whatever happens to find out first hand all about everything.

I love you Chubbie - have done my best - but failed.

Want to talk things over with you my sweet. Its five years now since we met.

Bill's diary entry for 10th April 1932. 'If it's gone from me I will end this life, I can't stand the strain much longer...' he writes. (*Daily News*)

8. Dangerous Liaisons

This was something Haden Clarke was good at. He had a natural way with women, and as an occupation it was a lot more palatable to him than writing. It is axiomatic of blocked writers that they find some distraction for themselves. Haden did. And emboldened by his success, he went further, suggesting a bob for her hair – she went for that too. He had advanced their intimacy, and delighted by his progress, he had given himself further opportunity to express his admiration for her. They were engaged in a subtle courtship dance…

And Haden's admiration for Chubbie was increased in its value by its newness, its freshness to her, in comparison to the tedious, assured professions of Lancaster's old love.

That night - of course - they got drunk. Haden, Chubbie later said, slept at the foot of her bed and she discovered him there in the morning – she tiptoed out and returned noisily, pretending to Haden that they had agreed to switch rooms the night before…

But Clarke was not such a fool! The memory of her warmth and her scent in the night would be upon him.

They went out again that night to another party; of course they did; they were both drunk again, they drank more at home, and kissed drunkenly on the lawn before staggering to the house where they had sex. That was in the third week in March.

Chubbie's letters to Lancaster now changed tone: they became curiously less irritable at Lancaster: now she was encouraging; she didn't wish for him to hasten his return. Her letters were no more frequent, but they had softened. She started calling him 'darling.'

Clarke was obviously seeking a displacement activity; women were always a displacement activity for him – but he proposed marriage to Chubbie the next day. And she eagerly accepted. Proposing marriage was something Haden Clarke had much practise at. They were drunk with passion and newfound love - and just drunk. Impetuously he asked, impetuously she accepted.

It was an absurd liaison and a betrayal by both, of course. But it took their minds off their woes, their tedium and constant hand to mouth existence - the uncertainty of the future. And in the ferment of the moment, of love or infatuation, there was the drone, the insistent, tedious, keening professions of love from Bill Lancaster:

'My sweetest...my darling' etc came his unwanted, intense letters, wearying in their painful devotion.

Chubbie delayed Lancaster's return, delayed reality, in spite of her clear view and knowledge by now, that Tancrel and Russell were crooks. She urged him to stay:

'It seems a pity to give up now...' she wrote.

Deceitfully – or at least self-servingly - she told him Haden couldn't write while he (Lancaster) and Shelton were present. It was probably true, but he could write no better in their absence either. She went further:

'Of course, I miss you like the very devil,' she wrote unconvincingly, 'but I do so want to get this book out and make enough money to buy a schooner and then we'll all ride out the Depression in the South Sea islands. How does that appeal to you, darling?'

It appealed immensely to Lancaster. Perhaps the 'all' betrayed her thoughts in this – it was clearly not an exclusive invitation. But she urged him to stay away until the book was written. His absence, quite clearly, was devoutly to be wished for. She stacked up further objections to his return. And her next letter was strewn with 'my darlings' – it was manifestly intended to keep the love-sick Lancaster, and his suspicions, at bay. She was seeking delay; to buy time.

In early April 1932 Russell had showed Lancaster the letters from his wife, which made plain her opinion that Haden and Chubbie were ginned-up and loved up. He rang Chubbie: no reply. When he finally did catch her with one of his incessant phone calls, she promptly handed the phone to Haden Clarke. They were having a bridge party: others at the party heard the conversation. Bill asked Clarke about the rumours he had heard of an affair: Clarke denied them flatly. But Lancaster was deeply unsettled:

'Much disturbed: ill with worry,' he wrote in his diary.

He started back for Miami.

He knew what was going on, and they knew he was aware of it since his conversation with Haden – but Lancaster chose to co-conspire with their denials to him. He wrote to Chubbie telling her he was longing to see her and kiss her again... His denial was astonishing. Chubbie and Haden must have been bemused. Had he bought Haden's flat, monosyllabic denials? Surely it was not possible?

Shelton, obviously struggling through his own alcoholic fug to comprehend Bill's unwillingness or inability to comprehend or grasp the truth, thought it prudent to warn Chubbie: he wired her:

'Tell Haden keep both feet on ground. Bill trusts him, but Russell upset half the Lancaster-Miller organisation by repeating scandal…'

They knew for certain now: Bill knew they were having an affair.

Shelton also tried to steel Bill for what was coming. But Lancaster was, at least at some level, in his own world; a world where chickens were free and bad cheques were a kind of gratis public fund for the impecunious. He wrote in his diary even now, on 7th April,

'If she would only say something nice, such as "don't worry. I still love you."'

But she didn't.

He remained generally upbeat and his face set against any possibility that he had been betrayed:

'I was sad you were drunk when I called on the phone. Do sober up, Chub, until I get back,' he wrote on 7th April, and –

'Have been through hell, sweetie,' he wrote to her, 'but see daylight at last… Mrs Russell wrote to Russell, but I told Russell "You don't know Chubbie. To hell with what you may say or think:" sweetheart, remember Port Darwin? We made it…' It was desperate, expressing hope where none was justified; he was digging deep to persuade himself, her, the gods who moved against him. By

9th April it was becoming hard even for Bill to maintain this parallel universe:

'Suffer the torments of the damned,' he wrote in his diary, 'Ways and means have to be found to get on east – east is where my life lies, everything I hold dear is there. If it's gone from me I will end this life, I can't stand the strain much longer.' (*Miami Herald*, 5th August 1932)

He was reaching a determination in his own mind. To Shelton, his companion, he could speak of nothing else. Shelton could only suggest he speak to Chubbie. He did, on 10th April and told her he had resigned from the LAA – Chubbie was muted, unemotional, remote – he was wound like a rubber band. She told him she had sent a letter to him via Shelton's father in St Louis. Haden had written also: letters awaited him in St Louis. It was ominous and he knew something was amiss. Yet, in spite of the clear signals he had received, he could still write to Chubbie the next day:

'You know, my sweet, the only thing in life that keeps me going is thoughts of you. I love you so sincerely that I will do anything I can to make you happy... What is this letter in St Louis? I am terribly eager to get there to receive it.' (*Miami Daily Herald*, 6th August 1932)

He borrowed $150 from a friend, Dorothy Upton, and he and Shelton started the journey back east. On 12th April his diary records

'As long as I have you I can fight and will win eventually!' (*Miami Daily News*, 6th August 1932)

They made Oklahoma City on 13th April; on 14th they were in Springfield, MO, finally flying in to St Louis on 15th April. Here the letters awaited him; two from Haden Clarke and two from Chubbie

Miller. He opened the letter from Chubbie first. There was no further scope for denial, even for Lancaster:

'The inconceivable has happened,' Chubbie wrote. 'Haden and I have fallen in love... I know that your one thought has been my happiness and feel that you will take it in the right way.'

Clarke's letter was longer:

'You doubtless have read Chubbie's letter, so there is no necessity for my relating again what has happened. I wish, however, to explain with absolute honesty my attitude towards the whole thing and I am hoping against hope that I may be able to justify my action in your mind and to regain, to some measure at least, the genuine friendship I am sure you felt for me. When you left you put a trust and confidence in me which I appreciated from the bottom of my heart. I considered your every interest my foremost duty, and my last thought was of anything that would harm or hurt you...

'Please believe that no other power on earth could have moved me to fail you and I would not have been swayed by this had I not been convinced beyond a shadow of a doubt that the thing was inevitable and unmistakably permanent.

'When this thing first dawned upon us a few days ago I weighed it carefully from every angle. No matter how I looked at it, I could find no possible course but the one I have taken. I did my damnedest to make friendship kill my love for

Chubbie, but it was a losing fight from the very beginning.

'No matter how I felt towards you this other thing was stronger.

'We both tried to talk each other out of it, but we could convince neither each other nor ourselves…I don't know what chance of happiness you and Chubbie had before this happened, but I am sufficiently sure of my ground to know with absolute finality that now it has happened neither Chubbie nor I can ever be other than miserable apart. I know it's going to be a hell of a blow to you, old boy, but I am faced with the obvious choice of hell for one of us and heaven for two of us…

'You have told me many times that your one aim was Chubbie's happiness. I don't know that my word means much to you now, but I give it that I will always do everything in my power to make her the happiest girl in the world. If I ever fail in this, I stand ready to answer to you for it…

'Nevertheless, your attitude is going to be a dominating factor in the happiness of both of us and I am extremely anxious to know what it is. I am far from hopeful in this direction, but please wire me immediately and write fully regardless…

'Our reason for not writing this immediately was by no manner or means a desire on our part to deceive you. We talked it over repeatedly and inevitably concluded there was nothing to be gained by upsetting you while the Mexican project was hanging fire. The night you called us up from Hollywood I felt like a snake, but there was a room full of people playing bridge at my elbow and it was entirely out of the question to do anything but to deny everything in emphatic monosyllables...

'Needless to say, this has been entirely confidential. I have communicated with my wife and have made arrangements for an immediate divorce. Chubbie and I plan to marry as soon as it is granted...

'Please think it all over sanely, Bill, and try to see your way clear to help us get it over with as smoothly as possible. If you do lose your head, I'm afraid I can do nothing but meet you halfway. It would break Chubbie's heart if either of us did anything violent, but the decision regarding this is entirely up to you.

Yours,

Haden' (*Miami Herald*, 6th August 1932)

The muse long absent from Haden Clarke, had brought him inspiration at last. It is a capable letter, filled with persuasive honesty, and also a great deal of deceit. The candid description of their regret at the hurt they must cause Bill is undoubtedly authentic – the dawning of their love for each other and their attempts to resist it, is not. We know from Chubbie's account, which is sufficiently scandalous to be truthful, that the two fell into a drunken sexual relationship, and that design (certainly on Haden's side) had played a part in this. Nor had their keeping the matter from Bill been due to Bill's being engaged in the LAA business, as Chubbie had sought quite deliberately to delay his return.

The obvious self-denial, the self-deception Lancaster had nursed within, in spite of all the contraindications and whispers of those about him, was now over. He was distraught. He sobbed piteously as he handed the letters to Shelton.

There it was, incontrovertibly laid out before him in black and white: Chubbie and Haden were to be married.

9. The Return to Miami

That night Bill tried to drown his sorrows in a pint of whisky. But he wasn't a drinker; it never worked for him as it did for others – for Shelton, for Haden and Chubbie. He just sank into a torpor of depression and retained a morose, brooding, insensate sobriety. Even after a pint of whisky. He was utterly broken – but by the morning he had recovered a semblance of dignity; he had a more immediate need in this business, and it seems he had a new plan: that was to act now to delay the pre-emptive finality of a wedding. He wired the new couple in apparent conciliatory tones:

'Am no dog in the manger, but hold your horses kids until I arrive. Insist on being best man and being friend of you both for life. Happiness of you my happiness. Hope arrive tomorrow night or Wednesday latest. Love Bill.'

Shelton senior loaned Lancaster $100 on a cheque he gave him, the circumstances under which it was given, later being disputed. That was in St Louis, and he went out later that day and paid $30 for a Colt .38. He bought ammunition for the gun, too. It delayed his departure for Miami because darkness prevented him from flying. He parted from Shelton and flew to Nashville alone on Tuesday 19th April, staying the night at a hotel. Here he opened the box of ammunition he had purchased, and he loaded the gun that evening…

Now his diary fell silent.

At dawn on 20th April he took off from Nashville, now alone with his thoughts. What they were is unknown. His diary is mute, and he had no confidante or companion who might subsequently be probed on this. He had little in the way of luggage; just the bare essentials he had flown with, a bunch of letters, his diary, and a loaded .38 revolver. He dropped off at Atlanta briefly, where he refuelled, and wired Chubbie to indicate he would arrive at 4.30 p.m. In fact, he was further delayed by headwinds before finally taking off for Miami Viking Airport, where he landed some time between 6.30 and 7 o'clock that evening.

Chubbie and Haden drove in the Lincoln to meet him, arriving at around 4.30 p.m. But owing to Lancaster's plane being delayed, they had to wait around. They sat in the car eating ice cream. It was a nervous wait for the couple. Bill had spoken by telephone to Chubbie from St Louis. He had been in an emotional state. What was said is unknown; but Chubbie subsequently said Lancaster told her about the gun he had purchased here. It was, though, one of three accounts she gave concerning the gun. Chubbie and Haden Clarke had a two hour wait at Viking Airport. At last Lancaster touched down in the Robin, and taxied his plane to an area where he parked it.

It was an awkward, tense meeting. Lancaster's apparently good tempered, jovial sounding wire of two days earlier, with its expressions of good will to 'you kids' seeking their delay in marrying until his arrival, had vanished. He was taut, watchful: there would be trouble.

The conversation and the events following this moment until 2.30 a.m. on 21st April, are entirely dependent on the accounts given by Chubbie Miller and Bill Lancaster. Only three people knew of them, and the following day, one of these was dead.

According to the accounts of the two surviving members of the trio, given in the various statements made to the State Attorney's Office, their meeting at the airport was amicable, they drove off in the Lincoln and stopped to buy cigarettes – Lancaster suggested alcohol, but Chubbie and Haden said they had given it up, because Haden had a 'malady.'[25] This was something Lancaster learned of here in the taxi for the first time, they afterwards claimed, so he decided not to buy drink and they just bought cigarettes. He also bought some steak for dinner from the meat market on Flagler Street, and there was a brief visit to a launderette for Haden to redeem some clothes and bed linen.

Further discussion of the matter of the forthcoming marriage occurred in the car:

'Chubbie, are you sure you know your own mind?' inquired Lancaster.

'Yes, Bill, I am,' she replied.

'Ever since I've known you my only desire has been your happiness,' he said, placidly.

He then turned to Haden in the car:

'Do you think you can make her happy?'

'I'm damn sure I can,' replied Haden Clarke, presumably not regarding his 'malady' as providing any kind of impediment to such a marriage. Lancaster then promised the couple $1,000

---

[25] As previously mentioned, the nature of this disease was never specified, although it is quite certain that it was either syphilis or gonorrhea.

($20,000 in 2022) on their wedding day, if they waited for a month to be certain they were doing the right thing. It seems his intention was to kill himself, Chubbie said later, and thus the insurance money on his life would come to her as his beneficiary. The matter is hazy and somewhat confusing as told by the two survivors, but it does seem that such a discussion took place in some form during that evening. Chubbie said they agreed to the delay. Lancaster went to bathe, while Haden Clarke and Chubbie cooked dinner.

Dinner was uneventful, courteous, according to both, but afterwards over coffee, Lancaster returned to the subject on his mind:

'Now, what's this really all about?'

Clarke said, 'Chubbie and I want to get married, it's as simple as that.'

An argument flared up after dinner, when Lancaster said to Haden Clarke:

'Haden, old man, I trusted you and you did this to me. You haven't behaved like a gentleman.'

Perhaps it was a strange notion for chicken rustlers and passers of bad cheques, but Lancaster had his code. Haden leapt to his feet and stood over Lancaster, saying:

'I resent that!'

It was confrontational, but Lancaster remained seated, quite equable.

'If you two are going to fight, I'm going to bed!' said Chubbie. She then left both men and went into the sitting room. She said that the two men followed her; she sat with Haden on the chaise longue, and Bill sat in an armchair. Things calmed down somewhat. Bill talked about going to see Huston about the LAA in the morning, according to

Chubbie; Bill said he mentioned to them that he had replaced Huston's lost gun and would return it to him.

Chubbie was overwrought and at some point Bill followed her to the kitchen, where she became upset. Here Haden Clarke discovered Bill comforting a tearful Chubbie –

'Leave her alone!' he told Lancaster, 'I won't have you trying to break down my wagon!'

'She always comes to me in times of trouble,' Bill returned, staking a counterclaim.

Clarke pulled Chubbie away and refused to let Bill speak to her alone. Chubbie went to her room – the men followed her like pesky teenagers, arguing again. At some point, according to Chubbie's statements, both men went out to buy cigarettes; Bill makes only one mention of this very late in his testimony in court, and given that the two men were clearly at loggerheads with each other, and that they had bought cigarettes on the way home from the airport, it seems to be a questionable event. A little later, Bill left the house with the dog Mickey and drove off in the Lincoln for 'five or ten minutes.' He returned to announce he would leave immediately, and stay in a hotel overnight, before returning to St Louis - but Chubbie told him to remain until the morning. He agreed to this and then went into the porch room, where Haden joined him a few minutes afterwards. It was about 15 minutes before midnight now. Both men were said to be sleeping in separate beds either side of a small bedside table. Chubbie said she visited them in the porch room and said good night, but Bill did not reply. He was sullen. She repeated this, and this time he said, 'good night.'

Later she heard both men talking and laughing. She settled into bed at 12.45 a.m. and read a detective story for about an hour. Then she turned off the light and went to sleep.

At some point, around 2 a.m., she was awoken by Lancaster banging on her door. He called out to her:

'A terrible thing has happened. Haden has shot himself!'

She said: 'There is no gun in the house!' according to their later version, and Lancaster told her he had 'brought one back with him for Huston.'

They went to the porch sleeping room and Lancaster said: 'Look! Haden left these notes.' She read Haden's brief note to her explaining his suicide and recommending his rival to her. Chubbie fetched a face flannel to wipe the blood from Haden's face. Accounts of what happened vary, perhaps this is understandable under the circumstances, events and emotions competing in the jumble of happenings feeding the narrative of that night. According to one version, Lancaster suggested destroying the suicide notes, but Chubbie demurred. Chubbie phoned Huston, who said he would call a doctor and ambulance and come himself. According to Huston, this phone call occurred at just before 2 a.m. – this is sometimes given in the newspapers of the time as 3 a.m., but the latter must be wrong. According to Ditsler, who logged the call at Philbrook's, he received a call for the ambulance service at 2.30 a.m. The ambulance arrived at the bungalow at 2.45 a.m. and the other accounts of timings are impossible unless an earlier timing of around 2 a.m. is accepted. It is also worth noting that Chubbie's initial statement said that Bill had called her 'after 2 a.m.,' which suggests an uncertainty about the time the shooting occurred, but probably that it occurred close to 2 a.m. This would seem to be confirmed by Bill's testimony in court:

Hawthorne asked him,

'It was before 2 a.m.?'

Lancaster replied: 'It was, perhaps.' (*Miami Daily News*, 11th August 1932)

Then, according to Chubbie, she remembered the name of Haden Clarke's doctor – Dr Carleton Deederer - and called him herself.

'Haden has shot himself. He's bleeding terribly. Please come at once,' she told Dr Deederer, and gave him the address.

The two ambulance men were the first to arrive and as a result it was the ambulance office that called the police – not Huston, Lancaster or Chubbie. The couple had realised one thing, though: although still alive, Clarke was a dead man; and they needed a lawyer.

10. The Defence of Bill Lancaster

Bill Lancaster's arrest for the murder of his rival, the lurid circumstances in which the three lived, and the fame of two of the triumvirate, created international interest in the case. There was a widespread misapprehension that Haden Clarke was himself an aviator, and he was frequently referred to as 'Haden Clarke, the airman.' He was not an airman, although he had enjoyed going up with Lancaster as his passenger on occasion during their short-lived acquaintance. There was natural hostility towards Lancaster in the US press to begin with, as Haden Clarke was a young, handsome American, who had won Mrs Miller's affections. It seemed – with some justification – the case was clear cut, from the facts known: Lancaster had resented his rival, and in a fit of extreme jealousy had killed him. Public opinion at the outset being adverse towards Lancaster, it made his case a difficult one to defend – his trial would likely result in a successful prosecution and a guilty verdict, with all the consequences that would flow from this. But all was not entirely lost: Lancaster was, through the offices of Mrs Clarke,[26] able to secure the services of James H Lathero (1903-1963), an able attorney who understood the

[26] When Lancaster visited Ida Clarke at the Everglades Hotel on 23rd April, following his release from custody by Hawthorne, he had looked her squarely in the eye, saying, 'I swear to you I had nothing to do with Haden's death.' She had believed him, at that point, but her convictions in the matter oscillated widely.

need to muster public opinion in his client's favour from the outset. He knew that even with the best efforts in court, it would be difficult to overturn the power of public sentiment against Lancaster, and that of the press which fuelled it, so Lathero began to formulate a strategy to counter this. First, he came up with a statement for Lancaster to issue, in the manner of a holding reply, to stem the tide of public hostility against him, and to slow its momentum:

'It comes as a great shock to me the fact that a technical charge of murder has been made against me. I am absolutely innocent, and I know that the outcomes will prove this. I have been treated with fairness by State Attorney Hawthorne, but there is a certain amount of circumstantial evidence against me. At the right and proper time an explanation will be made...' (*Daily Herald*, 4th May 1932)

In other words, Lancaster reserved his defence. Lathero had also been quick to ensure that no further antagonism should accrue from the fact that here was a foreigner who had murdered a good American boy, by speaking of the fairness of the State Attorney. It would not improve Lancaster's position and would likely exacerbate his predicament if he criticised the State prosecution or American system of justice. He had, of course, made absolutely clear, his denial of the charges proffered against him, describing these as merely 'technical.'

Chubbie Miller was re-interviewed by Hawthorne following the arrest of Lancaster and his confession that he had forged the letters. Had she known the letters were forged? She said she had not known this initially, but that Lancaster had informed her of this after they had both been released on 23rd April. He told her he had done it to allay any suspicions she might have of him. She believed him, she said.

Chubbie subsequently made a statement to the press, which was designed to shore up Lancaster's position, in which she confirmed her belief in his innocence. This was quite vital in view of the fact that she was the woman over whom the rival lovers had quarrelled – and, of course, that it was her fiancé who had been shot and killed:

'I am absolutely confident everything will come out right. I know the truth will be learnt and Captain Lancaster will be cleared. He is innocent and I know it. My faith in him remains unshaken. It has never wavered in the past, nor now, and it never will.' (*Daily News*, 4th May 1932)

It was a curious statement for a woman whose fiancé had just been killed, and whose former lover was standing accused of his murder. But there was no equivocation in her support for Lancaster, nor in her apparent conviction of his innocence. This was of great importance.

So much for the public relations aspect of Lancaster's defence. But James Lathero knew Lancaster would need an excellent advocate in court to argue his case, which was extremely problematic from a circumstantial point of view, and he decided to approach one of Miami's best attorneys to conduct the defence: James M Carson.[27] Carson had the reputation, it was

[27] James Milton Carson, b Kissimmee, Florida (1887-1950); he had attended the University of Florida 1903, receiving his BA in 1909 and LLB in Washington and Lee University 1910.

reported, of having never lost a criminal case in 22 years of practice; in fact he had only handled six criminal cases during this period, so was relatively inexperienced in this field of law. Nevertheless, he was an influential man – the son of a former Florida Senator, and a Democrat candidate himself for State Governor in 1928, he was also a professor of law at Miami University - and was pugnacious enough to defend this apparently hopeless case.

Naturally such a man was not keen to back a failure or to take on a case where the evidence was so compelling, because in spite of the claims of Lancaster in his statement concerning its being of a circumstantial nature, murder trials often are: murder is the darkest of human crimes and is therefore often committed as a solitary act under a cloak of concealment. But handwriting and forensic evidence, and the sheer weight of probabilities in the circumstances, made this a formidable case to defend. Carson knew it. Apparently, he refused to take the case initially, ('he's as guilty as hell!' Chubbie later claimed he declared when he met her), but was persuaded by her to visit Lancaster in jail. In fact, the approach to Carson was made by James Lathero. They met to discuss the case in early May and afterwards the two men visited Lancaster in his cell. He may have weighed up Lancaster's demeanour and candid insouciance and considered he could work well with such material - but there seems little doubt either, that Carson was genuinely persuaded that Lancaster was indeed innocent of killing Haden Clarke. In any case, he decided to accept the brief and agreed to act as counsel for the defence. His commitment thereafter to Lancaster's case was absolute. A defence fund of just $700 was available ($50,000 in 2022), a modest sum to defend a murder trial in the US.

Carson realised that he could not defend Lancaster with any hope of success, unless he was candid in regard to Chubbie's affair with both men. The prosecution would, in any case, make a great deal of this since the relationships between the three were the basis for the tragedy which had occurred in the early hours of 21st April. There would be no avoiding the lurid details of the relations openly acknowledged in the correspondence now in the hands of the public prosecutor and in Lancaster's diary. It was clear that Chubbie could not be spared any of the ensuing scandal – the cat was truly already out of the bag – but he told her he would do his utmost to present it in the best possible light in so far as this was possible. Chubbie agreed. There was little choice here.

'I'm afraid I'm going to have to make you the scarlet woman,' she said he told her.

'Will everything have to come out?' she inquired.

'Everything.'

'And there's no other way of saving him?'

'In my opinion, no,' Carson told her.

'Very well.'

This is surely a misrepresentation of the conversation that occurred between them – she had no choice in the matter, given that she was the prosecution's chief witness, and every detail would be presented to the court not by Carson, but by the State Attorney Hawthorne. The best that may be said is that Carson may have pointed out to her that she was in for a rough time, and he was not in a position to do anything other than concur with the prosecutor. Perhaps to mitigate the effects of the trial on her own image, she had, in this recollection, placed a favourable spin on her role so that it appeared to be one entirely of self-sacrifice.

Carson's main hopes of combatting the State case, though, lay in promoting an alternative theory of what had occurred: he decided that every effort must be made to promote the theory that Haden Clarke had committed suicide. After all, if Lancaster had not killed Clarke, then the story both he and Miller gave of Clarke's suicide must be true. This was the claim which Lancaster had made from the first, and it was implacably supported by Miller. To the public prosecutor, to the detectives involved, to the press and public, this had been a theory they had entertained at first; that they now chose to regard this as being untrue did not affect it as a viable hypothesis. On the one hand, every circumstance seemed to point to Lancaster's guilt: he had motive, means and opportunity, the holy trinity of guilty attributes – all three were brim-full of probability. How could Clarke have killed himself? It seemed wildly improbable that 1) a newly affianced man, one who had apparently seen off his love rival and won the hand of the woman he loved, had 2) taken a gun recently purchased by his rival with money he had recently borrowed - a gun which had curiously been loaded and left equidistant between the two men and within the reach of his hand - had 3) awoken in the night and shot himself at an almost impossible angle where he lay in an attitude of sleep.

For a defence to be successful, each of these circumstances would need to be imbued with sufficient uncertainty to make the scenario of suicide seem possible. Carson knew he couldn't do this without the full support of Chubbie – and this he had; Chubbie was willing to do all that was necessary to ensure Lancaster was acquitted. She betrayed not the least doubt of his innocence during any stage of the investigation, nor in public, nor would she at trial.

A series of articles, interviews and briefings for the press softened the press attitude, and in consequence, weakened the public determination against Lancaster. Lathero sought to present his client as a war hero, a gentleman, a man of honour – in fact the antithesis of Haden Clarke, whom he portrayed as a disreputable idler, a liar, womaniser, and a drug addict who suffered from a shameful malady. It was most necessary that every vice that could be attributed to Clarke be played up to the hilt, and every virtue Lancaster possessed be offered in contrast, so that Lancaster's own faults were diminished by comparison.

The acquisition of Carson to defend Lancaster at trial was a great coup for the defence: perhaps things were not so hopeless after all.

The other actions Lathero took were to seek reasons why Haden Clarke might commit suicide. In this he asked Chubbie to provide him with a list of possible reasons for this. She did:

1) Remorse at the situation he had created, after his promise to Bill Lancaster.

2) Doubt of himself and me. Fear that the past five years would prove too strong a bond and I would return to Bill.
3) Financial worries.
4) Doubts of his ability to write the book and make money with his writing. He talked constantly of this; his writings were all returned.
5) Intense sexual life over many years, suddenly discontinuing.
6) The fact he was young and he had placed too much burden of responsibility on him.
7) His physical condition.
8) The fact that he was very temperamental and emotional; that he rose to great heights of joy, and sank to the depths of despair. (*Miami Daily News*, 7th May 1932)

Chubbie signed this list, and it was sent to the State Attorney's office. It had little impact there, but it provided the basis for the defence case, that Clarke had committed suicide. It further had the benefit, of course, of coming from the dead man's fiancé.

Mrs Ida Clarke, Haden's mother, cognizant of developments in the case, had initially accepted Lancaster's assurance to her that he had not killed her son, although she claimed he also said, 'he was so upset he sometimes thought he had killed Haden.' (*Miami Daily News*, 7th May 1932). She had initially believed him to be innocent. Lancaster was a persuasive man, with a pleasing, gentlemanly demeanour and excellent manners. He did not have the appearance of a murderer. But she had soon thereafter altered her mind again. With Lancaster's arrest, and the news that her son had not written the suicide notes (a fact which she had been the first to suspect), it was inevitable she would again begin to have doubts. It naturally caused her to review her acceptance of Bill's personal assurances to her: whatever failings her son may have had, Haden had an aversion to guns, he was a writer and lover, not a gunman. She had already had cause to doubt Haden's notes, and the confirmation that these were forgeries, as well as the revelation concerning the love triangle her son had been involved in, (she had known nothing of her son's relationship with Mrs Miller, she said) caused her to suspect Lancaster may indeed have killed Haden. On 7th May she indicated to the *Miami Daily News* that she would request that an autopsy be carried out on her son's body:

'I believe my son was beaten about the head with a revolver before he was shot,' she said, alluding to Dr Deederer having told her that Haden Clarke had bruising, a fracture at the base of the skull, and 'three unnatural bumps' on the left side of his head.

'Dr Deederer told me Thursday he was convinced these conditions were not the result of a suicidal shot. I make no accusations, but I want all facts in the case brought out.' (*Miami Daily News*, 7th May 1932)

Hawthorne said in response to this, that he would make no official statement on the matter until he received Mrs Clarke's request:

'If I find there is sufficient reason for disinterring the body, I shall order it done,' he said. (*Miami Daily News*, 7th May 1932)

This was a bombshell. But Carson and Lathero acted swiftly: they saw the advantage of making a pre-emptive request, thus making it possible to claim in court that the autopsy was Lancaster's idea – in the same way that Lancaster had admitted to forging the letters, after he had been discovered, but pre-empted the fact, or proof of this. Now Carson could similarly claim that the autopsy was his client's idea – it was not strictly true, but Carson calculated that it offset any risk such a strategy might entail.

Permission for the exhumation of the body of Haden Clarke was given by circuit judge Henry F Atkinson, and a Medical Commission was appointed, which would oversee the conduct of the autopsy and produce a report on this. The Medical Commission consisted of three doctors, representatives of each constituent interest: Dr M H Tallman for the court, Dr Donald F Gowe for the State, and Dr Percy Dodge[28] for the Defence.

The autopsy on Haden Clarke was carried out on Tuesday 31st May at Jackson Memorial Hospital. Dodge had already nailed his colours to the mast in contradicting the initial findings of Dr Deederer concerning powder burns at the wound site, and their implication for the proximity of the weapon to the head. The results of the autopsy did little but demonstrate that Haden Clarke had been shot in the right temple, at such an angle that the

[28] Percy Lorraine Dodge (1883-1963), b Nova Scotia; Boston State Hospital, Worcester Insane Asylum, Hudson River State Hospital New York, served in WW1 and afterwards US Veterans Hospital, Boston; moved to Miami in 1927 as a result of arthritis. He seemed to list a series of ailments – at the time of the trial he was suffering from heart disease. He lived to the age of 80 in spite of these illnesses.

bullet had exited near the top of the head on the left side, its having travelled in a trajectory from front to back and in an upwards direction. The doctors for the court and the State offered no opinion on whether or not the wound could have been self-administered, but the defence representative, Dr Dodge, retained by the defence, dissented, asserting that the gun could have been fired by the victim and further, that in his opinion, Haden Clarke was of such a character and state of mind that this was probable. This was an extraordinary judgement and quite beyond his remit: Dodge was basing his assessment on no personal or independent knowledge of Clarke, but on an unchallenged description of Haden Clarke's character given to him by the defence. This was based entirely on what Lancaster and Miller had told them of Haden Clarke. In any case. it was something of a stalemate. Whenever multiple experts meet with divergent interests, it usually is. It may be that the embalming process had interfered with the ability of the Commission to make other observations, because their report seems to have been less thorough than the circumstances warranted.

In his 8 feet by 10 feet cell, which was situated on the 22nd floor of the Dade County Courthouse, Lancaster paced up and down and exercised, in an attempt to keep fit. Chubbie was initially allowed to visit Lancaster daily, but following his indictment by Grand Jury, she was restricted to visits of just 60 minutes each week. She brought him clothes, magazines, and food - he was allowed to have food delivered from outside – and he had a radio, books and had two photos of Chubbie for company.

Chubbie was indefatigable in her resolution, and she made prodigious efforts on Lancaster's behalf. She was in constant contact with the press and put together, with his aid, a mini biography for him, which she circulated to the press; she also circulated testimonials he had received in the past from Lord Powers Court of Enniskerry and other British luminaries, with a view to boosting Lancaster's personal standing in the public purview. She had her own troubles, too – she was arrested on 22nd June on illegal immigration charges and was held briefly in a cell on the floor above Lancaster's. She posted bail of $1,000 and was released: it was determined thereafter that immigration matters concerning Lancaster and herself, would be held in abeyance until after the trial. Mark Tancrel, erstwhile President of the Latin American Airways, was less fortunate in his attempts to obtain bail: he was charged with impersonating a US naval officer, but could not raise the $2,000 required of him, and was held at the County Jail.

Perhaps feeling vulnerable, and having time to reflect, Lancaster wrote to his daughter Pat on 21st June. She could barely remember her father, having not seen him since she was five years old in October 1927. Now she was ten years old. Nina, her younger sister, who was now five years old, had no recollection of her father at all as she had been just six months old at the time of his departure from Croydon Airport. His letter to Pat was touching, but betrayed little in the way of remorse for his neglect of her:

'Mr Dearest Pat,

'I want you to understand a little of the thoughts and actions of 'old Bill' during the five years that have passed since you waved goodbye to a small aeroplane on the aerodrome at Croydon.

'At the present time my small kingdom consists of a room ten feet by eight in a gaol. Not a nice place, in spite of being on the twenty-second floor of the Town Hall, and commanding a view of the sea, and the beach, and the boats. The gaolers are not inhuman people, and treat me very well. Fortunately some friends still remain, and I have my food brought to me from the outside world. I have a radio which I can turn on and imagine I am far away. Sometimes when certain strains of old songs or operatic music come from the loudspeakers I lean back and conjure up memories of those days that have gone before. India, Australia, New York, and England.

'Of course, some people will have condemned me already, and will have said that I am lost to the world, at least the world as I would have you know it. A world of brightness, of ambitions, of love. But this is not so, because they put me in gaol without real cause. They accused me of something that I did not do. And the newspapers carried stories of the circumstances as they would like them to be (to sell their papers), not as they really were.

'Soon an opportunity will be given me to tell the true story, and to produce the evidence which will support the story. Then things will be much better, because I shall be released from the gaol, and everyone will say I was treated badly.

'Your mother, dear sweet person that she is, wrote a letter to the lawyer who is helping me with my case, and she told him of two ways to put forward a defence. She did not know the true story but had just read warped reports printed in the newspapers. Still, it was kind of her to obtain the opinion of some learned lawyer in England.

'Your mother, Pat, is one of the nicest mothers in the whole world for a little girl to have, and I hope you will always love her very much, and be sweet to her, helping and loving her so that she too will love you so much.

'You see darling, old Bill knows. He has wandered all over the world and met many people. But never has he met anyone nicer than your mother. Always think of this, and try to do things which will make your mother happy, and glad that she has you for her little girl. When Nina Ann grows as big as you are now, you must tell her too.

'Some day you may meet me again, flying an aeroplane back to the same field that I flew away from. I have tried very hard to make this possible during the last five years, but somehow the days, the months, and years have come and gone, and still I have no aeroplane in which to fly back. I wonder if you would be very excited and joyful if this did happen.

'I think of you often, and wonder how tall you have grown, and what you are doing, and if you are becoming a clever girl. London, where you are, is the nicest town in all the world. America is not really a nice place to live in. American people are so insincere and crude. Of course, not all of them. I have some American friends who are just as nice as anyone in England.

'Perhaps I had better tell you a little of the true story which will be told in a little while for all the world to know. You see they said I shot a man and killed him. But this man shot himself, because he did not want to live any more. He was not a nice man at all. He had no money, and he was a failure. He drank to excess, and he used dope which undermined his constitution. Well, he went from bad to worse, and finally he decided he had nothing more to live for, so he took his own life.

'Now he was my friend, so I did not want everyone to know what kind of a man he was. But now I am afraid everything will come out, as there are other people who knew all about this, and they insist on telling, as they think they should do this for my sake.

'Then the doctors had to confer over the case, and exhume this man, so as to be able to express an opinion as to what caused his death. They were very clever doctors, and I had to pay a lot of money for their services. But they talked and talked, and examined everything, and finally agreed (all of them) that this man took his own life.

'All of this is not a very nice thing to talk about, and you will have to ask your mother to explain it all to you. She has probably been very worried about it all. For remember darling, if you ever do wrong, or are accused publicly of doing wrong, it hurts people who are your relations, or friends, as in my case now. But when the truth is made known, and it is shown that you really did not do wrong, in a measure things are put right.

'When you write, address your letter to the army & navy club, New York city. Kiss Nina Ann and mother for me. And remember my thoughts are of you darling. By the grace of God, and the love of your mother, you will grow up to be like her and never be in a situation such as I now find myself in.

'Goodbye darling until my next letter.

Bill'

It was a letter from a stranger. Self-serving to a degree and self-deluding, he seems to be trying to persuade himself; and above all his letter betrays not the smallest interest in her, in what she is doing, in her life, her schoolwork and education, her interests and friends; the things that form a ten-year-old child's world. It is expiation, not the contrition of an absent, neglectful father. It could have been written to a distant relative. In truth, he has no idea of how to speak to Pat because he does not know her. Bill seems to look on the world as though from his private cockpit and no-one is very real down there. He speaks of his daughter seeing him again, her pleasure at this – his trial and situation; his daughter is a dot on the ground far below. It is also a letter written with Kiki in mind. His excessive praise of her, his explanations are principally directed to her: he wants to ensure that she is on his side. There is a great deal to antagonise her in the business; a great deal that might – should – arouse her suspicions of him; he is quite conscious of this and of the fact that he might need her at trial. Carson was determined upon bringing her into the defence equation at this time and wrote separately to Kiki seeking her support. He also intimated that Kiki should give no interviews, and asked her to attend the trial unknown to the prosecution, to speak favourably of Bill and their past life. But Kiki fended off this suggestion, pointing out she had to work for her living, and she also alluded to the lack of support her children had received, saying she could not afford the trip. Carson understandably realized she could do as much damage as she could do good and dropped the matter. In fact, Kiki had privately taken advice of counsel in London who advised her it would be neither prudent nor useful for her to attend the trial.

Lancaster wrote to Kiki too, on 4th July:

'Your letter of 4th July reached me this afternoon. It is one of the few things that are worthwhile that have come to me for such an age.

'When Haden Clarke shot himself he placed me in a ghastly position, which I made even worse by trying to get him to sign notes which I had typed – self-preservation instincts caused me to do this. I did no wrong in the matter.

'Trial is now set for 2nd August.[29] The authorities have been unfair, but NOT as unfair as the Miami newspapers. It is going to be an ordeal, but I am fortified by the knowledge that I am innocent of the charge.

'Unless there is unfairness, which is not unlikely, the courts here are rotten, I shall be cleared in an honourable way. James Carson, my chief lawyer, is a learned man, a "gentleman."

'I have been terribly handicapped by a lack of money. In America "justice" is a matter of dollars and cents. Have been 3 months in gaol the whole time in a cell 10 feet by 8 feet. They are setting the

[29] The trial had been set tentatively for 5th July, but owing to Carson falling ill while attending a Democratic Convention in Chicago, it was delayed until 26th July, and then firmed-up for 2nd August.

court in the typical American manner (for a gloating public), wired so that everything can immediately be given out. The various newspaper syndicates sending special representatives etc.

'You can depend on my keeping my chin up! No white feathers around. Just annoyance. I suffer greatly at the thought of such harm as may be done to you and the babes through all this.

'Will write again before the trial. Appreciated the photos sent by Pat. Kiss the babes for me.

B'

Chubbie gave further interviews prior to the trial, which sought to further soften the public attitude to Lancaster, whilst subtly disparaging Haden Clarke:

'My love for Captain Lancaster was worn out before I met Haden, though I consider Lancaster to be the finest human being. Haden and I suddenly loved with the maddest rapture, hysterically. He came and helped me with my autobiography. We hardly worked; we loved madly and insanely. Both of us were broke. Haden always said, "God will provide," I usually did. We were delighted in each other and hated separation. I could scarcely buy food, and the lights were often out... In great sorrow, I am realizing the great wrong Haden did me. I planned to marry him...'

11. The Trial of Bill Lancaster

The trial of Bill Lancaster began in Miami on 2nd August 1932 before Justice Henry Fulton Atkinson (1861 - 1938). The prosecution was led by the State Attorney Nathaniel Vernon Hawthorne, and James Milton Carson led for the defence. The court, situated on the 6th floor of the Dade County civic buildings on Flagler Street, was oversubscribed - as murder trials always are, especially those in which sex and celebrities feature prominently. It was estimated that nearly 2,000 people tried to get into court; it became a rowdy affair and beyond the control of court bailiffs, who called in the police to help manage the situation. The press was out in force, too; photographers jockeyed for position, and there was a vibrancy in the atmosphere of the court as the protagonists in the drama arrived. Wearing a light brown suit, Lancaster, who was described as being pale from his incarceration, but nevertheless in relaxed good humour, took centre stage. The other person whose presence attracted much attention was Chubbie Miller, dressed in white for the occasion. She seemed tense, nervous, aquiver with anticipation. She exchanged an anxious glance with Lancaster, whose lingering gaze betrayed something of his great affection for her, and sought to impart a certain reassurance also. They both smiled. If Lancaster showed any anxiety, it was on her behalf, not his own.

An early blow for the defence was the absence of Dr Percy Dodge. His assertion that suicide by Clarke was 'eminently probable' was a powerful point in Lancaster's favour. Dodge was in poor health, on this occasion suffering 'heart trouble' the court was informed. Carson sought to have the trial postponed until 15th September, arguing Dodge was a vital witness in the defence case, but Judge Atkinson denied this. The administration of the law could not be dictated by the matter of illness of an expert witness. In any case, as Judge Atkinson pointed out, although the doctor might not be able to speak to his evidence and be examined on this, his opinion was available and would be presented to the court in the Report of the Medical Commission on the autopsy. His absence was not, therefore, material.

The selection of the jury, the first business of the morning, was completed in a timely fashion by 2 p.m. The two points of possible contention in jury selection in the case were 1. that Lancaster was British and 2. that he had been living with a woman who was not his wife. Close questioning of the beliefs and opinions of the pool of one hundred possible jurors did not expose any inherent prejudices on either count amongst the twelve men selected, so this matter was dispensed with quickly. Throughout the selection process, Lancaster gazed interestedly at proceedings and at those present in court, his inquisitors - those who were to exercise formal and informal judgement on his actions. The excitement was palpable in the courtroom; there was something of the atmosphere of the theatre before the curtain is rung up on a first night.

Hawthorne opened the proceedings with a statement of the prosecution case. He spoke of the background to the case, of the change of fortunes the couple had suffered since the Depression; of Lancaster's all-consuming passion for Mrs Miller, which had reached a point of crisis when he had learned the dead man, Haden Clarke, had taken her from him. A man he trusted implicitly had betrayed him by taking from him the thing he cared most about, he said. Lancaster had heard rumours during his absence out west in pursuit of a business venture; he knew that Chubbie drank, and frequently got drunk. He was known to say, Hawthorne said, 'Chubbie has two personalities; Chubbie drunk and Chubbie sober, but I love both Chubbies.' (*Miami Herald*, 3rd August 1932) The rumours he heard out west became fact and confirmed his darkest fears, which he committed to his diary. Upon learning of the affair, he had been heard to say:

'I'll get rid of him,' in referring to Haden Clarke, and,

'I'll kill the son of a bitch.'

He had also said he'd 'seen hundreds of dead men during the war, and one more won't matter.'

Having received letters from Chubbie Miller and Haden Clarke in St Louis, during his return trip to Miami, he had borrowed $100 and bought a pistol and a box of cartridges. On the night before his return to Miami, at Nashville, he had loaded the gun in his hotel room.

The atmosphere, said Hawthorne, had been tense on his arrival at Viking Airport at Miami, where he met Clarke and Miller. At dinner things had been difficult and he had said he would leave, but was prevailed upon to remain until the morning. At around 2 a.m. Ernest Huston, Lancaster's friend and attorney, and also treasurer of the Latin American Airways, had received a call informing him that Clarke had shot himself. When the ambulance arrived, the driver found Haden Clarke barely alive and Chubbie 'hysterical.' Lancaster was agitated but controlled, and his primary concern seemed to be whether or not Clarke would be able to talk again. That was a curious concern, Hawthorne suggested.

Lancaster had since admitted to forging the suicide notes, which he initially claimed had been written by Clarke and discovered by himself on the typewriter table; he had requested of the attorney Huston that he say the pistol was his. It had, said Hawthorne, been wiped clean of fingerprints.

The prosecution's case was straightforward enough: Lancaster was besotted with Chubbie Miller, and finding himself usurped by Haden Clarke he had become jealous and enraged. He had returned to Miami affecting to be happy for the deceitful couple, and feigned acceptance of their impending marriage - but this was a ruse: his purchase of the gun before he hurried back from St Louis, and his loading it on the eve of his return, proved this. On his arrival at Miami, he had quarrelled with Haden Clarke; there had been a stand-off, and that same evening Lancaster had shot his love rival with his pistol, forging suicide notes purporting to be from the dead man.

This was the gist of the State's case against Lancaster. It could hardly have been stronger, and the State prosecutors had every reason to be confident that they would prove their case.

But attorney James Carson was personally and professionally convinced Lancaster was not guilty, and he intended to mount a robust defence from the outset: he presented Lancaster as a soldier and a gentleman; his character was impeccable; his love for Mrs Miller unshakeable, and Haden Clarke was his friend. He was an unselfish man, noble in his attributes: all the evidence pointed to Clarke having committed suicide. That he did so was not surprising, said Carson: Haden Clarke was a drug addict; he had spoken of money worries; he had grossly exaggerated his writing qualifications and lied that he had a degree from Colombia University; he was somewhat degenerate in his pursuit of women too, and he was being treated for a 'vile disease.' He had also spoken of suicide previously - and ultimately, he had shot himself because he had reached an impasse in his life.

Carson conceded that some of the circumstances aroused the greatest suspicion towards Lancaster – he referred to the suicide notes Lancaster admitted to forging – but he said the defence would 'prove' these were written by Lancaster after he discovered Haden Clarke had shot himself, and had been written solely to allay any suspicions Chubbie might have in the matter, not to deflect police suspicions from himself.

Lancaster and Clarke did not quarrel that night, Carson said, in spite of all the tensions. When Lancaster had been woken by the pistol shot and discovered Clarke had shot himself and was dying, he was afraid of how Mrs Miller would perceive the situation. He therefore wrote the two notes, two notes which he acknowledged were a 'colossally foolish' error – but, said Carson, without these notes, there would be no indictment.

Clarke, he said, had been buried without an autopsy and inquest being conducted, which they most certainly should have been according to the laws of the State of Florida, their omission being a stain on the State Attorney - and Lancaster had immediately agreed to request an autopsy, just as he had volunteered the information that he had penned the suicide notes himself. Carson was keen to imply Lancaster was responsible for the disinterment and the volunteering of the admission that the notes were written by himself. In fact, he was a beat behind in both matters – acting quickly to forestall these events when it became inevitable they were about to expose him.

Carson turned his attention to Haden Clarke: in January he had been living in New Orleans, drinking heavily and smoking marijuana; he suffered from a debilitating physical condition, and he spoke of suicide, he said. He spoke to two friends of shooting oneself behind the right ear – near to where he was found shot. Furthermore, the defence would prove that the gun had not been fired from a distance as Dr Deederer had initially – and wrongly – claimed, but had been held tightly against Haden Clarke's head, which showed that the shot was self-inflicted, as otherwise instinctive flinching would have occurred had the gun been presented in this manner by a third person. He concluded by inviting the jury -

'In listening to the evidence, not only to see whether it fits the picture of guilt but in meaning and circumstances, to decide for yourself whether the circumstance is consistent with the presumption of innocence which the law affords the defendant.' (*Miami Herald*, 3rd August 1932)

The primary speeches done, the scene was set: now 40 witnesses would be called at the trial – the State to prove its case, to substantiate its claims that Haden Clarke had been murdered by Bill Lancaster, and the defence to repudiate it. More than 24 of the witnesses were for the defence, to show that Clarke was of a disposition to commit suicide and had done so – and that Bill Lancaster's only crime was in writing suicide notes to allay any suspicions that Mrs Miller might have of him.

The first witnesses called were those of the State: Ernest Huston, the attorney and treasurer/secretary of the LAA was first up. He told the court that he had been called by Chubbie Miller at about 2 a.m. on 21st April and that she told him Clarke had been shot and asked him to come to the house at once. He called an ambulance and a doctor, he said. On his arrival at the house at around 3.15 a.m. she said, 'Thank God you're here!' and he went upstairs to the porch room. Lancaster was sitting on the stairs on the landing, grim-faced, and said:

'It's terrible, isn't it?'

Huston said he saw Haden Clarke lying in the bed moaning. It was at once apparent that Haden Clarke was dying. Lancaster showed him the suicide notes and the two men went downstairs to the living room where Chubbie and the ambulance driver, Ditsler, were. Chubbie had said there would be a scandal if the notes were discovered, and Lancaster suggested their destruction. Huston said he had warned against this.

Questioned by Hawthorne about the gun, he said that he had asked Lancaster if the gun was the .38 he had loaned him, and he was told it was not. Huston was reluctant to answer these questions, but he said Lancaster had asked him if he could claim the gun belonged to Huston rather than to himself. He had refused this. He had similarly told Lancaster he could not say the gun belonged to the LAA.

Cross-examined by Carson, Huston said that Lancaster's bed was 'mussed,' not smooth and he denied, when shown a photo of the bed with smoothed out pillow and bedclothes, that this was as he recalled it being on the night of the tragedy. Carson suggested that when Lancaster expressed anxiety as to whether or not Haden would speak again, he had actually added the words 'so he could tell why he did it?' Huston agreed that this rider had been added to the words. It was a useful point secured for the defence, having the effect of lessening the damage of Lancaster's apparent anxiety as to whether or not Haden Clarke would be able to speak again. It neutralised this point somewhat, as it could now be used to serve both prosecution and defence cases. Carson would claim consistently at trial that Lancaster's anxiety was that Clarke should be able to speak again, so that he could explain why he had shot himself, rather than its being an anxiety as to what Clarke might reveal if he spoke.

Huston said that Clarke's bed was a single bed against the wall on the east side of the sun porch, and he had seen the gun partially concealed under the middle of the body. He said the other bed was parallel to it and they were two feet apart. Huston said he had known Clarke, and had been consulted informally by him concerning divorce from his wife, about two weeks prior to his death.

Charles P Ditsler (1908-1943), the ambulance driver from Philbrook's Funeral Home was the second witness to be called. He told the court he had received a call at 2.30 a.m. and went to the bungalow where he was met by Lancaster at the door.

'I examined Clarke. Captain Lancaster asked me if I thought Clarke would ever talk again. I told him I believed not.' (*Miami Daily News*, 3rd August 1932)

Chubbie Miller, he said, had vigorously objected to the removal of Clarke, saying a doctor was on his way. When Huston arrived, Mrs Miller continued to object to Clarke's removal. In consequence of this refusal, when Ditsler went downstairs to call his office, Mrs Miller had asked him if he was going to call the police? He said his office had already done so. She and Lancaster continued to raise objections to the removal of Clarke – he said this impasse was finally broken when his supervisor, Mr Olon Charles Yeargin (1904-1960), arrived and gave his authority for this. He, Ditsler, was there for 45 minutes before Clarke was removed in the ambulance, which was done over the continuing protests of Lancaster and Miller. He could not recall, however, when questioned by Carson, whether or not the body of Clarke might have brushed against the wall while it was being removed from the house and thus this might have been responsible for the bruises evident on the head and right shoulder of Clarke. Ditsler, however, thought that his recollection was correct in that Lancaster had expressed his anxiety as to whether or not Clarke would speak again, but did not recall the use of the explanatory phrase 'so he could say why he did it,' although he conceded that it might have been said. The Assistant Manager, Mr Olon Yeargin, confirmed his colleague's account and indicated it was he who had ordered Haden Clarke to be taken to hospital. Mrs Miller, he said, still protested against his removal.

The emergency policeman, Earl Hudson (1907-1970), told the court that he had received a call from Jackson Memorial Hospital before 3 a.m. on 21st April regarding an attempted suicide. He arrived at the hospital before Lancaster and Miller and when they appeared, with the victim, Lancaster had asked him repeatedly if he thought Haden Clarke would recover consciousness long enough to be able to talk. He also said Lancaster told him Haden Clarke 'had contracted a disease which preyed heavily on his mind.' He said he had found and secured a number of letters he had discovered at the bungalow, including a number from Haden Clarke's girlfriend, Peggy Brown. He said he knew of Lancaster and Haden Clarke because he (Hudson) was married to Peggy Brown's sister – and Peggy had visited his house several times with Haden Clarke.

Hudson said Ditsler alerted him to the suicide notes, but when he asked for them, Mrs Miller had brought him only one. He asked for the second one and she replied that it was personal – he insisted that she hand it over and she fetched it. Under cross-examination by Carson, Hudson conceded that when Lancaster had asked if he thought

Haden Clarke would regain consciousness, he had added 'so he could tell us how it happened.' Lancaster told Hudson the gun belonged to the LAA.

Meanwhile Carson was playing a rear-guard action which was to prove decisive in altering public perceptions of the case: Chubbie gave an interview to the International News Service (INS) in which she told her side of the story – it was clearly a careful collaborative effort between Chubbie, INS journalists and Carson – who personally approved the final draft. Carson, like Lathero, was acutely aware of the need to swing public opinion in behind Lancaster. The case he had carefully constructed needed a fair wind to make it sail. It had another purpose also: the $300 paid by the INS to herself and Bill, who wrote a companion piece, went to the attorneys Carson and Lathero. The article, which was widely syndicated, duly appeared on the morning of Wednesday, 3rd August, the second day of the trial, and the day on which Chubbie would make her first appearance on the witness stand. It anticipated her by hours, and was a clear statement of the testimony she would give:

'I have always considered my intimacies and my liquor drinking my own affair,' it began. 'But when the life of as fine a man as Bill Lancaster is at stake I must not let any reticence on my part prevent his vindication. I know him better than almost anybody else and I know he is innocent...his innocence must be established even at the expense of my own reputation.' (*Miami Daily News*, 3rd August 1932)

She went on to cover their trip to Australia in 1927, their first intimacies which began in Persia that year and continued until 6th March of 1932, when Bill took employment with the LAA to try to make some money for them.

'Bill knew when he left it was dangerous to my discretion for me to drink too much liquor, but he thought that since Haden Clarke and I were busy writing a book which we thought would be our financial salvation he could leave us together with me under Haden's protection.

'We did not do as well at writing as we did at drinking.

'My love for Haden seemed to be too much for me and also seemed to exclude the possibility of our doing any work on the book we were supposed to be writing...We could not concentrate on writing or anything except each other.'

After two weeks of 'violent love making we discovered Haden's physical condition made it necessary for him to quit drinking... I quit drinking too, so that two weeks before Bill came home we were sober as well as broke.'

She averred Haden Clarke committed suicide and signed off with 'my drinking days are over.' (*Miami Daily News*, 3rd August 1932)

James H Lathero was a wily attorney, whom Mrs Clarke recommended to Lancaster. (*Daily Mirror*)

Judge Henry Fulton Atkinson was an experienced judge who did his best to keep the partisan gallery under control. He even indicated he knew of planned demonstrations in Lancaster's favour.

Woman in white: Chubbie Miller in the witness box. Her testimony was riddled with contradictions, but her support for Lancaster was vital. (*Daily Mirror*)

James Carson (left) with Lancaster in court. (*Miami Daily News*)

12. The Scarlet Woman

Chubbie Miller's appearance was the subject of great interest: a celebrity, whose exploits as an aviator were famed, she had been catapulted to the very first rank of public attention by the case – not in any way she would wish for, of course. Her exploits as a flyer were now thoroughly overshadowed by a titillating lifestyle and manner of living, which excited curiosity and moral indignation in equal measure. Her interviews and statements to the press, and the careful briefings supplied by Lancaster's lawyers, had softened the public indignation towards her to an extent, and her appearance in the INS syndicated newspapers the very morning of her court appearance played somewhat sympathetically too. She was a woman wronged in her view, and when she appeared on the witness stand, diminutive, sombre, but defiantly resolute, there was a great deal of sympathy for her as well as prurient fascination. Dressed in white, she spoke in barely an audible voice, and was described as being 'a diminutive 85-pound aviatrix' by the *Miami Daily News*. Elsewhere she was described as being 'less than 100 pounds.' She was clearly of light build, anyway.

Although a state witness in her first appearance (she would appear for the defence later), Hawthorne regarded her as a hostile witness and indicated he intended to treat her as such during his examination of her. Under his guidance she gave details of the events leading up to the tragedy. She said she had taken the lease on the Coral Gables bungalow on 1st January; she and Lancaster had moved in on that day and Haden Clarke a little over a month later in early February. She said that a man named Jack French had been living with them for that first month, but moved out soon after Haden Clarke moved in.

'Mrs Miller, were you engaged to Lancaster?' Hawthorne inquired.

'You can't be engaged to someone who is already married, but I intended to marry him,' she replied. (*Miami Daily News*, 3rd August 1932)

She said she had changed her mind when she met Haden Clarke. Hawthorne led her carefully through the affair which she said began 10-14 days after Lancaster left, and how Lancaster had come to know of it by degrees:

'Did you anticipate trouble when Lancaster received the letters [in St Louis]?' he asked.

'Not trouble. I knew he would be upset.'

'Did he intimate he was upset by telephone and letter?'

'Yes.'

Hawthorne then guided her through the tensions which had been present on Lancaster's return to Miami at between 6 and 7 p.m. on 20th April.

'He seemed very sad,' she said, but his greeting to them was friendly – he kissed her. Hawthorne asked how he had greeted Haden and what his reaction to him had been?

'Cordial,' she replied.

At dinner she said Bill had said to Haden, 'I trusted you and you did this to me. It was not the act of a gentleman.'

Haden grew angry, she said, jumped to his feet and knocked his chair back against the wall.

Hawthorne: What did Lancaster do?

Chubbie: He remained seated.

Hawthorne: He didn't get up?

Chubbie: No.

Hawthorne: Did you all retire at the same time?

Chubbie: Yes, at a quarter to one.

Hawthorne: After you went to bed did you hear them talking?

Chubbie: Yes, I could merely hear the murmur of their voices.

She said she was awakened by Lancaster hammering on her locked bedroom door – she had heard no shot – and he told her Clarke had shot himself. She said,

'Don't be ridiculous, there is not a gun in the house. Bill said, "Yes, there is, I brought one back with me!"' (*Miami Herald*, 4th August 1932)

When she went into the porch room she saw the gun under Clarke's body and pulled it out about 2 inches by the nozzle. She said Lancaster attempted to get an ambulance and called Huston.[30] Later she called for a doctor via the operator. She said she had accepted the assertion that he had shot himself, as a statement of fact, and not

[30] Accounts of who called Huston vary: Lancaster said it was himself, Huston said it was Chubbie; Chubbie said it was her on at least one occasion; and Lancaster on another.

enquired why he might have done so. She also said she and Haden had discussed a suicide pact two weeks earlier, but that they all went to bed on friendly terms.

Hawthorne asked her why her bedroom door was locked.

Chubbie: Because Haden told me to lock it so Bill would not be able to get in to talk me out of the marriage.

Hawthorne: What was his language when he told you that?

Chubbie: 'Lock the door so that dirty son of a bitch won't be able to talk you out of it.'

Hawthorne then asked her directly if she knew who had killed Clarke?

'I am convinced he killed himself,' she replied steadily.

Asked why he would do this, she referred to his 'drinking and his violent temper,' and to his mother's nagging him.

Hawthorne queried this, referring to Chubbie's statement in his office that he rarely drank, was not aggressive, never lost his temper unless he was drunk, and was of gentle temperament, generally.

She said she had been trying to 'shield his memory.'

Hawthorne's chief object here was to highlight the inconsistencies of Chubbie's statements and to show she was not a truthful witness. From here he moved to the implications of this:

'Are you not equally anxious to protect Lancaster? In trying to save Lancaster did you not say that you would issue a statement to the newspapers that you killed Clarke yourself if Lancaster was held?'[31]

She could only acknowledge that she had said this.

'Was that statement made for the purpose of helping Lancaster out of his difficulties?'

'Yes.'

She claimed Clarke had flown into a temper when he heard from his wife that the divorce would not happen for one year, and asked her where he would get $100 from for a quick Miami divorce? This was something Bill had said he advised Clarke he must tell Chubbie 'in the morning' of their bedtime chat. One of them was mistaken or lying.

If Hawthorne missed the significance of this, then Carson did not: he was quick upon the danger here:

'But he tried to object when Bill wanted the wedding postponed for a month?' he queried. She agreed. Carson saw in this inconsistency, only evidence of Clarke's neurotic mind at work.

Lancaster was, according to Press reports, extremely anxious during this examination of Chubbie, which was attributed, favourably, to his concern for her.

Carson's cross-examination for the defence focused explicitly on the character of Clarke and his predisposition to suicide. Again, Lancaster looked anxious.

At least two Important letters from Chubbie Miller were missing – the two she had sent to

---

[31] 'I would sign a statement that I killed Clarke myself if I thought it would help Bill out of this trouble,' she was reported as saying (*Daily Herald*, 5th August 1932).

Lancaster from St Louis informing him that she and Clarke had been having an affair and were intending to marry. The prosecution had claimed Lancaster must have destroyed these following Clarke's shooting – a careful tidy up must have followed the shooting, Hawthorne suggested, which included writing the suicide notes and removing dangerous evidence. But Carson now countered this by claiming it was police carelessness that was responsible for the missing correspondence, citing a telegram from Haden Clarke's wife concerning the divorce, which Chubbie said she had found screwed up in the hall following the police search. Chubbie said Lancaster had gone out alone for about half an hour. It was during his absence she and Clarke had discussed suicide over their guilt at their betrayal of him. She said Clarke had a nervous, violent temper and that he talked of suicide 'quite a bit.' *The Miami Herald* noted that in her earlier testimony Mrs Miller had said that she and Haden only discussed suicide once, about two weeks before, but not that it had been discussed as a way out of their troubles on the evening of 20th April. *The Miami Daily News* also picked up on this, referring to the 'contradictions' in Mrs Miller's testimony.

Chubbie said Lancaster had planned suicide and this was to be the source of the $1,000 he told her he would give her as a wedding present. She informed him the insurance company had failed days earlier. Later,

'I said I was getting tired and said, "Good night, chaps." Haden answered, but Bill was looking at his mail. I felt wretched about Bill and didn't want him to feel he was going out of my life entirely.' (*Miami Herald*, 4th August 1932)

Under cross-examination she said she had heard laughter from the room next door. She also said she had no fear of violence between the two men, in spite of their sharing a room and sleeping in beds just three feet apart. The judge interceded with his own question, asking what she thought had happened to Clarke when she went to the porch room and saw Clarke's condition?

'I thought he had had a haemorrhage,' she replied.

Picking up on this, Hawthorne inquired,

'When the judge asked you a moment ago you answered your first thought was that he had had a haemorrhage. Why did you say that?'

Chubbie: Haden told me some time before that he was suffering from ulcers of the stomach. A friend of his a few days before had been taken to hospital in a dying condition from that cause.

Hawthorne: (with disbelief) From a bullet wound?

Chubbie: No.

Hawthorne: Then you doubted Lancaster?

Chubbie: No, I just couldn't believe it.

She said they frequently discussed suicide and that the best place to shoot oneself was to the left and rear of the right ear, according to Clarke.

Hawthorne: And Lancaster had told you Haden had shot himself, yet you still believed it was a haemorrhage?

Chubbie: I believed that until Bill told me there was a gun in the house.[32]

Referring to Haden Clarke's being aggressive and having a bad temper, she said that Clarke's wife had told him she had divorced him in November 1931 and remarried, then on the morning of 19th April he had received a telegram from her saying she had made this up – he must wait for a final decree. Clarke flew into a rage, she claimed, and said 'Where am I going to get $100 to start divorce proceedings in Miami?'

Hawthorne again queried this:

'But he tried to object when Bill wanted to postpone the wedding?'

Chubbie: Yes.

She had no answer to his suggestion of the obvious inconsistency here. She said Clarke's feet were striking against the bed's iron rail and Lancaster took his pillow and placed it under his feet, but the ambulance man Ditsler told him not to as it would make the blood run to his head. This was similar to the claim Lancaster had made in this respect - it provided an explanation as to why the bed did not look to have been slept in, although Ditsler had already denied that this had occurred.

Carson's cross-examination of Chubbie was benign; he took her through the same points Hawthorne had, but with a different purpose. He focused on drawing what positives he could from her testimony. Of their meeting with Bill at Viking

---

[32] When Bill told her this seems to be a movable feast. Here she is, once again, clearly indicating it occurred on a later occasion, not at the door to her room.

Airport in Miami on the afternoon of 20th April, she said that she and Haden sat in the car eating ice cream. When Lancaster arrived, he greeted her with 'Hello darling.'

Carson: What was his greeting to Haden?

Chubbie: He said, 'Hello, old man.'

She said Bill spoke to a man about the plane. It was $2 for hangar storage, and $1 for outside parking: he took the latter. Then he retrieved his luggage from the plane. All three of them got into the front seat of the Lincoln and drove to a drugstore for cigarettes. Lancaster gave $5 to Haden for this and told him to keep the change.

Carson: Was there anything said about drinking?

Chubbie: Yes, Bill asked me if there was any liquor in the house and I told him that there was not, and we started towards a bootlegger's. I told Bill that Haden was not drinking and Bill asked why. I told him he couldn't on account of his physical condition... I told him I had promised Haden I wouldn't drink until he could...' (*Miami Herald*, 5th August 1932)

They then stopped at a market and bought groceries which Haden paid for with the change from the $5. On the way back to the bungalow, they also called at a laundry to collect house linen and some of Haden's things. Bill paid for the laundry, which upset Haden.

At the bungalow Chubbie prepared dinner and Haden cooked the steak. The two men squabbled, and Chubbie sent them out for cigarettes.[33] On their return they continued arguing in her bedroom. Bill said he would leave the house, stay in a hotel and fly to St Louis in the morning, but they persuaded him to stay the night, after which things settled down.

Bill wanted to talk to her alone, but Haden Clarke refused to allow it. She then asked Bill to leave them alone and Bill went out for 'five or ten minutes' with the dog.[34]

Questioned about how she had learned of the shooting, she said that when she awoke, Bill was pounding on the door, and she opened it – the light shone in from the porch room.

'An awful thing has happened. Haden has shot himself,' he told her. She rushed to Haden and asked him to speak to her. Then she said she was told by Lancaster he had brought a gun back with him – then, seemingly oblivious to the glaring contradiction in her statement, she said she had known of the purchase of the gun *because he had spoken to her of it from St Louis.*

Chubbie's first appearance was notable for its many contradictions, some of which may be attributed to errors of recollection, others to variations in newspaper transcriptions of the court proceedings - but the contradictions in her statements are so substantial they suggest she is not telling the truth. She had been an

[33] This was the second time they had bought cigarettes, according to Chubbie. The fact that the two men – who were at each other's throats - went out together suggests a bootlegger's was the real purpose of the trip: Haden because he knew the bootlegger's and Lancaster because he had the money to pay.

[34] She had told Hawthorne it was 'half an hour.'

uncomfortable witness, and Lancaster's anxiety on her behalf was noted by those present.

Dr Deederer, questioned by Assistant State Attorney Henry Jones, told the court he had received a call from Chubbie saying 'Doctor, Haden has shot himself. Can you come right away? He's bleeding terribly.' She gave him the address and eventually he found his way there. Clarke had been removed by the ambulance by this time and he followed to the hospital in his car. Here he examined Clarke. Deederer said he found a bullet hole midway and three inches above a line between the right ear hole and the right eye. The exit point was above the left ear but near the top of the head.

John O. Barker, Miami police fingerprint expert, said he found smudged, but unidentifiable fingerprints on the gun barrel. In cross-examination, Carson elicited from him that wiping the gun clean of blood might have removed fingerprints.

The lateness of the hour led to an adjournment.

The following morning was 4th August. Hawthorne began by reading Lancaster's second statement to the court. Carson had arranged for Bill Lancaster's story, the companion piece to Chubbie's of the previous day, to appear in INS syndicated newspapers. In this he spoke of Haden's 'physical condition' and of protestations he made 'vigorously' to Haden concerning this.

Jack F Russell of the LAA was the first witness called. Hawthorne led him through his statement concerning how worried Lancaster had been about Chubbie's financial situation and her neglect of writing to him. He then came to the letter Russell had received from his wife, which indicated that Haden Clarke and Chubbie were in a relationship. Russell said he had told Lancaster he had lost out with her –

'Bill asked if I thought Haden had double-crossed him... I said I thought he had. Bill said: "I'll get rid of him!"'

A further adjournment followed, and Carson's cross-examination of Russell began on 5th August: he questioned the authenticity of the letter and effectively did what he could to undermine Russell – it was not difficult: he was currently serving six months in prison for conspiring to smuggle aliens across the border into the US. It clearly damaged Russell as a witness for the prosecution. To ensure the central point of Russell's testimony was upheld - that Lancaster had indeed been shown such a letter - Hawthorne introduced Lancaster's diary and the letters between the three principals, by way of corroboration. He read these to the court; they confirmed a pitiful narrative of Lancaster's gradual descent into a condition of despair and jealousy, which spoke to his state of mind, as the affair between Chubbie and Haden became known to him.

It was effective for its purpose, but it also elicited great sympathy for Lancaster in his predicament – an unwanted side effect as far as the State was concerned. The mood in court had swung noticeably in Lancaster's favour, and it was remarked upon in the press.

On 6th August the other associate and President of the LAA, Mark Tancrel, was called to testify. He too had been indicted – in his case for impersonating a US navy captain. It tarnished his testimony.[35] He said Lancaster's end of the deal was to produce two planes and pilots for them – but that he had produced only one plane which was in poor condition. He said he had overheard Lancaster speaking to a man named Ince at the Hilton Hotel in El Paso, Texas:

'I don't think Haden Clarke has double-crossed me, but if he has – well, I've seen a lot of dead men and one more won't make any difference,' he had heard him say. Tancrel also said that subsequently, at Nogales, Lancaster had said:

'I'm tendering my resignation. You fellows can paddle your own canoe.'

Lancaster had inquired if he, Tancrel, had seen the letter from Russell's wife. He told him that he had, and Lancaster said he would, 'get rid of that son of a bitch,' referring to Haden Clarke. Later, after resigning from the LAA venture, he had further said to Tancrel:

'Russell showed me a letter in LA and told me all about it. I'm going back east to get rid of that lousy bastard!'

But Tancrel's testimony was challenged by Carson, who used his potential impending criminal status and his being a fantasist, against him. He asked him if he was a captain? Tancrel replied that he was a licensed captain in the merchant marine. He denied he was, or had ever claimed to be, a member of the paperhangers' union, but agreed he had said something about having 'papered my own

---

[35] Born in Mauritius of French extraction, Mark Gabriel Tancrel was to be acquitted of impersonating a US naval captain in October 1932, the judge ruling that as a licenced captain in the mercantile marine, he was entitled to call himself 'captain' and to wear the uniform of one.

home thousands of times.' Carson was intent upon making the most of this casual unsustainable exaggeration:

Carson: Thousands?

Tancrel: Not that many. No paperhanger in his lifetime could hang that much wallpaper. I've papered my own home many times.

Next, the forensic evidence was heard; its confusing contradictory opinions had the net effect of their cancelling each other out. The embalmer from WH Combs' Funeral Home, K.B. Bess, said he found no powder on Clarke's head wound, which he said was unusual in a suicide case - but Carson queried this, declaring Bess unqualified to make this judgement.

Earl Hudson, the emergency police officer who had examined the scene, said that Lancaster and Chubbie Miller had been in the bedroom when he found the gun, and attorney Huston 'somewhere in the house.' He said there had been blood on the gun; he had picked it up with his handkerchief and placed it in a box he found on a table at the foot of Lancaster's bed. He had then taken this to J.O. Barker for fingerprint testing back at police HQ.

Carson made much of the fact that Hudson's sister-in-law, Peggy Brown, had been Haden Clarke's girlfriend. He also suggested that Hudson might have provided the illegal alcohol for Chubbie and Haden Clarke's parties, filched from police-raided stocks - which Hudson hotly denied. Carson's purpose in this was intended to sow doubt on the character of Hudson, before attacking his testimony itself. This he now did: the gun had been wiped clean of fingerprints, according to the police, and the implications flowing from this were extremely damaging to Lancaster: Clarke's fingerprints should have been found on the gun if he had fired it; if it had been wiped clean, then it suggested it had been done for the purpose of concealment by a third person. It was vital, therefore, for the defence, to challenge this evidence.

Carson suggested that Hudson had picked up the gun using a handkerchief, but had placed it directly into his pocket – not, as he claimed, into the box first because the box was too large for his pocket. It certainly seemed doubtful that he could have slipped the box into his pocket without difficulty, and the attorney Huston had referred only to his placing it in his handkerchief and then his pocket. It was a clear point to the defence. Carson laboured it, referring to the claim humorously on at least two other occasions, in passing. Whatever the truth of Hudson's evidence concerning his collection of the gun, it was thoroughly nullified by Carson's insistent, contemptuous cross-examination of him.

It was another hot day in Miami. In adjourning proceedings, and releasing the jury for the weekend, the judge informed them they could go to Miami Beach for a swim if they wished. It is not known if they had suitable beachwear for this – over the pond this was a topic of great interest that year. George Ward Price, took a firm stance on the matter in an article in the *Sunday People* on 7th August, advising that the sun had life and health-giving properties which should overcome any prudish considerations. He reported that nude swimming and sunbathing was common in both Germany and France, and that a well-known Swiss doctor had informed him:

'The sun is the best massage and muscle-building agent in the world.'

A noted admirer of Germans, Mr Ward Price also regretted that the average German youth could flatten his puny British counterpart on this account. Nevertheless he wore a full upper and lower body costume when he visited the swimming baths himself, he assured his readers.

13. Chubbie Miller is Recalled

On Monday morning, Hawthorne recalled Chubbie Miller to the witness stand. Her statements and the contradictions therein were widely noted. Now his intention was to double-down on Chubbie – to show her to be a liar, willing to forego the truth for Lancaster's sake.

Once again, he took Chubbie through the events of the night of 20th April. She said Lancaster went to his room 'to read his letters, Clarke and I sat downstairs talking... Then I made a fool suggestion. I said, "I wish we could end it."' (*Daily News*, 8th August 1932) After this, things became amicable between Lancaster and Clarke, she said. Later she had heard Haden Clarke laughing with Lancaster after she had gone to bed.

Hawthorne: What was your belief when you were shown the alleged suicide notes?

Chubbie: I had no belief.

Hawthorne: Didn't you tell me in my office that you were positive that Bill didn't write them?

Chubbie: I don't remember saying that.

Hawthorne: Didn't I say to you in my office, 'are you as sure about the notes as you are that Lancaster didn't kill Haden Clarke?'

Chubbie: You didn't ask me that.

Hawthorne: Then you knew Lancaster had written the notes?

Chubbie: No.

Hawthorne: Were you shown the discrepancies existing in the notes?

Chubbie: Yes.

Hawthorne: Did you not say that Lancaster didn't and couldn't have written them? Did you say the language made you know Lancaster didn't type the notes?

Chubbie: Yes.

Hawthorne: Didn't you assert that Lancaster's code of honour wouldn't have permitted him to write those notes?

Chubbie: I did state that.

Hawthorne: Then the first time you knew of the forgery was when you asked Captain Lancaster directly at the house after your release?

Chubbie: Yes.

Hawthorne: If you had asked him if he had killed Haden Clarke and had received the answer yes, would that have surprised you more than the admission of forgery?

Chubbie: Most decidedly.

Hawthorne: Although you stated to me previously that you were positive that Lancaster had not written the notes as you were that he had not killed Haden Clarke?

He paused while the jury worked out the implications of this; then:

'Do you still love Haden Clarke?' he asked.

Chubbie: No.

Hawthorne: Do you love Lancaster?

Chubbie: No.

Hawthorne: When did your affection for Captain Lancaster die?

Chubbie: About two years ago.

Hawthorne: Did it die a natural death?

Chubbie: Yes. I am still intensely fond of him.

Hawthorne: Was there anything Lancaster did to cause a natural death of your love for him?

Chubbie: No.

Now his purpose in this line of questioning became clear:

Hawthorne: Then why did you deliberately betray him in every letter, telegram, and telephone message to him? Weren't you a traitor to him during all that time when he was sending you even single dollar bills in his letters?

Hawthorne was now scoring heavily off Chubbie's veracity, and character – and most importantly against her truthfulness as a witness.

Hawthorne: Weren't you a deliberate traitor to Lancaster in all those letters, in all those telegrams, all those times you said, 'all my love to you?'

Chubbie: You don't understand a feeling that exists between Captain Lancaster and myself... We were pals, not ordinary friends...

Chubbie was wilting under the insistent questioning of Hawthorne, but he didn't relent.

Hawthorne: So you no longer love the memory of Haden Clarke?

Chubbie: (sobbing) No I have been completely disillusioned.

Hawthorne: By what?

Chubbie: Proofs.

Hawthorne: Are you referring to his illness?

Chubbie: Among other things.

She said he had lied to her.

Hawthorne: Did he lie about his love for you?

Chubbie: No – he lied about his age, his university degree. He told me he had never had that malady before: he lied to me about things he had done.

Hawthorne: Then the principal thing that killed your love for Haden Clarke was because he was a liar?

It seemed a curious question, but Hawthorne's question had a purpose. Again, Chubbie had walked into Hawthorne's neat parlour...

Chubbie: Yes...

Hawthorne: Do you know Lancaster pleaded guilty to a crime for which he was not guilty to save you?

Chubbie: He always tried to save me, to help me.

Hawthorne: You don't love him even though you have said you will die for him?

Chubbie: Yes.

Hawthorne: Would you lie for him?

Chubbie: No.

Hawthorne was eliciting a string of inconsistencies from Chubbie, which she seemed only vaguely to be aware of – and they continued:

Hawthorne: One of the things you admire about Lancaster is his code of honour?

Chubbie: Yes, he is one of the finest men I ever knew.

Hawthorne: He'd steal for you, wouldn't he?

Chubbie: No. He doesn't steal.

Hawthorne: Didn't he steal a chicken for you?

Chubbie: Yes.

Hawthorne: A rabbit?

Chubbie: Yes.

Hawthorne: A duck?

Chubbie: No – we had a duck. (laughter)[36]

---

[36] This is one of those areas in which the lack of an official transcription of court proceedings leads to a variety of reports of what precisely was said here. None of the reports make much sense and it is unclear whether she implied they had not had a duck, they already had a duck, or she was correcting her initial denial by saying

It was clearly at least several chickens, rabbits *and* ducks, as Lancaster's diary records this. And her ordeal was not yet over as Hawthorne now sought to impugn both her and Lancaster's own morals.

Hawthorne: Do you know Lancaster has a wife from whom he is not divorced?

Chubbie: Yes.

Hawthorne: And two little girls?

Chubbie: Yes.

Having made the point that Lancaster was not an honourable man in the generally accepted understanding of the term, he proceeded to draw the implications of this from it:

Hawthorne: If Lancaster committed perjury to save you from the penalties of the law after you'd been drinking, did that increase your admiration for him?

Chubbie was struggling to find the answers such questions required without doubling back on herself.

Hawthorne: You said earlier that you intended to marry Lancaster, that you believed it was inevitable?

Chubbie: Yes. I always felt that when Bill was free from his wife in England I would marry him.

Hawthorne: But you weren't in love with him?

---

she had indeed had a duck. The amusement elicited in response to her questions, was presumably the unintentional comical image conjured of the theft of a procession of local livestock.

Chubbie: Being in love and just loving a person are two different things. I was not thrilled or infatuated with Lancaster, just terribly fond of him.

Hawthorne: Were you infatuated with Haden Clarke?

Chubbie: Yes.

Hawthorne: Now you do not even love his memory?

Chubbie: No... (she began to sob again) Unfortunately no....

She was also asked if she had contracted Haden Clarke's 'malady.' She said she had not.[37]

She left the witness stand 'semi-hysterical' according to Reuters' report, crying out

'They're trying to crucify me!' (*Daily Mirror*, 9th August 1932)

Hawthorne was done. If Hawthorne had drawn his points from Chubbie Miller with admirable forensic ruthlessness, had shown her to be a liar, of low morals, and deficient in constancy, she had at least elicited great sympathy for what she had endured on the witness stand. Carson changed tack in his cross-examination of Chubbie – he worked to draw from her Clarke's hot temperament, his rages, and the fact that Peggy Brown had supplied a great deal of the liquor to the house. He also drew from Chubbie, by way of

[37] Chubbie had been examined in early May for signs of having contracted the disease and was found not to be suffering from it. What tests were employed to determine this is not known, so repeated tests may have been required to ensure it did not subsequently manifest itself.

restitution for the damage Hawthorne had done to her character, that she had sent £30 a month to Mrs Lancaster after the flight to Australia – a third of their earnings. Perhaps this claim, its duration and accuracy would not bear too close an inspection, but there was no-one there to challenge it.

Carson now sought to alter course, drawing the minds of the jurors from the drama of Chubbie's appearance and its flawed nature, by recalling officer Hudson to account for the missing letters – having identified a weakness in Hudson, he was working to pin any discrepancies on him. The prosecution alleged that Lancaster and Miller had burnt or destroyed the missing letters, but Carson insinuated that Hudson was neglectful in his duties and had mislaid or lost them. Hudson declared that he had turned over everything he found to the State Attorney's office. Carson looked sceptical.

Attorney Ernest Huston was then recalled to the witness stand. He wanted to offer a counterbalance to Chubbie's testimony, which spoke chiefly to motive.

Ernest Huston said he 'now recalled' that Lancaster had said the gun was *technically* Huston's. It was a fine point! He also said he had impressed on Lancaster when he loaned it to him, that he valued the gun, as it had been given to him by an 'old friend,' and wanted it back – this was his first assertion of these points, which suggest, at the very least, a measure of prompting had taken place in the interim. Further, he said Lancaster had promised to take the best care of it, and if anything happened to it he would replace it. In the early hours of 21st April, he said, it was Chubbie Miller who called him, and that she requested an ambulance and a doctor. He also described watching Earl Hudson wrap the gun in a handkerchief and place it in his pocket: *there was no box*. It was good to ground things again.[38]

Carson: Was there blood on the gun?

Huston: It was running with blood.

A good strong image and a possible reason for wiping the revolver was offered here: wet with blood, this might have had the effect of removing fingerprints, as Barker had conceded. Again, it was a new detail supplied by Huston.

John B Rowland, the State Attorney's investigator now took the stand: he said he had pointed out to Lancaster several similarities between the typing of the notes and copies of Lancaster's typing of other notes. He said Lancaster had expressed astonishment:

'Why Mr Rowland,' he had exclaimed, 'Isn't that a coincidence? I can't understand that.'

He had then suggested to Rowland that he should submit the notes to handwriting experts in New York and offered to help him find one!

Rowland said he had located the bullet in the blood-soaked pillow later in the morning of the tragedy.

---

[38] It is difficult to make sense of Huston's evidence. He was a respected attorney, as far as we know, and there was no obvious reason why he should suddenly recall such improbable supplementary points in Lancaster's favour: his previous statements to Hawthorne and his previous testimony to the court, had failed to make any mention of these points, though their importance is plain enough.

Carson's cross-examination took the form of an attack on Rowland's competence – he now suggested the missing letters from Chubbie to Bill in St Louis, had been lost by Rowland or by the State, not destroyed by Lancaster or Chubbie. Rowland denied this and said he had never seen the letters at any point.

At 2.50 that afternoon, Hawthorne rested the case for the prosecution. The defence case was now to be made – and it would be challenged too.

James Carson opened dramatically, asking for all the 'circumstantial' evidence and exhibits except those of Dr Deederer and the gun, the bullet and the photo of Haden Clarke to be stricken from the record. It was a request to disallow the majority of the prosecution case.

Judge Atkinson, unsurprisingly, rejected this. It was a useful gambit to open the defence case by implying the prosecution evidence was so worthless and insubstantial that it ought to be dismissed from consideration by the jury.

14. Bill Lancaster's Story

Lancaster took the witness stand on 8th August. James Carson devoted the first day to questioning his client on his life and background. He led him through his childhood and schooldays in England, his RAF service, followed by his marriage and the relationship with his wife. Lancaster described his meeting with Chubbie Miller in Baker Street, London, their subsequent meeting at the Authors' Club the following day, their flight to Australia in 1927 and other experiences in aviation. He said his wife had 'private means' - which was not true in the strict understanding of the phrase - and he claimed Mrs Miller and he sent a third of their income to Kiki, bearing witness to Chubbie's earlier testimony: this was not strictly true either – but it would meet no demurral from Kiki, who was not present to be cross-examined on this, and who in any case was anxious to see her husband acquitted. In fact, Kiki derived her income from working herself, and Lancaster's parents provided further for her and the children. Lancaster's earnings since 1927 had been erratic, and since 1929 negligible. What money Chubbie sent Kiki is unknown – only Chubbie refers to it, and Kiki's and the Lancasters' hostility towards Mrs Miller does not suggest any sense of gratitude – however grudgingly given – was felt to be due to her.

Lancaster's life in the US was detailed up until the advent of the LAA scheme which had resulted in his leaving Coral Gables on 6th March - and in his leaving Chubbie alone with Haden Clarke. It was a lengthy introduction to Lancaster's background, and the court adjourned here until 9th August, when Carson began his examination in chief of Lancaster:

'Captain Lancaster – did you kill Haden Clarke?' he asked, opening with a traditional defence gambit.

'No, I did not,' Lancaster replied.

He turned directly to the relationship Lancaster had with Chubbie. There was no avoiding this – he knew Hawthorne would put Lancaster under considerable pressure over this, so he had to make the best he could of it and try to pre-empt anything Hawthorne might say. On the face of it, Lancaster had deceived his wife and betrayed her; he had abandoned her and their daughters without provision and apparently given them little enough thought thereafter. It would not play well in court, and Carson realised he needed to present this as a more benign occurrence, if Lancaster was to win the sympathy of the jury.

'When did you first find yourself in love with Mrs Keith Miller?' he asked.

'Mrs Keith Miller and I suffered many dangerous trials on the trip to Australia. I grew to admire her character. We suffered many things together. I am sure I was intensely in love with her on our arrival.'

He admitted that by the time they had reached the Persian Gulf the two were in a sexual relationship.

Carson: Was it physical passion or unselfish love?

Lancaster: Both.

Carson: In Australia, on how many occasions did you have intimate relations with Mrs Keith Miller?

Lancaster: I can't remember, although I am sure it was not many.

He said there had been fewer opportunities, but that his love for Chubbie had increased over the years, and their physical intimacy continued up until the day he left Miami on LAA business on 6th March.

Carson then turned to the arrival of Haden Clarke on the scene: it was to be the start of the gradual deconstruction of Clarke's character, which he had already commenced in the articles issued to the press by Chubbie and Bill. Clarke's vices and vicissitudes were to be cruelly exposed.

'When did you first meet Haden Clarke?' he asked.

Lancaster: (consulting his diary) February 9th, 1932. We had met in New York before, he told me, but I didn't remember him.

Carson: You roomed together from the first day?

Lancaster: Yes.

Carson: Did any other person share a room with Clarke except yourself?

Lancaster: Yes, women.

Carson: How many times?

Lancaster: On at least three occasions.

On further questioning he admitted he shared Mrs Miller's bedroom when Haden had visits from his women. Peggy Brown had spent several nights there, he thought.

Carson then turned to Haden Clarke's writing. He asked him how much writing Clarke did, to which Lancaster replied, 'Very little.' Coaxed by Carson, Lancaster said Haden Clarke had exhibited a temper on a number of occasions.

Carson: Was there drinking at the house?

Lancaster: Yes.

Carson: By whom?

Lancaster: By all of us.

Under close examination on this point, he admitted most of the drinking was done by Haden and Chubbie, himself less so. He said Peggy Brown brought flasks of alcohol to the house and that she had said she thought she and Haden (whom she called Charlie) would be married.[39]

Lancaster also said that the day before his trip west, he had a talk with Clarke:

'I told Haden Clarke of my love for Chubbie, of our intimacy over a five-year period, and asked him to protect her and watch over her while I was gone. I asked him not to let her drink and I asked him not to drink. His reply to me was: "Bill, I will care for her in such a way as to make you remember my friendship for ever."'

---

[39] Nora Alice Peggy Brown (1909-1980) was actually married at this time to Wendell Brown, but then both Haden and Lancaster were married men also! Peggy remained married – happily, it seems - for the rest of her life until her death in 1980. It must be assumed that the affair with Haden Clarke took place during an interlude of some sort in her marriage.

Thus Carson had, by this line of questioning, established that Haden Clarke was lazy, a womaniser, a drunk and delinquent. Of course, even if this were all true, he could take it only so far - one would wonder why Lancaster indulged the friendship of such a man; and why he would entrust the woman he professed to love to his care. It was a delicate line to tread.

Lancaster also said:

'I told him of Mrs Keith Miller's occasional weakness while drinking and asked him to keep on the water wagon and assist her while I was away.

Carson: What was the result of these 'occasional weaknesses'?

Lancaster: Her conduct at these times would not be her normal conduct.

Carson: Did you give him details of this abnormal conduct?

Lancaster: Yes, I did.

He said he had not previously spoken of his and Mrs Keith Miller's intimacy and on being asked whether Haden Clarke was surprised at this revelation he said he 'didn't know.' Presumably Lancaster was being delicate in this matter, as he had already indicated that he was sleeping in Mrs Keith Miller's room when Haden had his women to stay. For Haden Clarke to be 'surprised' at this confession of their intimacy would therefore be absurd.

The three men, Tancrel, Lancaster and Shelton were seen off at the airfield by Clarke, Peggy

Brown, and Mrs Miller on 6th March, Lancaster told him.

Attention now turned to the contract Lancaster had signed with Mark Tancrel in Ernest Huston's office before leaving. He spoke of his suspicions of Tancrel and his failure to find naval records for him, which Tancrel had dismissed by saying these had been destroyed in a fire. He said that as Tancrel had given him $200 up front, he felt obliged to give him the benefit of the doubt. He said he trusted Tancrel's confederate, Russell, because he had never 'posed as anything – at one time he showed me his honourable discharge from the army.' He had doubted the LAA venture from the outset and at El Paso he had learned of the plan to smuggle 'Chinamen' across the Mexican border. He had told Russell then he would have nothing to do with any illegal activities. When they mentioned dope smuggling, he had expressed his disgust and said he would return to Miami.

Lancaster's character was thus set in contrast to that of Haden Clarke. The defence now reinforced this by calling four aviators and a businessman to testify to Lancaster's good character:

Captain Frank Upton, Congressional Medal of Honor recipient; Lieutenant A Irving Bayer, British Aviator; Rex Gilmartin, WW1 flying ace; Clyde Pangborn, Aviator; and Keith Bon, a retired rubber broker from Singapore - all dutifully took the stand to give accounts of Lancaster as a man of honour and a gentleman. Aviators' character references – like job references – are, perhaps, light weight tributes, but they contributed to a general impression that Lancaster was a man held in regard by his peers.

Lancaster's own conduct on the stand was more important than any of these testimonials – and in this he scored highly. His appearance was always that of a gentleman – well-spoken and unassumingly polite in character, Lancaster presented himself as something of a caricature of the British flying ace breed. It was a role he knew how to play. His speech was littered with bluff jargon: 'stay on the water wagon,' 'paddle your own canoe,' and so forth. It all played into a character type he nurtured. It was evident the public gallery liked him. They expressed their approval of each point he made by stamping their feet appreciatively. Hawthorne looked exasperated; and the judge made numerous interventions. Lancaster's supporters in court had formed something of a claque.

Lancaster said that on receiving the letter at St Louis he had behaved 'like a schoolboy.' He had borrowed $100 ($2,000 in 2022) from Gentry Shelton's father and bought a gun to replace the one he had sold that Huston had loaned him. He had loaded the gun in Nashville, the evening before flying to Miami.

He said the meeting at Viking Airport with Chubbie and Haden Clarke was cordial, echoing Chubbie's description of the event.

Wednesday 10th August was Lancaster's third and final day on the stand giving evidence on his own behalf in response to the careful contrived questions of his own counsel. For three days Carson had sought to depict Lancaster as a man of good character and fundamental decency. But even so, it was still necessary to address some of the less favourable aspects of Lancaster's conduct.

Carson did so now: he asked him about 'foraging' for food and Lancaster agreed that he had 'foraged' for chickens and rabbits.

He flatly denied the claims by Tancrel and Russell concerning the threats they alleged he had expressed to them with regard to Haden Clarke. Had he said he would 'get that lousy bastard?' inquired Carson. He had not.

'The entire testimony of both Tancrel and Russell was a tissue of lies,' he replied.

He said he had loaded the gun because that was the condition in which Huston had loaned him his gun.

He said that Chubbie *had agreed to delay the marriage for four weeks or until Clarke obtained his divorce.*[40] He also said he told Clarke he wished to speak to Chubbie alone and Clarke replied that it was up to Chubbie.

'Did you talk to her privately?'

'No, she refused.'

There was clearly no suggestion of coercion by Clarke here, which Chubbie had claimed to be the case.

He said that there had been an argument after dinner between himself and Haden Clarke, and that he had left the house *to buy cigarettes.*[41] Upon

---

[40] This is important. It is completely at variance with the notion that Chubbie had claimed that she had wished Clarke to be cured of his malady before marrying him. His testimony on this point makes no mention that Haden's malady was known or factored into the decision to delay marriage. Nor is there any suggestion that this was known or figured in their discussions at this point.

[41] If this is so, then cigarettes were bought on three occasions that evening: when returning from Viking Airport, when Chubbie 'sent them out to get cigarettes,' and when Lancaster apparently went out

his return Chubbie and Haden Clarke were reclining together on the chaise longue, and he had gone to his room, sorting out his mail, where Clarke had joined him later. Lancaster said Mrs Miller came and took the alarm clock, then bid them goodnight. Drawn out by his attorney, he said he had not told Hawthorne of the conversation that occurred between the two men because he wished to protect Haden Clarke's memory.[42]

'I do not want to tell of that conversation now and I will not unless it is absolutely necessary,' he said. It was a clever ploy in which Lancaster was absolved of any responsibility for what he might now reveal of a detrimental nature concerning Clarke.

'On my shoulders rests responsibility for the conduct of your defence – please answer my question!' Carson admonished him, loftily. Lancaster, thus neatly absolved of any possible accusations of treachery, did so:

'Haden talked of his illness. He was almost in tears. He expressed his great remorse and regret over what had happened between himself and Chubbie. Previously we had discussed the beginning of their intimacy.' Lancaster also said Haden told him he had had the malady for some time.

---

alone to do so.

[42] In fact, he had discussed Haden Clarke's illness with Hawthorne when giving his statement, which nullifies this motive he offered; he had also offered this as the reason Haden had shot himself to Fitzhugh Lee and Hudson at the hospital.

Carson: Was there any discussion then regarding the permanence of Clarke's and Chubbie's love for each other?

Lancaster: Yes, he was very frank. He said: 'I have had many affairs in my life but this time I am absolutely in love. I shall do everything in my power to make her happy. Now I have something to work for.' I was impressed with his sincerity.

Carson: Was the question of his age discussed?

Lancaster: Yes, he said 'I'm sorry but I'm not 31.' He said he was either 26 or 27. I can't remember which, and he asked if I thought it would make any difference to Chubbie.[43]

Carson: Did you discuss any of his other false claims?

Lancaster: Only about the book. He said he didn't know whether he would be able to put it over. I remember the phrase he used – he said he didn't know if he could 'make the grade.' He also told me he didn't have a degree.

Lancaster told the court that Haden Clarke said he had difficulty making money through his writing and showed Lancaster a telegram from his wife saying it would cost $50 to $100 to get a divorce – which he didn't have.[44]

---

[43] Lancaster knew very well now that Clarke had been 26, as this was noted in the newspapers and in court, but his expression of uncertainty as to the age Haden gave him on the evening of 20th April was designed to lend an appearance of veracity to this conversation. It is worth noting also that only Lancaster and Miller claimed Haden Clarke maintained this fiction about his age.

[44] Chubbie claimed to be aware of this and said Clarke had spoken to

Haden Clarke was a veritable chatterbox! Considering the two men had been at loggerheads after dinner, almost at blows, and Lancaster had tried to leave, Haden Clarke was now blabbing about anything and everything.

Lancaster said he told Clarke he must tell Chubbie 'What he had told me tonight, and that if she loved him she would overlook his misstatements.'

Then he said he changed the subject to Tancrel's story about being a US navy officer and carrying a paper hangers' union card, claiming to have hung 'thousands of square miles of wallpaper.' This was, according to Lancaster, responsible for an abrupt change of mood and some hilarity ensued between the two improbable bedfellows.

Lancaster, perhaps conscious of the improbable nature of this conversation between the two adversaries, said Haden Clarke treated him as a 'father confessor.'

According to Lancaster this bonhomie finally ended with:

'I was lying back on my bed yawning, and I said, "Let's talk it over in the morning with Chubbie." I can remember his last words:

"You're the whitest man I ever met, Bill."

'Then I turned off the lights. It was brilliant moonlight that night.'

He said the gun he had bought in St. Louis was lying on a table between the two men's beds. The

---

her of it. Lancaster's conversation suggests it had been withheld from Chubbie. The fact that Chubbie had agreed to delay the marriage for the month in the car drive home, also indicates she had no knowledge of the telegram.

reason for the gun being out was because Haden Clarke inquired about it after Lancaster had spoken earlier about visiting Huston in the morning to return it. The next thing he was aware of was being 'awakened by a noise...a bang. When I first came to, I was under the impression a window had fallen. I called out, "What's that, Haden?"'

'And what did you hear then?'

The courtroom was spellbound, rapt in its attention. They were in the presence of the tragedy, witnesses to the fatal moment: either a murder or a suicide had now occurred. There was a thrilled silence, as Haden Clarke in his death throes was conjured before their eyes.

'A gurgling sound came from Haden's bed. I turned on the light and looked at Haden's bed. I could see something had happened. He had blood running over his face.'

'Did you see the pistol?'

'No. I said to him, "what have you done?"'

'His right arm was bent upward at the elbow, with the hand turned in toward the body. Then I saw the pistol half under his body.'

'When and where did you last see the gun?'

'On the table between our beds. Haden had picked it up and I told him to be careful, it was loaded. We had talked about my buying the gun to replace Huston's, earlier in the evening.' Yet more friendly conversation between the loquacious Haden Clarke and Lancaster.

'What did you do?'

'I asked him a second time to speak to me. He just moaned... I looked around for a note indicating what had happened... I sat down at the typewriter. It took me about five minutes. I then took a pencil and the notes and went to the bed and asked Haden to speak to me again. I asked him to try to sign the notes; there was no answer but a groan, and Clarke's head moved feebly back and forth. Then I shouted "Chubbie" and got no reply. Then I did something I shouldn't have done. I scribbled "Haden" on one note and wrote "H" on the other.' (*Daily Mirror*, 11th August 1932)

The account was as ingenious as it was improbable: the forgeries had been exposed, but his account of the conversation (a late addition to his version of events) managed to convey friendship and mutual respect; the actual words used in the notes were words he attributed to Clarke in that conversation; and he had, by his account, simply put Haden Clarke's sentiments into print for him, intending for him to sign them: his single error and wrong was, therefore, in signing the notes himself.

Finally, asked by Carson about the pistol, Lancaster said that police officer Hudson had picked this up with a handkerchief, and placed it directly into his pocket: there was no box.

Carson's work was done.

During a total of 9 hours and 10 minutes over the course of three days, he had taken Lancaster through an account of his life, his relationships and the events of the April night which had resulted in Haden Clarke's death. He had accounted for everything in one manner or another, and Lancaster's position was much fortified. But it was now the State Attorney Hawthorne's turn to probe Lancaster's account: the defence knew it would be a different matter entirely.

15. Lancaster's Ordeal

It was a hot day when Vernon Hawthorne stood up in the Florida courtroom to begin his cross examination of Bill Lancaster. The heat, intensified by the murmur of bodies in the tightly packed room, was accompanied by the high whine of occasional mosquitoes flying lone sorties, and the shuffle of people, stale and close in the confined space. Hawthorne looked hard at Lancaster on the stand:

'Captain Lancaster,' he said. 'The first question asked of you this morning was "Did you kill Haden Clarke?" Your answer was in the negative. Who did kill him?'

Lancaster: Haden Clarke committed suicide.

Hawthorne: In your presence?

Lancaster: I didn't see him.

Hawthorne: Was it in your presence?

Lancaster: I must have been in the room with him...

Hawthorne then read the suicide note addressed to Lancaster out loud to the court. When he had finished he looked up at Lancaster:

'This is on Latin American Airways stationery. Did you write that note?'

'Yes,' said Lancaster.

'Positive?'

'Yes.'

He then read the second letter, the one addressed to Chubbie, to the court. Again, he looked up from the letter and queried:

'Is that your work?'

'Yes,' replied Lancaster.

'Positive?'

'Yes.'

Hawthorne: Are you as positive today it is yours as you were on April 23rd that it wasn't?

Lancaster: Yes.

Hawthorne: Did anyone ask you in my office on that date if you wrote those notes?

Lancaster: No.

Hawthorne: Didn't Jones? [Assistant State Attorney Henry Jones]

Lancaster: No.

Hawthorne: Did you afterwards send word to Jones that you were sorry you didn't tell him the truth about the notes when he asked you?

Lancaster: I didn't mean that. I meant I was sorry that I acted a lie.

Hawthorne: When you were shown these notes in my office and the discrepancies between the typing of Clarke and the typing of the notes and the similarity between them and your own, what did you say?

Lancaster: I believe I said, 'Isn't that a coincidence?'

Hawthorne: What else did you say?

Lancaster: I can't recall.

Hawthorne: When you were examined in my office were you being subjected to abuse or discourtesy by anyone?

Lancaster: No.

Hawthorne: Were you more excited in my office than when you wrote those notes beside Clarke's body?

Lancaster: I was less excited.

Hawthorne: What else did you say about these notes?

Lancaster: I suggested getting outside experts to look at them...

Hawthorne: What was your purpose in suggesting that?

Lancaster: To put you off the scent.

Hawthorne had here established 1) that Lancaster was capable of falsehood; 2) that he was extremely clever in bluffing the matter of a lie; 3) that his apparent volunteering the information that he had written the notes, was not because he wished to tell the truth, but done in the certain knowledge that he had been discovered.

His objectives secured, Hawthorne made no further comment on this. Instead, he turned to the matter of the revolver. Lancaster told him he had bought the gun at a sporting goods store in St Louis for $30 and registered it with a local sheriff there.

Hawthorne: Did you give a cheque to Gentry Shelton Snr?

Lancaster: Yes, for $100.

Hawthorne: On what bank was that cheque drawn?

Lancaster: On my bank. I gave that cheque with the understanding it was not to be presented.

Hawthorne: Then he betrayed your trust, Captain Lancaster, by presenting that cheque?

Lancaster: No, he didn't present the cheque.

Hawthorne: Would you recognise that cheque?

Lancaster: I certainly would.

Hawthorne: Examine this and see if you can identify it.

Here he handed Lancaster a piece of paper.

Lancaster (studying the paper): That looks like a photostat copy of my cheque.

Hawthorne: And on the back is Mr Gentry Shelton Snr's endorsement. On the front is marked 'Returned First National Bank. Account closed.'

Lancaster: Until this moment I didn't know that cheque had been presented.

Hawthorne: Then he has betrayed your trust?

Lancaster: Yes, very much so.

Hawthorne: Why did you give him the cheque? Why not an IOU?

Lancaster: His son asked me to.

Hawthorne: So you gave him a cheque on a bank where you had no account?

Lancaster: The account was closed since I have been in jail. I didn't close it.

Hawthorne: Then the bank has betrayed you too?

In spite of the prosecution scoring off Lancaster to good effect in these exchanges, the mood in court was markedly in his favour. The newspapers, fickle arbiters of public opinion and purveyors of dubious fact, had altered their view; his character was now admired. The articles and interviews given by Chubbie, and the drip-feed of favourable stories and press briefings by Lathero, had tilted the scales decidedly in Lancaster's favour. On one occasion when the spectators in court roused themselves in Lancaster's approval, the judge was indignant – 'this is not a vaudeville show!' he exclaimed. The mood of the audience was now changed: Lancaster had correctly observed in his letter to Kiki just a month previously, that the justice system in America was theatre. His own performance and every aspect of the trial's stage management by Lathero and Carson was being employed to excellent effect.

Hawthorne soldiered on – it was becoming a struggle for him to play his part before a hostile audience. He was the pantomime villain in their eyes. He asked Lancaster when he had loaded the gun, and Lancaster replied he had done so in Nashville on the evening prior to his return to Miami.

Hawthorne: Your diary shows there was a dire need of funds at home. Weren't Haden Clarke and Chubbie uppermost in your mind?

Lancaster: No. I was afraid she might have been harmed.

Hawthorne: By whom?

Lancaster: Haden.

Hawthorne: In what way?

Lancaster: He might have taken advantage of her because she drank.

Hawthorne: The reason you were so worried about Chubbie was because you loved her better than anything in the world, wasn't it?

Lancaster: Yes.

Hawthorne: Would you lie for her?

Lancaster: I have.

Hawthorne: Would you steal for her?

Lancaster: I have stolen for her.

Hawthorne: Would you kill for her?

Lancaster: I would.

Hawthorne: Did you?

Lancaster: I did not.

Lancaster's handling of these questions was deft. He had not made the error of attempting to deny the lesser offences (i.e. lying and theft) only to have the truth of these drawn from him. This candid approach had enabled him to make the damaging assertion that he would kill for her seem a virtue, by his lack of hesitation in the matter – perfectly setting up his denial that he had done so. He had shown his hand as the stakes rose, to be a royal flush of truth: the list of truths he had volunteered invested the consequential matter of his word that he had not killed Haden Clarke with the same stamp of authenticity. Hawthorne had failed to draw the conclusion he had hoped from this suite of questions. The audience beamed.

He then asked:

'You met Chubbie in London?'

Lancaster: Yes.

Hawthorne: Ever meet her husband?

Lancaster: Yes, in Australia.

Hawthorne: Were they divorced?

Lancaster: No, separated.

Wearily, he turned to the matter of Lancaster's desertion of his wife and children – surely it would win the audience to his side – Lancaster must be condemned on this account if on no other... but Carson objected to this because it had no bearing on the matter of the charge against Lancaster: Judge Atkinson upheld his objection. It was a serious blow to the State's case, as his desertion of his wife and children impacted directly on Lancaster's claims to be an honourable man - and on the impression Lancaster, Chubbie, and the defence both in and out of court had worked hard to foster. The subject was now permanently out of bounds.

Hawthorne obtained a little more traction on the subject of Clarke's 'malady,' which Lancaster claimed Clarke had told him of himself.

Hawthorne: You found out before you got home and from the lips of Clarke that he had a serious malady?

Lancaster: You are quite right.

Hawthorne: Did the love affair of Clarke and Chubbie still appear quite beautiful to you?

Lancaster: Yes.

Hawthorne: The knowledge of this malady didn't affect you?

Lancaster: No. They were very much in love; I saw only that.

Having forced his quarry into an improbable assertion, Hawthorne played this for all it was worth:
'Then when you learned of the intimacies between them, while you were away, it still appeared beautiful to you?' he asked.

Lancaster: There was a beautiful side to it...

And –

Hawthorne: You left Chubbie with Clarke, a drinker, and she was a drinker too?

Lancaster: Yes, but his reputation was good.

Hawthorne: According to your standards, Captain Lancaster? Hadn't he used your house as a house of prostitution?

It was a step too far by Hawthorne.

Lancaster: No.

Hawthorne: Hadn't he stayed there three nights with a woman to whom he was not married?

Lancaster: Yes. That was not prostitution.

Hawthorne: But he had used your home as a house of debauchery, hadn't he?

Lancaster, under increasing pressure, said that Haden spent nights with girls, but said it was not done with his consent – he had simply not objected to it:

'I didn't consent, but I didn't hold it against him,' he said.

Hawthorne: It was beautiful to you?

Lancaster: No. I didn't think Mrs Keith Miller should allow it and I remarked to her about it.

Clearly Mrs Keith Miller was in charge of the house and knew of Haden's lovers. Hawthorne next turned to another matter:

Hawthorne: Did you write an entry in your diary for January 7th?

Lancaster: Yes.

Hawthorne: (reading) 'Fined $50 with a suspended license on a complaint filed by driver of Buick. American justice is all wet. The evidence given was insufficient to convict me, but, like all American courts, they are subject to the inefficiency of the court officials and police.' What did you mean when you wrote 'American justice is all wet'?

Lancaster: I had been found guilty of something I hadn't done. I now realise I should not have written it. I'm sorry you don't like it.

'Being an American, I don't like any of it!' snapped Hawthorne, probably hoping to muster some patriotic indignation from the American jury. Then:

Hawthorne: Did you ever utter threats concerning Clarke in front of Tancrel and Russell?

Lancaster: No.

Hawthorne: Did you tell Gentry Shelton you had seen a hundred die under machine gun fire, and you wouldn't mind seeing another dead man?

Lancaster: No.

Hawthorne: Shelton is not here, is he?

Shelton had not shown in court to the State prosecutor's chagrin. He could not be questioned on this matter, nor on a great many other matters to which he was said to have been a witness. But he had made a written statement to investigators in Miami in May – unfortunately, owing to his absence from court, the contents of this are unknown, although Hawthorne clearly implies here that Lancaster did indeed issue the threats Tancrel and Russell accused him of. Lancaster admitted Russell had shown him letters from his wife in LA, but claimed he had told Russell he trusted Chubbie.

'Did you tell Gentry Shelton you would see Haden Clarke dead before he would marry Chubbie?' he asked him.

'I did not. That night I drank a pint of Scotch... I might have uttered threats. I said, "If he hurts Chubbie, he'll have to answer to me."'

It was a better spin on a matter on which Shelton's account could not be probed, and on which Tancrel's identical corroboration was distrusted, but it placed Lancaster in a new difficulty. Hawthorne was quick upon it:

Hawthorne: Would you consider his [Clarke's] behaviour as harming her?

Lancaster: I would, but when I arrived, I overlooked it.

And:

Hawthorne: Would you consider Haden Clarke a man of calm or flighty nature?

Lancaster: He was a man who would act on impulse.

Hawthorne: Yet you left your gun in his plain view and where he could easily reach it?

Lancaster: I never thought of that...

Then:

Hawthorne: He went to bed laughing?

Lancaster: Yes, he laughed at the story of Tancrel's paper-hanging exploits.

Hawthorne: And his last words were?

Lancaster: 'Bill, you're the whitest man I know.'

Hawthorne: And in the storm and strain you wrote the notes before calling the doctor?

Lancaster: Yes.

Hawthorne: You saw people die in the war?

Lancaster: Yes, quite a few.

Hawthorne: Did you remember a person with a similar head wound live or talk again?

Lancaster: Yes, I have known it.

Hawthorne wanted to draw attention to the importance of urgency in obtaining medical treatment for Haden Clarke. He hoped to emphasise this and Lancaster's delay by his next question:

'How long did it take you to type the notes?' he asked.

Lancaster: Five minutes.

Hawthorne: How long was it from the time the shot was fired until the time you called Mrs Keith Miller?

Lancaster: No more than eight minutes.

He then asked Lancaster to demonstrate in court how he had typed the notes, and Lancaster obliged, while being timed: it took him two and a half minutes. It had been a mistake to request this of Lancaster – it has surely never more truly been said that a lawyer should never ask a question to which he does not already know the answer! It was a damp squib to the prosecution's attempt to damage Lancaster's account, and had the specific effect of undermining the prosecutor's attempt to show unnatural dilatoriness on Lancaster's part, in seeking medical attention for Clarke.

Lancaster's ordeal was over. It had been a slog, but his showing had been exemplary; he had triumphed - he had evaded the traps Hawthorne had set for him deftly, as Chubbie had walked blindly into them. A great deal of what should have been damning evidence was ameliorated. The evidence of Shelton had been obviated by his absence from court, and the questions relating to Lancaster's desertion of his wife and children had been disallowed. On such trivialities, the verdict might depend. The press and public opinion now clearly favoured Lancaster, and in the courtroom there was unbridled support for him, expressed by the stamping of feet, applause and vocal approval – the judge had admonished those in attendance on a number of occasions and he admonished them again in the absence of the jury, prior to opening proceedings on the morning of Thursday 11th August: once again he warned the spectators to remain silent during the session. He said he had learned there was to be 'another demonstration in Lancaster's favor today,' and that he would not allow it. The claque was muted, for a while at least.

*

Back in England the Lancasters were following their son's trial closely. They were feeling confident also – or at least they were putting a brave face on things:

'My son had no fear, and he has no fear,' said Mr Lancaster senior to the *Daily Herald* reporter. 'He was captain of his boxing team when he was in the RAF in which he spent nine years. He rode in a bronco competition at the White City. Nothing could stop him.

'Now he writes from Miami with the same old courage he has shown all through his life. Both my boys were splendid youngsters. The younger joined up as an airman before he was 17 and was shot down behind German lines.' (*Daily Herald*, 11th August 1932)

Lancaster's parents were largely confined to their home in Crystal Palace and were frequently doorstepped by reporters lying in wait outside their home.

This was a period of considerable anxiety for them.

*

It was not the only news capturing the public's attention back in Britain, though. The *Sunday Mirror* reported that a Mrs Andrews from Wareham, Dorset, whose husband Arthur had gone missing, was much relieved to receive a letter from him. Apparently he had left the house on the evening of 15th February carrying the cat and saying he was going to drown it – he didn't return. The cat was discovered safe and sound two days later, a mile and a half away – but Arthur Andrews was missing. Fears of his neighbours that he may have drowned himself instead of the cat, however, were unfounded. Mrs Andrews gratifyingly received a letter from her husband in early August, informing her he had been terribly ill and lost his memory. He was also, it seems, being cared for on a remote island off the Canadian coast by a French woman called Yvonne, who was 'sort of queen of the island.'

'I can't tell you where I am,' wrote the unfortunate man. 'No more than I can gather it is off the Canadian coast. How I came here I can't find out. I have been very ill, and my memory is a blank. I can only remember you, dear, and Jimmie.' (Jimmie was his son.)

'Yvonne,' the 23-year-old French Queen of the remote island, had fallen in love with him, apparently - but he was having none of it.

Mrs Andrews, at once relieved to find her beloved husband was alive, handed his letter to the local police. Fortunately the police were able to find her husband. It seems he was mistaken as to his whereabouts – he was in fact living in a hostel in Bristol, where a policeman escorted him to the train station and placed him on a train home. His wife was waiting for him here for what was surely a joyful reunion. (*Sunday Mirror*, 10th August 1932)

16. The Trial Nears its End

The case was drawing to its close, the main witnesses had been heard – a few additional witnesses were called to corroborate, clarify or rebut items of previous testimony and dispute.

Dick Lavender, a roommate of Haden Clarke from New Orleans, testified he had met Haden in a New Orleans speakeasy, and they had roomed together in Canal Street for a few weeks. He said that he and Haden drank a great deal and Haden Clarke smoked marijuana 'torpedoes' – although he himself did not. He also said Haden Clarke had unprotected sex with women in spite of his 'malady' – an ailment he had suffered with for some time and had had several treatments for. He said when he challenged Clarke on this, he had retorted he didn't care because 'someone gave it to me.' Lavender also said Clarke discussed suicide with him and had once told him he knew where to shoot oneself to effect certain death – this was behind the ear. The two men rode freight trains from New Orleans to Miami, and at Daytona Beach, Clarke had taken some of Lavender's money and decamped. Hawthorne's cross-examination of this new witness was scathing. He sought to show Lavender to be disreputable and an untruthful witness.

Hawthorne: What are you doing now?

Lavender: Nothing.

Hawthorne: You got two cheques for a total of $24?

Lavender: Yes.

Hawthorne: Who were they from?

Lavender: The U.S. government, the Veterans' Bureau.

Hawthorne: How long have you been getting government cheques?

Lavender: Since right after the war. [14 years]

Hawthorne: Did you have to hold Haden down while on the trip to prevent him from committing suicide?

Lavender: No, he held me down. I was the one he thought was going to commit suicide.

Hawthorne: Oh, you were the one with suicidal thoughts?

Lavender: Yes.

Thomas S Jefferson, Justice of the Peace, was called by the defence to explain why an inquest had not been held. He said the State Attorney's office had requested a postponement pending the completion of the murder inquiries. As the matter had been before a Grand Jury he deemed it unnecessary to proceed with the inquest subsequently.

The owner of New Haven Restaurant, 104 S Miami Avenue, Mrs Alma Throup (1889-1986), was called by the defence to testify that she had known Clarke 4-6 weeks and he was often broke and had complained he would like to leave, but said he had fallen in love. She loaned him a dime on one occasion, which he said he would repay but didn't.

Richard Richardson, an aspiring playwright, who had known Clarke for about a year, said Haden was a heavy drinker. He said he had discussed with Clarke the best way of shooting oneself, and Clarke had said the place to do it was behind the right ear. It was tenuous stuff, and his testimony was not wholly helpful to the defence case either, because under cross-examination he added that Clarke had intimated that 'shooting oneself in the temple was inadvisable, because it often resulted only in blindness'! It was difficult to know whose point he had proved.

Carson claimed Clarke had been bigamously married in 1931 to a woman from New York named Virginia, from whom letters were found in the Coral Gables bungalow.[45] Miss Peggy Brown, his most recent girlfriend/fiancé, was shown also to be married, but this line of argument was obviously limited by the fact that it hardly improved the characters of Lancaster, who was married, and Chubbie, who had been having an affair simultaneously with two married men and had been married herself during one of these affairs!

The autopsy report gave little intelligence either. Dr Tallman produced Haden Clarke's skull in court, which caused a thrill in the proceedings. It was reported that many women left court in distress; Mrs Clarke and Chubbie Miller were not present in court on this occasion. The jury passed the skull

---

[45] There was no evidence of this – the woman was Virginia Van Wert (b 1908) who was a widowed hairdresser, and became engaged to Clarke. In her letters she expressed great passion for Haden.

amongst their number, gingerly, each examining it carefully. Bill Lancaster leaned forward and gazed at the skull of his friend with great interest and apparent curiosity. Perhaps he was trying to reconstruct the features of his friend, whom he had flown with, and fished, and rustled chickens and rabbits from neighbouring houses with – and with whom he had quarrelled three months before. What would he say if he could articulate these bones now? Haden Clarke was silent still: he just grinned, the eternal rictus of the dead.

Then the defence called Dr Albert Hamilton (1860-1938). His appearance on the witness stand was notable: he proclaimed himself to be by profession an analytical chemist. In fact, he was everything, but chiefly something of a self-vaunting showman, a braggart and self-appointed expert in anything that might turn a profit for him. Since the 1880s he had been parlaying highly dubious expertise to the highest bidder as a witness for hire – and since 1913 he had been exposed in successive trials as a fraud. His evidence resulted in Charles Stielow, a labourer from West Shelby in New York, receiving a death sentence in 1915, and his subsequently spending five years in Sing-Sing before Hamilton's deception was discovered, and Stielow was reprieved. Yet Hamilton continued uncensured and unabashed. He was shameless. In 1921 he was a forensic witness in the Sacco/Vanzetti trial and was caught trying to switch gun parts in court.[46] He shrugged this off

[46] Nicola Sacco (1891-1927) and Bartolomeo Vanzetti (1888-1927) were Italian immigrant anarchists who were executed for an armed robbery and murder in 1927. A highly controversial case both at the time and since, the two men were pardoned by proclamation of the

too. A report into his conduct on this occasion was scathing, but ultimately no action was taken against him.

In 1932 Carson hired him as an expert witness – apparently Hamilton was not remunerated for this beyond his expenses, but Hamilton duly informed the press of his arrival, and liberally handed out his photograph to reporters, in case they wished to write an article about him! He supplied them with a glowing account of himself and his cases, which resulted in highly laudatory articles being published on 'the Sherlock Holmes of forensics, Dr Hamilton,' and 'Ballistics Marvel.' Naturally Carson was more than happy to present him to the court as Dr Hamilton, of 47 years' experience as a 'ballistics expert and nationally known criminologist.' He was neither a doctor nor a ballistics expert in any accredited sense, and his atrocious record as a man who had been known to offer his services to both prosecution and defence counsels, offering to supply precisely the opposite evidence to each, should have disqualified him from any courtroom. Nevertheless, 'Dr' Hamilton – whose reputation in other states seems not to have been as well known in Florida, gave evidence now with aplomb and breath-taking assuredness:

'There was but one, and only one conclusion that could be arrived at from the [autopsy] examination,' he told the court, 'And that was that the shot was self-inflicted, a close, hard contact shot at the instant the gun was hard against the head and head hard against the gun.'

'Was it suicide or homicide?' asked Carson.

Massachusetts Governor Michael Dukakis in 1977.

'Absolutely suicide. There is not a scintilla of evidence to support a theory of homicide or murder.'

There was never equivocation in Hamilton's pronouncements: they were decrees absolute. His great value as an expert witness was his certainty in all his pronouncements.

He pointed to 'subcutaneous ballooning' as a proof of suicide. He had discovered brain tissue and hairs on the nozzle of the gun, he said.

Hawthorne questioned Hamilton about his qualifications – was he a doctor? Hamilton was quite unfazed; he claimed lawyers called him Dr, not he. It was not for him to discourage them. Hawthorne questioned him in detail, too, on his involvement in the Sacco/Vanzetti case and read a report to the court concerning Hamilton's conduct in this. Although not conclusive of Hamilton's guilt in the matter of switching barrels, it did suggest, at the very least, he had been careless to the point of criminality. A Dade County investigator, C.A. Peterson, was asked about Hamilton's reputation. His understatement was revealing:

Hawthorne: Do you know of his reputation as an expert?

Peterson: Yes, I know his reputation.

Hawthorne: Is it good or bad?

Peterson: Bad.

Hawthorne: In view of your last statement would you believe him on oath?

Peterson: No, I would not.

Three other expert witnesses were subsequently called by the prosecution to identify the 'hairs' found by Hamilton on the gun nozzle as being cotton fibres and to testify that no brain tissue had been discovered on the gun barrel. Hawthorne requested of the judge that 'Dr' Hamilton's testimony be struck from the record – but Judge Atkinson refused this: Hamilton had done some damage. His disagreement with two other doctors concerning its not being possible to tell who had fired the shot, was similarly uncompromising:

'I found nothing to support anything but suicide. I say this not as an opinion, but actual knowledge,' he declared. A jury loves an expert witness who supplies them with such unqualified certainty! By contrast, doctors Gowe, Walter C Jones, Tallman and Stewart could offer no professional opinion as to who had held the gun.

On the afternoon of 12th August, the judge, jury and Bill Lancaster visited the scene of the alleged crime at Coral Gables. The next morning Lancaster was permitted to make a statement to the court that on the visit of the previous day, the beds had not been situated as close together as they had been on the night of the shooting. He also said he recalled now seeing Haden Clarke's missing letter on a table after Haden had been removed to hospital. The reason he recalled this was, he said, because he had used the letter to copy Haden's signature for the suicide notes. Hawthorne asked him if this was the case, why had he previously maintained that when Haden couldn't sign the letters, he had '*scribbled* Haden on one and H on the other'? Lancaster was described in the *Miami*

Daily News as 'becoming confused' here. It was a rare misstep.

Joseph Ince, a former RAF pilot, appeared for the defence and denied Tancrel's claim that he had seen Lancaster display resentment towards Haden Clarke at El Paso.

It was Hawthorne's turn to call some additional witnesses in rebuttal. Vladimir Virrick (1893-1978), described in court as an architect, was the first of these. He was well-acquainted with Clarke and typically played bridge with him twice each week, he said. He had been present at the bridge party 'five to seven days before Haden's death,' when Chubbie and Haden had received the telephone call from Lancaster asking him if he and Chubbie were having an affair. That was, he thought, about 14th-16th April. He also said Chubbie 'was not sober.' (*Miami Daily News*, 15th August 1932). Virrick said he had never seen Clarke depressed, but that on the occasion of the phone call Clarke had expressed concern after he had hung up the phone:

'I think there will be trouble, damn it. He's coming...'

Paul Prufert (1889-1949), also present at the same bridge party, confirmed this:

'There'll be trouble – that son of a bitch is coming back...' was his candid recollection of Haden's words.

Hawthorne: Was Mrs Miller drunk or sober?

Prufert: Well, she wasn't sober.

Prufert also agreed with Virrick that Clarke was never depressed or moody either. Both men said he was 'happy go lucky.' Prufert said he often played bridge and chess with Clarke and had never seen him depressed or downhearted.

A man called Brown, who had employed and known Clarke for over two years, and had spent a month on a trip with him, was asked by Hawthorne whether he had ever seen Clarke depressed.

Brown: No, he never thought of yesterday or tomorrow.

Hawthorne: Did you ever see him with his mother?

Brown: Yes.

He said he had seen Clarke get impatient with her.

Hawthorne: Did you ever seen him in rages directed against her?

Brown: No.

He said he had last seen Haden Clarke on 5 April.

Hawthorne: Did finances depress him?

Brown: No, he was always more or less hard-up.

A man named Jorgenson was called and said he had known Clarke for four years.

Hawthorne: Intimately?

Jorgenson: Yes.

Hawthorne: Did you observe his general demeanour in this period?

Jorgenson: Yes. He appeared to be happy-go-lucky.

Hawthorne: Did you ever see Clarke depressed?

Jorgenson: Never.

A Mr Schauffler, structural engineer, who'd known Clarke well for two years said he had never seen him depressed or worried about anything. A Mr Belchan, consulting engineer, who frequently went on fishing trips with Haden, also called him happy-go-lucky.

Hawthorne: Did he ever show any signs of being depressed?

Schauffler: No, furthest from that.

A mechanic, James Enrico, from Viking Airport in Miami, was then called and reported that the meeting between Clarke and Lancaster on the evening of 20th April had not been cordial, as Lancaster and Miller claimed: the two men did not shake hands. It was a cold, tense stand-off.

Mrs Ida Clarke, Haden's mother, had been due to take the stand and this event was awaited with great interest – but the audience was to be disappointed: she was said to be in a state of collapse and unable to appear. It was a disappointment to the prosecution too, as they had hoped to rebut Chubbie's claims that Haden was at odds with his mother, which the defence had proposed may have been a motive for his suicide. They hoped also to counter claims of depression on Haden's part, and to establish Haden's antipathy to guns and suicide. It seems in addition, that Mrs Clarke had said that Lancaster had told her that he sometimes 'thought he might have killed Haden.' This fascinating claim of hers was never tested; nor the claim she made that Lancaster had asked her to voice her conviction he had had nothing to do with her son's death – something she had refused to do.

The evidence had now been heard – the prosecution and defence cases had been presented and probed. Now the speeches of respective counsel would be heard.

On 15th August Assistant State Attorney Henry M. Jones addressed the jury:

'Consider the three persons who were in the Keith Miller house at the time of the tragedy,' he said. One now lies in a Miami cemetery, his lips sealed by death.[47] A second, the defendant here on trial for his life, is the most interested person in the world in the outcome of the trial...

'You are reasonable men. Will you be guided by self-serving professions of innocence or by facts presented to you?'

He went on to say Clarke was 'cock of the walk' upon Lancaster's return: he had won the lady and vanquished his rival. There was also the fact that Haden Clarke of all people, a man who wrote with eloquence, had not left a note: he would have done so. Huston owed Lancaster $250, the defence had claimed – yet Lancaster bought him a gun he had loaned him, on money drawn on a bad cheque.

He spoke first of Lancaster's character, and he referred to Chubbie as a 'fallen woman':

---

[47] Presumably excluding his skull which was in a box in the courtroom on the evidence table.

'When a woman loses her virtue, she loses all. She also, it seems, loses the power to tell the truth.'

The motive for killing Haden Clarke was Lancaster's, said Jones; sex was the motive – beneath the veneer of civilisation there was the 'animal in all of us... The greater a man's love for a woman, the greater his motive for killing his rival.'

Every word of Lancaster's diary proved his all-consuming love for Chubbie Miller:

'He didn't even attempt his own life, in spite of his saying he would in his diary...He gave worthless cheques to all, but would buy a revolver to replace that which he had borrowed.'

In addition, three of the four letters written to Lancaster at St Louis were missing. The defence claimed the State had destroyed them – why would the State destroy them, he asked. In whose interest could it possibly be?

Of Lancaster, he said:

'He is a supreme actor, shrewd beyond degree – cold, calculating. Why did he say 'Get more experts' when it was suggested the letters were forgeries? That's the man who tells you of his honour.

'He shot Haden Clarke in his head while he slept,' he told the jury. 'It was the most dastardly and ignominious murder ever committed.'

After shooting him, Lancaster did not call a doctor or Chubbie, but in cold blood he forged two notes. The key clue was the angle at which the bullet had gone through Haden Clarke's skull:

'When you get there in the jury room, lie down on the floor and see if you can shoot yourself through the head where this man was shot.'

The bullet entered the right temple and exited above the left ear. Clarke would have had to depress the trigger with his thumb. But the bullet was, Jones said, 'exactly as one might expect had the shot been fired by someone standing between the two beds.' (*Miami Daily News*, 16th August 1932)

At 4.28 p.m. Carson began his address to the jury. He opened with the eulogy of Senator John W Daniels for the Confederate general, Robert E Lee: he characterised Lancaster as being like Robert E. Lee, whom he clearly admired, and never more so than in the adversity he suffered following his defeat:

'William Newton Lancaster, 4,000 miles from his home, facing an American jury upon a charge of murder in the first degree, having gone through periods of financial distress, deprivation, and almost starvation, and having for many months paced the narrow confines of his lonely cell, deserted by many, but not by all of his friends, stands forth above those who have surrounded him in such pure sweetness, strength, unselfishness, and sheer nobility of character, so that we can only begin to appreciate it when we see it shine like a brilliant diamond, against the muck and dirt and filth which form the solid background of this trial.' If Robert E. Lee stood ghost-like in the wings of the theatre of justice, before the jurors' eyes, proud and undefeated, he might have baulked at the comparison.

Carson reminded the jury that Lancaster was not charged with adultery or passing bad cheques, or stealing chickens, ducks or rabbits, but with murder. The State case was circumstantial and based very much on the notion that if Lancaster did not kill Haden Clarke, then he ought to have done. He pointed out that the attorney Ernest Huston had mitigated the evidence of the gun –

'This is the gun I bought to replace the one you loaned me and therefore it is technically yours...' Lancaster had told him.

Huston's account of Lancaster's asking if Haden Clarke would talk again, was likewise explained by the addition of the rider, 'so he can tell us why he did it.' Then there was the pillow which Huston said had been 'mussed' in contrast to the evidence of the State police.

Against this was officer Earl Hudson's slipshod testimony, his faulty memory evinced by various slips he had made.

The missing letters from Chubbie which Lancaster received at St Louis, were lost or mislaid by the police and investigators, not by Lancaster. The discovery by Chubbie and Lancaster of a crumpled-up telegram apparently overlooked by detectives, clearly showed their incompetence in this respect.

Earl Hudson had misled the court concerning his sister-in-law 'Miss Peggy Brown,' whom he had been forced to admit was a married woman. In comparison, Chubbie Miller's testimony was unimpeachable. Lancaster's admission to forging the notes was his own, made by him unprompted and in good faith. Tancrel and Russell were vindictive liars. Of Tancrel, he said: 'Mr, Captain, Admiral and General, Ambassador Tancrel, the man who had papered his own house thousands of times...' This humorous effect was grotesque exaggeration, and its purpose was to destroy

Tancrel's character and therefore every aspect of his testimony. The audience chuckled appreciatively.

Carson's address continued on the following morning, 16th August. He said that although the circumstances looked suspicious, the prosecution case rested on five circumstances:

1. Lancaster's love for Chubbie.
2. The threats he made against Haden Clarke to Tancrel and Russell.
3. Lancaster's purchase of a revolver in St Louis.
4. The forgery of the suicide notes.
5. Lancaster's asking whether Clarke would be able to speak again.

All these points, said Carson, had been satisfactorily dealt with - conclusively so – and the prosecution case had completely failed. In fact, it had proved the opposite of that which it intended – that Clarke had indeed committed suicide. It was the only possible conclusion to draw from the evidence.

Carson blamed Chubbie for the sordid elements of the case:

'There are women who, due to some pathological condition, are utterly unable to live up to the standards of virtue and chastity which you and I have been taught to believe constitutes the crowning virtue of the set to which our mothers belong…'

But he softened the effect of this by referring to -

'This woman's bravery in bringing into the glaring light of public opinion in the interests of truth, matters she had thought to be forever hidden, is an outstanding point of this trial.' (*Daily News*, 17th August 1932)

Carson appealed for Lancaster's acquittal on the basis that he was a gentleman, a war hero, a man who exhibited scrupulous fairness to all in his life. He said that because a man from Kissimmee would murder his love rival, it did not mean that an 'honourable Englishman would do so'! He implied Earl Hudson was a rather stupid cop; fingerprint expert Barker found no fingerprints on the gun because Hudson had wiped it clean; J.F. Russell and Mark Tancrel were felons – nothing they said could or should be trusted. He reiterated the eight reasons Chubbie had written down for the defence as being the reasons why Clarke had committed suicide: remorse, doubt that Jessie would remain with him; doubts concerning his writing ability; the cessation of his sex-life; the great responsibility placed upon him; his illness; his mood swings; and financial worries. Clarke's was 'an honour suicide' declared Carson, because 'there was nothing else for him to do.'

Clarke was weak, unstable, mixed up in many affairs, indulged dope habits: a failure. The fact that Lancaster had signed the motion for the disinterment and autopsy proved his innocence. What had he to fear? That autopsy had showed the gun to be tight against Clarke's head when it was fired, and it showed that he had indeed committed suicide. Its peculiar trajectory and the position at which it was fired was explained by the fact he had turned his head so that the bullet would not hit the 'whitest man he had ever met.' The suicide notes were written and intended solely for Chubbie and proved there was no premeditation. Hawthorne, the

State Attorney, saw an opportunity to make a name for himself, he said, in pursuing such a hopeless case. The quick burial, and the omission of an autopsy, were black marks against him. He suggested the jury could do no other than to find Lancaster not guilty of murdering his friend, Haden Clarke.

Now Hawthorne addressed the jury for the closing summation: it was the prosecution's final opportunity of framing the matter of Clarke's death as a murder committed out of rage and jealousy. He spoke of Carson's defaming everyone in court who was connected with the State case. All were rascals and perjurers in his view. Even the Clerk of the Circuit Court's integrity had been impugned, concerning the cotton fibres which Hamilton had mis-identified as hairs.

Clarke, he said, was the winner the night he was shot – he was not in the least bit depressed or suicidal. And referring to Lancaster:

'The gun goes off and he thinks, he says, a window slammed. I submit that the report of a .38 calibre pistol held less than 3 feet away from your head would burst your eardrums.'

And -

'There is not a single fact or circumstance, when the rule of common reason is applied, that does not point to the guilt of this defendant. Every page in his diary points to his guilt. His own testimony, that he bought a gun while Chubbie was hungry and that he loaded the gun the night before he arrived in Miami, points to his guilt. A guilty conscience needs no accuser, and the fact that he wrote those notes when Clarke was dying doesn't sound so good. Lancaster asked Huston if he could say the death gun was his. Over and over again he asked if Clarke would be able to speak again - these things point to his guilt.'

Hawthorne alluded to the position of the gun when it was discharged as sealing the fact that Lancaster alone fired it, he said. The bullet had been fired in a place in the head where the defence's own witness had said Haden Clarke had said it should not. The autopsy showed only that the victim died of a gunshot wound, the gun being held at close range – nothing more than this. It was murder.

The State witnesses attacked by Carson may have had deficiencies – but they were not the State's choice, they were there because they were Lancaster's choice of companion. The State could only rely on those companions as witnesses to events. Russell had said he spoke to Lancaster about the affair and Lancaster's own diary confirmed the truth of this.

The missing letters Chubbie sent to St Louis were last seen by Lancaster – the State had not seen them at all, and the inference must be that Lancaster had destroyed them by way of concealment for what they might reveal.

'Haden Clarke was not depressed or suicidal. To the victor belongs the spoils – and Haden Clarke was at the top that night; Haden Clarke was in the driver's seat that night. Haden Clarke...told Lancaster he was the head man at the house that night. Lancaster, realizing this, said he would leave the house, go to a hotel, and start back for St Louis in the morning. Lancaster foresaw trouble; Haden Clarke expected it...'

And -

'At the house he [Lancaster] threatens to commit suicide – he might or he might not have meant that threat. It may have been to sell Chubbie on his love for her. But she tells him she loves Haden Clarke.

'Clarke forbids Chubbie from speaking with Lancaster alone, and Lancaster threatens: "If I don't talk alone with her tonight, I'll talk with her in the morning!"'

'Chubbie comes into the sleeping porch and says, "Good night, chaps," and Bill doesn't speak. Then she says "goodnight" again...'

Acutely conscious that Lancaster had the sympathy of those within the court and those without; that the newspapers had turned in his favour, and that the conduct of the gallery of spectators in the court made abundantly clear their support for Lancaster, Hawthorne closed his address with:

'You are a trial jury, not a pardon board. Do not let sympathy or emotion play a part. Decide simply if Haden Clarke committed suicide or if William Newton Lancaster killed him.' (*Miami Daily News*, 17th August 1932)

The arguments had been made; the evidence had now been heard.

It was 11.30 a.m. Wednesday 17th August when Hawthorne concluded his words to the jury. There was a sense of resignation in his demeanour – from the certainty of a conviction, his evidence against Lancaster had been whittled away, diminished until a cloud of doubt hung over it; but equally important was the sympathy that Carson had succeeded in securing for Lancaster, and the sense of the great wrong he had been done by

Chubbie Miller and Haden Clarke. Such things play powerfully on human emotions, right and wrong: the deep-seated morality of ordinary intelligent human beings, interferes with the inviolable principles of the law where the two diverge. Those in court knew it. After a brief recess, Judge Atkinson charged the jury and sent them out for the final act in the trial and the drama: to decide whose case had been made. Did Haden Clarke commit suicide, or was he murdered by Bill Lancaster?

17. The Verdict

The atmosphere in court was tense. The result of months of inquiry, and of legal process was about to reach its conclusion. The decision, whatever the press, the public or anyone else thought on the matter, was the jury's alone. But a jury is not insulated from the wall of opinion outside, nor from the mood within a courtroom. They willed the jury to acquit, strained their collective will against a guilty verdict: they dared them to find Lancaster guilty.

It was 6.30 p.m. in England when the jury retired. It was reported to be the hottest day of the year there. It was hotter at night than at mid-day and at midnight still 73F (20 Celsius). People crowded down to the beach, even at night. There were floodlights set up on the south coast beaches to facilitate this. At Barking Park, in East London, the outdoor swimming pool was open 7 days a week, including Sunday, until 11 p.m. each night.

All thoughts turned to the sea, which insulates the island, and gives refuge from the heat. At Margate councillors were in session that week on matters of grave local concern. They were outraged by the 'bathing slips' being worn by young female bathers and a serious debate raged in the council chamber. Alderman Venner complained of their attire:

'As time has gone on it has slipped further and further...' he warned.

Councillor Abbott said he had been looking all over town for the sea and sunbathing offenders and had found none.

'Go to Palm Bay,' Councillor Fasham advised him.

Councillor Abbott: I took my glasses and a camera.

Councillor Hine helpfully pointed out that the local museum contained pictures of bathers at Margate 200 years ago who wore less than slips!

Three elderly councillors, Graville, Collins and Abbott, custodians of Margate's morals, armed with binoculars, went off to survey the beach for possible offenders and pronounced themselves satisfied:

'I remarked to myself how wonderfully fit and tanned the girls looked,' one told the *Daily Mirror*, 'And that, of course, was partly thanks to these costumes. Nobody could wish for anything better.'

Fifty miles to the west of Margate, Bill Lancaster's parents endured the heat indoors at their Crystal Palace home, and waited for news of their son's fate. It was a long evening.

The jury was out for over five hours. It was no easy task facing them. Their first attempt at a ballot failed to produce a result: the circumstances were undoubtedly damning, Lancaster's account was unsettling, and aspects of it unlikely, even unbelievable. Who amongst them could believe that Haden Clarke had committed suicide? After long arduous discussions, and unable to arrive at a decision, they returned to seek clarification from the judge on the definition of what constituted 'reasonable doubt' and asked to see the exhibits again – the skull and the gun were surely on their mind here – but James Carson objected to this request, anonymously: the jury could not know which party had objected to their request. They clearly wanted to see if it was possible for Clarke to have committed suicide – to lie on the floor, gun in hand as Jones had exhorted them to do, and see for themselves if they could do it; to check this against the angle and path the bullet had followed through Clarke's skull. Carson knew if he refused them, the element of uncertainty they had now declared in this matter, was assured; it would be sustained: they could only acquit Lancaster.

The jurors returned to the jury room non-plussed and empty-handed. The confidence of the defence was now soaring; triumph was waiting in the wings. This time the jurors' absence was a brief one: no more than 20 minutes' delay. News of the jury's impending return electrified those awaiting the denouement. They filed back into the courtroom; all eyes were upon them. There was nothing to indicate what they had decided. They did not look at Lancaster. The gallery quietened, pent upon the verdict: it was a tense moment. The confidence of Lancaster shrank suddenly, as he braced himself; that of the defence team faltered upon the imminence of the verdict. Chubbie waited outside, in quiet terror of what might be. It is always so when the process of justice holds a person's life in the balance. When the variable act of human decision intrudes upon the moment so keenly. It was the ultimate moment of drama. There was absolute silence. The foreman of the jury handed the Clerk to the Circuit Court, E B Leatherman, a note. Without delay, and without any expression, the Clerk read it to the court briskly:

'Not guilty,' he declared.

The court erupted in cheers, shouting, stamping of feet; a roar of approval rent the air. It was vaudeville again. There was no equivocation in this case as to the favour of sentiment in court. As is usual and traditional on such occasions, the judge tried to restore the dignity of the court. But he was hardly heard, still less obeyed. He had no authority in the court of human emotion. The stage was stormed.

Lancaster beamed, delighted; moments afterwards he made a short address to the jury, bowing, and thanking them, for their decision. He posed for photographs with the judge and jury before heading on out of the court. Chubbie was waiting for him near the courtroom door, beyond in the lobby: she heard the thunderous cheer within and knew its import. Her eyes were shining with delight as she greeted him. Outside he was mobbed by back-clapping, beaming well-wishers, whom he acknowledged with smiling good will. It felt like Port Darwin again – but without the rain.

Outside it was brilliant sunshine. Reporters crowded in to catch the words of the acquitted man, a man who moments earlier had stood in peril of his life but now had triumphed. He spoke to them as they jostled him in good humour, shook hands with anyone and everyone. He was now cock of the walk:

'I have been convinced all along that my innocence would be established, and I will always be grateful to Mr Carson and Mr Lathero for their splendid defence of me. My trial has been eminently fair, and I have been treated cordially at all times.'

Asked if his future now included marriage to Chubbie, Lancaster protested:

'Don't ask me that! First of all I need to get a job – though what that might be I cannot tell.'

Outside the sun was hot, but the air seemed fresh to Lancaster. It was new.

Hawthorne was taciturn; he had lost. He betrayed no signs of his feelings, paused only briefly to speak to reporters:

'The performance of my duty to the best of my ability is sufficient compensation. The jury, the only agency provided by law to determine the issue, has rendered its verdict, and I accept it without regret.' (*Miami Daily News*, 18th August 1932)

The principals had left the stage, the reporters hurried off to tender their reviews to impatient editors; the crowd drifted away, carrying with them a murmur of the day's events and their own witness to them. The show was over.

*

It was almost midnight in England. Bill Lancaster's parents received the news in their Crystal Palace home in Park Road, relayed to them by a friend. Their relief was palpable.

'It has been a terrible ordeal, but now, thank goodness, it is over. Although we were very tired, we decided to stay up all night to hear what had happened,' said Mr Lancaster to a reporter from the Daily Mirror.

'We knew our boy was innocent all along, and that knowledge has sustained us,' added his wife. (*Daily Mirror*, 13th August 1932)

State Attorney Hawthorne put Lancaster under relentless pressure, but Lancaster was a formidable witness and made few errors. (*Miami Daily News*)

James Carson was a pugnacious political animal, who coaxed the best from his client. (*Miami Daily News*)

BALLISTIC MARVEL

DR. ALBERT HAMILTON

A legend in his own mind: the term 'ballistic marvel' was one of many 'Dr' Albert H Hamilton accorded to himself. Hamilton plagued US courtrooms for over 40 years, offering his services to whichever side would pay him. His great value for counsel was his certainty in all things. (*Miami Daily News*).

A montage of happiness following Lancaster's acquittal: top left, Carson congratulates Lancaster; top right, Joseph Ince does likewise; bottom right, Lancaster thanks the jury foreman; bottom left, Judge Atkinson speaks with Lancaster. The centre picture of Chubbie's delight is clear! (*Miami Daily News*)

Lancaster with his mother in New York some weeks after the trial. (*Daily News*)

Many remained skeptical that Haden Clarke (above) committed suicide. (*Miami Herald*)

18. The Problems with Lancaster and Miller's story.

Bill Lancaster was a free man. The great wheel of fortune had paused in his favour; and the gods had deigned to spare him. The case against him had been a powerful one and yet it had failed. There were a number of reasons for this.

Hawthorne believed collusion between counsel for the defence and Lancaster and Miller - beyond what professional duty required - was chiefly responsible for the difficulties in procuring a guilty verdict. That was partly true: Carson and Lathero with the energetic assistance of Lancaster and Miller had made prodigious, sometimes questionable, efforts to counter every point of the State case. When it was necessary to show that the missing letters had been mislaid or destroyed by the State, rather than by Lancaster or Miller, Lancaster gave fresh evidence late in the trial which involved his suddenly 'recalling' having seen one of the letters on a table after Haden had been taken to hospital, but before the police had conducted their search. When it was necessary to provide a strong reason why Lancaster had bought a gun to replace the one which Huston had lent him, Huston 'recalled' he had impressed on Lancaster that he wanted it back, and said Lancaster had assured him he would buy him a new one if he lost it – although neither man had ever mentioned this previously. There were so many instances of improbable evidence emerging at the 11th hour to plug a particular hole in the defence case, that it is necessary to run a gauntlet of improbabilities to believe them.

But collusion was only a part of the prosecutor's failure to win the case. It was, overall, a fine balanced victory: the evidence against Lancaster was compelling; circumstantial for the most part, as it tends to be for murder trials because of the nature of the crime, but probably enough to secure a conviction in 1932. There is no doubt Lancaster had won the war of character and the goodwill of all in both the court of law and the court of public opinion, but the ultimate arbiter of the matter was the jury: what would it decide as it attempted to wrestle with the warring imperatives of head and heart? The fact that they deliberated for five hours, and that they sought clarification from the judge on the matter of 'reasonable doubt,' suggests it was a battle that was not easily decided. But the very fact that they sought clarification on reasonable doubt, also suggests that it was there in some measure. The debate in the jury room was clearly not whether Lancaster had killed Clarke, but whether there was *sufficient reason for believing he did not*. That seems an odd way of putting it, but when all the niceties are set aside, this is what remained.

The psychology and dynamics of a jury can never be ignored – great advocates knew it then as they know it now. An appeal to a jury based purely on the evidence is an unrealistic ideal, because with the best of intentions human beings are subject to their own prejudices; have their own beliefs and understanding of the world to be affirmed. They do not leave them at the door to the jury room, as if they were a pair of muddy shoes. A good advocate knows this; and a great advocate depends upon it.

The principal grounds on which the prosecution case failed were 1.the characters of Lancaster and Clarke; 2. the efforts of the defence attorneys; 3. the testimony given by the witnesses; 4. the crucial missing witnesses; and 5. the defects and omissions of the prosecution.

As regards the first of these, the characters of the principals, Lancaster had successfully portrayed himself throughout the trial as a soldier, a war hero and a gentleman, and this played a major part in his deliverance. His constant attentive concern for Mrs Miller, and his anxiety on her behalf, were visible to all in court; so was his calmness, his implacability under the intense pressure of cross-examination – and his impeccable delivery of the most improbable aspects of his testimony. These won the hearts of the public, press and jury. It was sufficient to nudge him over that fine line between a guilty and not-guilty verdict – which for him meant the difference between life and death.

By contrast, the jury was persuaded that Haden Clarke was a drug addict; possibly a bigamist; idle; dissolute; a womaniser with an unpleasant disease, who seemed not to care whom he shared his malady with; and he was an interloper who had seduced his friend's lover.

Chubbie's testimony is conflicting on Haden's character: she said he never worried about money, simply said 'the Lord will provide,' but it was she who had to. That seems to be a good assessment of Clarke's personality, and it aligns with the testimony of most of the character witnesses who knew him. He seems to have been careless, dilatory and bone-idle. Unable to get down to work and apply himself to writing, he was happy to while away his days fishing and flying with Lancaster or Shelton. The rest of the time he spent drinking or playing cards. He was a man who really couldn't care less whether or not he passed on his 'malady' to one of the women he seduced – 'someone gave it to me,' he reasoned. There is little to suggest he was moody or bad-tempered as a rule. His own mother said he hated guns; he despised suicide. He was indolent; idle - not an anxious, driven character. But against all of this, Chubbie tried to claim Haden had a violent temper, flew into rages, was anxious and nervous in temperament. The only other person who supported this claim was Bill Lancaster. A string of witnesses denied it.

The jury was ultimately persuaded that Bill Lancaster was the antithesis of Haden Clarke. There was a feeling - as Carson had observed in respect of the prosecution case - that if Lancaster didn't kill Haden Clarke, then he should have: in fact, that Haden Clarke probably deserved it.

Then there was the matter of the attorneys for the defence - Lathero and Carson - who had left no stone unturned in their campaign to redeem the character of Lancaster, and undermine the State's case against him. By fair means and foul they secured their objective. Their budget, furnished mostly by Bill's parents, and by articles published under Bill's and Chubbie's names, was not unlimited, but working within these constraints they assembled a range of witnesses who effectively stood in direct opposition to those of the State.[48]

Carson attacked anyone connected with the prosecution case – Hawthorne was only pursuing the case from personal ambition, he said; he implied the Clerk of the Circuit Court had been negligent in his handling of the evidence regarding fibres on the gun. He attacked police officer Hudson, declaring him to lack intelligence as well as integrity; and was prepared to suggest he was the source of the illegal alcohol supplied to the bungalow at Coral Gables. Carson was prepared to say anything which might procure Lancaster's acquittal. Lawyers sometimes are – but to be quite fair in the matter, he probably believed that Lancaster was innocent to the point where he had convinced himself that the ends in this case justified the means.

Chubbie Miller, as chief witness, was key to the defence: she was the lover of both men, and the fiancé of the man who had died - and the fact that she was adamant that Bill Lancaster was innocent was vital. She was quite prepared to lie for Lancaster and to declare her belief in his innocence without a quiver of doubt. Had the dead man's fiancé been Bill's accuser, or shown the least doubt in him, it would have played badly with the jury and public. But Chubbie didn't do this.

Huston too, played his part in Lancaster's acquittal. His evidence and role in the Lancaster/Miller affair is not wholly satisfactory. There was no suggestion made in court that Huston was anything other than a respectable lawyer, but a great deal of the case and the facts

[48] By declaring Lancaster's insolvency the defence was able to leverage payment of expenses to witnesses by the State to supplement its funding.

pertaining to it hung upon his word. He it was, who insisted that Lancaster had added the words 'so he can tell us why he did it,' or words to this effect, to Lancaster's anxious inquiry as to whether or not Clarke would ever speak again. Others were less certain that he did use those words. Their effect was to mitigate Lancaster's apparent anxiety that Clarke might speak again, and their motive thus became ambiguous.

And Huston served Lancaster's defence in another crucial way: it was the potent evidence of the purchase of the gun as a replacement for that which Huston had previously loaned Lancaster and which was used to kill Clarke, which was corroborated by Huston. He was prepared to swear on oath that he had impressed on Lancaster that he set some store on its return. It had sentimental value. In suggesting this and doing so only at a *later stage* of court proceedings, it offered a cogent reason why Lancaster might spend a third of the money he had 'borrowed' from Shelton Snr to buy a new one. Without Huston's testimony on the gun the jury might have felt entitled to agree with the prosecution, that the gun was a most unnecessary purchase.

Nor did Huston – curiously for a man of law – call the police on hearing Haden Clarke had shot himself. He knew very well the importance of this and yet did not. He called an ambulance. His delay in arriving at the house may indicate his reluctance to become involved. He told the court he received Chubbie's call at 2 a.m., but he arrived at 3.15 a.m. As previously noted, there are questions concerning the timing – in many accounts Huston seems to give the time of the phone call from

Chubbie as 3 a.m. This is impossible: Ditsler said he logged the call from Huston at 2.30 a.m. He arrived at approximately 2.45 a.m. His timings tally with those of Yeargin, and the call being received by Emergency Police Officer Hudson 'before 3 a.m.' about an attempted suicide. In her first statement, Chubbie had described the time of Lancaster's awaking her as 'after 2,' and Lancaster agreed with Hawthorne that the shooting occurred 'before 2 a.m.' All these factors point to a time of around 2 a.m. when Huston received the call from the bungalow. He lived just 4 miles (10 minutes) from the Coral Gables address. Why then, did it take him 75 minutes to arrive at the bungalow?

It was also Ditsler, not Huston, who informed police of the suicide notes from Clarke – he had not, it seems, demurred at Chubbie's injunction 'not to mention the notes to the police.'

Huston was Secretary and Treasurer of the LAA and established the 6-way agreement. He knew both Lancaster and Miller quite well, as both had discussed with him Lancaster's desire to obtain a divorce from Kiki. There is, at least, a contributory culpability on his part, for the dubious enterprise: if Lancaster was suspicious of Tancrel and Russell and of the LAA scheme from the outset, then surely Huston, in drawing up the agreement and acting as its treasurer, would not have been less so.

Nor did Huston's contribution to the defence case end here. He was prepared to swear that the bed Lancaster had slept in was 'mussed' – thus crucially subverting the police claim that it had the appearance of having not been slept in.

Huston it was who corroborated Lancaster's claim that police officer Earl Hudson had put the bloodied revolver in his pocket wrapped only in a handkerchief, thus effectively destroying the State suggestion that Lancaster had wiped the gun clean of fingerprints. And yet would police officer Hudson have placed a bloodied gun in his pocket, and collected the box for it separately, carrying the latter in his hand and the gun in his pocket? Huston said that officer Hudson did, but it seems to militate against every normal human instinct to place a gun 'running with blood' in one's pocket, wrapped only in a handkerchief. If the box was available, which it was, then why did policeman Earl Hudson not use it to store the gun in? He claimed he did, but Huston and Lancaster stated that he did not. There is an apparent disparity here which is troubling.

Against all this and to his credit, Huston refused Lancaster's request that he tell police the gun was his. But refusing to implicate himself in a lie which might easily be exposed (the gun's certificate was in Lancaster's name in St Louis) confers no great credit on him. Hawthorne, in fact, suggested there had been more conversation between the two men concerning the gun, but Huston denied categorically that when asked by Lancaster, if he could say the gun was his, he had replied 'leave me out of it!'

There was a great deal about Huston's testimony that is unsatisfactory. And yet why would he lie? There is no record of any other link between himself and Lancaster which might make this probable – I am unable to find any record of his being a freemason, for instance. Lancaster used his masonic connections wherever he could; it lubricated his social and business worlds: it is quite consistent with his means of operating, that on arrival in Miami and needing an attorney, he would seek out one through his masonic connections. If so, then Huston might feel obligated to go further than he otherwise might to secure Lancaster's acquittal. But there is no evidence for this. It seems probable that he, like Carson, simply liked Lancaster, and had a personal conviction of his innocence - and so believed the promise was worth the lie. After all, the fact that he gave Lancaster his gun when he must have known the LAA venture was dubious in some way, appears to indicate a friendly concern for Lancaster's safety.

Then there were the general witnesses whose testimony was heard and on which much of the prosecution case depended. In this the prosecution case was severely hampered by the rogue's gallery of witnesses they were forced to rely on. The jury would likely consider felons (or felons-in-waiting) like Tancrel and Russell could hardly be depended on where a man's life was at stake - and even some officials, whose testimony should have been dependable, seemed doubtful: Officer Hudson's relationship to Haden Clarke's girlfriend Peggy Brown, who supplied an endless stream of hooch for the residents of the bungalow, was unfortunate. Did Hudson supply the illegal alcohol to her as the defence implied he did? No evidence for this was offered, but the suspicion of it was enough to damage Hudson further. He was thoroughly discredited.[49]

---

[49] Earl Hudson had only a few months remaining in the Miami police

Against the obvious defects of the prosecution witnesses that Hawthorne had to contend with, was an equally squalid set of defence witnesses who often seemed more plausible by comparison: 'Dr' Hamilton in particular, was unquestionably an unscrupulous fraud, but he gave an excellent impression in articulating with a certainty no other 'expert' would dare to proffer, that Haden Clarke had committed suicide. Hawthorne's efforts to have his testimony struck from the record failed; and though Hamilton's unsavoury reputation was exposed to the jury, the damage was done. The impression of his thoughts, of his certainty, loitered around the forensic evidence table. In fact, besides the careful equivocation of the doctors of the Medical Commission and other expert witnesses, his certainty stood out like a beacon of truth. It was his stock in trade – it was what he was good at. In 1989, Dr Joe Davis, then Dade County's Chief Medical Examiner gave his view on Hamilton's testimony in the case:

'I wouldn't trust this guy as far as I could throw an elephant,' he said. In particular, Hamilton's assertion that a 'sealed contact' shot implied suicide was incorrect: 'His whole premise was phony. It is possible for someone to walk up to you, put the gun against your head and pull the trigger, before you're even aware he pulled the trigger. Especially if you're sleeping.' (John Dorschner, *Miami Herald*, 1st October 1989)[50]

---

force. In January 1933 he attempted to arrest two men and was shot in the spine and eye. He received a pension and a glass eye from the State of Florida, and worked as a security guard for the City Hospital thereafter, until his death in 1970.

[50] Colin Evans, *A Question of Evidence: The Casebook of Great*

The absence of important witnesses was also an important factor in the failure of the prosecution to secure a conviction. Where was Peggy Brown? She had vital evidence concerning Clarke and his character, on the relations between those in the house. Where had she obtained the liquor from, which she helpfully brought to the bungalow regularly? She undoubtedly believed herself to be Haden Clarke's fiancé – but she was not the only woman who had believed this! Presumably she was unaware of Haden Clarke's 'malady' either... Even more important, was Lancaster really staying in the same room as Haden Clarke, if not when she was there, then when she was not? She would surely have been able to tell whether he normally slept in the same room or elsewhere in the house. Lancaster, although naturally coy on the matter, suggests that he normally slept in Mrs Miller's room. This would be the natural assumption – but his word was accepted that he had slept in the same room with Haden Clarke on the one night when it seems improbable in the extreme that he would do so. Had Peggy Brown given evidence to the effect that Lancaster did not normally sleep in the same room, that he never slept in that room to her knowledge – i.e. the porch room – it would have opened up a strong possibility, even a likelihood, that Lancaster was sleeping in the room downstairs – the room which Jack French had previously occupied, and which was now vacant, or else on the sofa. As they retired, according to Chubbie, Haden said 'I don't want that son of a

---

Forensic Controversies from Napoleon to O.J Simpson, Wiley, 2003 – gives an excellent appraisal of Hamilton's character.

bitch trying to talk you out of marriage.' If that was so, it seems utterly beyond comprehension or belief to imagine Haden proceeding to his bedroom and tucking himself up in his bed 3 feet from this man – a man whom he loathed with an intensity only love rivals can - and chatting amiably for the next hour about everything under the sun. It is quite implausible.

And where was Shelton? He was the only person who was with all three of the main protagonists in the house, who had been with all three for almost the entire period they were together: he drank with Haden and Chubbie through most of February up until early March, when he departed with Lancaster and Tancrel on the LAA escapade. What did he know of Haden and his habits? Of Chubbie - of the dynamics between the three? Lancaster's diary refers to Shelton's astute comment 'There are two Chubbies: Chubbie sober and Chubbie drunk.' What were the exact qualities of a drunken Chubbie? He knew. He witnessed the growing anxiety Lancaster felt during his absence out west – his obsession with Chubbie working on him like a virus. He knew of the affair between Chubbie and Haden – knew of it before Lancaster did; he was witness to Lancaster's moods, his threats, his depression; he was with him in St Louis where Lancaster bought the .38 gun. What communication passed between them? He was sufficiently alarmed at the situation and Lancaster's mood, to cable Chubbie to tip her off regarding the impending debacle, in advance of Lancaster's return. He was the most important witness after Chubbie – in fact more so, because any lying he might be prepared to undertake on Lancaster's behalf would presumably have its limits. He would also have been able to indicate whether or not Lancaster ever used the porch room. We can never know what Shelton might have been obliged to reveal under cross-examination - because he wasn't there. His absence was costly for the State case. Hawthorne seemed to suggest to Lancaster that Shelton's failure to turn up in court was at Lancaster's behest – but there was certainly no proof of this. Whatever its cause, it is likely that Shelton's absence benefited Lancaster.

Apart from all of these problems, the conduct of the prosecution was, without doubt, wanting: so many opportunities were missed; lines of questioning were pursued to mere innuendo and seldom to the point of resolution - such opportunities were thus squandered. Questions were asked which never should have been: the time taken for Lancaster to write the notes on the typewriter was an unforgivable error: he carried out the demonstration in such an expeditious fashion, that it proved the exact opposite of that which Hawthorne sought to prove: there was ample time for Lancaster to write the notes. Hawthorne seems not to have thought this through. Had he tried this in his own office before employing it as a test in court, he would have quickly appreciated that it *was* possible, and avoided the demonstration which served only to undermine his own case. But he didn't do this. He gifted the defence a perfect and memorable visual demonstration of a point which favoured Lancaster. Although it had little real relevance to the practical consequences of the killing, it had the effect of vaguely suggesting the prosecution case was ill-founded, and that Lancaster was in some way proved truthful. And coming, as it did, right at the end of Hawthorne's cross-examination of Lancaster, it left a cloud of doubt hanging over the prosecution case.

It was one of a number of Hawthorne's failures. On numerous occasions, he asked Chubbie or Lancaster a question to which he thought he had a clear answer established by prior statement – only for them to deny a particular assertion. He would press on regardless, perhaps changing tack, when what was obviously required was for him to prove the point by reference to a signed statement previously made by one of the couple. He didn't seem to have the sources upon which his questions were based to hand. It left a measure of uncertainty as to what had been said.

All of these things, taken in sum, made it possible, against every strand of circumstantial evidence the prosecution offered to the contrary, that there was sufficient reasonable doubt to justify a not guilty verdict. Ultimately, the jury was persuaded that if Bill Lancaster was not innocent, then he should be. And they found him so.

19. Suicide or Murder?

There were and there are only four possibilities that explain the death of Haden Clarke that April night in 1932, if we rule out, as we must, those of accident, or murder by an outside intruder. These are:

1. Murder by Chubbie Miller.
2. Murder by Lancaster and Miller.
3. Suicide by Haden Clarke.
4. Murder by Lancaster.

The first two possibilities were quickly dismissed by the State Attorney Hawthorne – he believed Chubbie, or at least he believed the core of her statement; he believed her grief at Clarke's demise, and he could not conceive of a conspiracy between Lancaster, as the ex-lover, and Chubbie Miller, as the fiancé. He did, however, believe that Chubbie was lying to protect Lancaster, and as time went on he became convinced of it. He thus fashioned the matter as being either option 3 or option 4 – that is, either suicide by Haden Clarke or murder by Bill Lancaster.

Taking the possibility of suicide by Clarke himself, as the defence did, it is highly problematic - perhaps even impossible:

- First. That he had succeeded in dislodging his rival from his position in Chubbie's affections, effectively removes the chief motive for his suicide – his opponent was vanquished; Lancaster was to leave the house in the morning. Nor was there anything to suggest this situation had been overturned. It may be, as Lancaster suggested, he feared this outcome – but that is a very tenuous reason for suicide.

- Second. The likelihood of Clarke shooting himself in the head while tucked up in bed in the middle of the night is difficult to accept; Carson cited instances in which this had happened, but in the present circumstances, and given the character of Haden Clarke, his age, and the other factors which militated against this having occurred, it is highly improbable. He could have picked up the revolver and walked out into the moonlight and shot himself – but he didn't. He shot himself while in a position which suggested he was at repose, while his fiancé slept next door and his friend in a bed adjacent to his. Is this believable? No - not without some significant mental gymnastics.
- Third. That he shot himself with a revolver conveniently located, equidistant between his love rival and himself on a bedside table just 18 inches (45 cms) from his grasp, is not only improbable, it is quite absurd. Would Lancaster really have left the gun in reach of a man with whom he had nearly come to blows just hours earlier? A man with whom he had quarrelled - and with such resentment and latent hostility simmering between them? The presence of the gun lying loaded and exposed on the bedside table between their beds, seems to be a

contrivance designed to provide Clarke with the ease of access, and therefore the *means*, of killing himself. The claim that he had been playing with it earlier in the evening and Lancaster had told him to 'be careful – it's loaded' was opportunistic. It is profoundly counterintuitive. Mrs Clarke said Haden had a lifelong revulsion of guns, and she cited numerous examples of this. There is no reason to disbelieve her.

- Fourth. The likelihood that he should commit suicide without leaving a note for his fiancé is also difficult to accept. He had made no attempt to explain his actions; no final declaration of love or despair was forthcoming, of relinquishment or guilt – no attempt to sort his affairs, no apology: none of the things people who commit suicide usually do. So glaring was this omission and so obvious, that Lancaster knew he would have to try to remedy this deficiency by writing the notes one would expect in such a case. That is revealing.
- Fifth. That no fingerprints at all were found on the handle or trigger of the gun, but were found smudged and unrecognisable on the barrel end, suggests that the gun had been wiped clean and placed beneath Clarke by a third person. The notion that Hudson had wiped the gun clean was a possibility, but never very convincing for the removal of all fingerprints, even from the trigger. Why would Hudson wipe the gun and then take it to Barker at HQ for fingerprint testing? The likelihood remains that the gun was

purposely wiped to conceal the identity of the person who had held it.

- Finally, the angle of the wound to Haden Clarke's head was, as Hawthorne pointed out, almost impossible to administer to oneself. Henry Jones memorably invited the jury to lie down on the floor of the jury room and try this for themselves. They almost certainly did this, and sought the skull and .38 revolver to inform their experiments, and to replicate as accurately as possible the conditions required for Haden Clarke to have been capable of this. They were thwarted by Carson's astute refusal to permit them to review the physical objects. He probably understood their intention and forestalled it. He knew its dangers.

Note.

In respect of this latter point made by the prosecution, it is still possible to take up Jones' challenge to the jury, by using a replica gun, and adhering to the skull measurements gleaned from the autopsy report of the Medical Commission. It is worth doing. I have tried this and found *it is* possible – but I have found that holding the gun at the required angle involves either bending the wrist to such an acute angle that the fingers are deprived of strength, or else of using the thumb to release the trigger, the butt of the gun being held in compression against the four opposing fingers. In the former attitude it is simply not possible to pull the trigger if the full trigger-pull weight must be engaged.[51] However, by cocking the gun first, the necessary leverage can – just about - be applied to the trigger to fire the gun. The question must be, why would Clarke contrive to fire the gun at such an awkward angle? Would he not simply fire the gun at a natural right to left trajectory which would produce the same effect – death? A further problem with this assumption is that if the gun was fired from such an insecure grip at this angle, then the recoil which occurs in the uppermost (live) chamber of the revolver, would cause the gun to cock in an upward direction – effectively the gun sight would tilt upwards. That effect can only be resisted to a point – in a loose grip, such as that which Clarke would have to have employed at that angle, the effect would have been exaggerated: the bullet would have gone along the top of the skull, taking it even further from its intended path. Alternatively, the use of the thumb to release a cocked or uncocked trigger presents the gun in a highly unstable attitude and would render the results of discharging it highly unpredictable. If the defence's own witness is to be believed, then Clarke possessed a conviction regarding the uncertain outcome of shooting a bullet into the temple. It seems highly unlikely that he would take such a chance, especially when a further element of uncertainty is introduced. He seems to have been quite aware of the dangers of doing so. In contrast, the gun held against a sleeping man's head by a third person, now with a firm, straight-wristed grip, would deliver a bullet along the precise path which was evident in Clarke's case.

---

[51] A colt .38 revolver is a long barrelled heavy weapon, with a trigger pull of 8 to 14 lbs.

The inescapable conclusion is that Clarke was shot by a third person, not by himself.

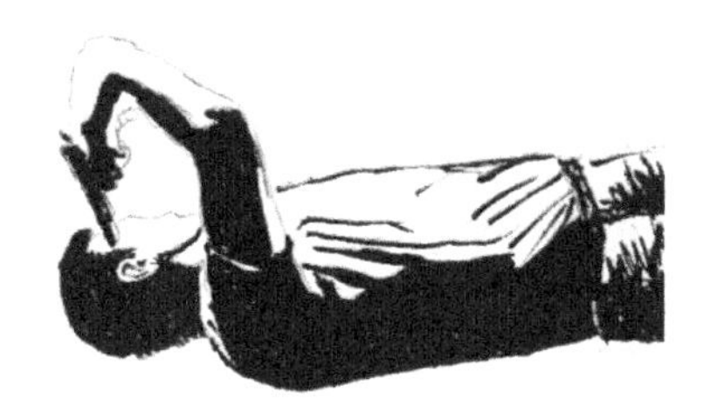

Position of hand required where right-handed person uses thumb to pull trigger.

Position of wrist required for right-handed person to shoot oneself in temple.

If these points taken individually do not make it impossible that Clarke could have committed suicide, then taken together, they almost certainly do. And they make it sufficiently secure, in my view, to place the matter beyond a reasonable doubt that he was shot by a third person. A jury is not required to arrive at a verdict that is certain; that is unrealistic, and the law is framed only to require that a matter be placed to a standard beyond a reasonable human doubt. That is a high enough standard for our purpose here: Haden Clarke did not shoot himself.

If the notion of Clarke's suicide is incredible, then we are left with the second possibility governing his death. That is the alternative offered by the prosecution case: that Lancaster committed the murder - and prima facie this could hardly have been a stronger hypothesis. Look at the evidence – the facts of the case as we know them to be:

1. Mrs Miller was growing closer to Clarke and Bill Lancaster was aware of this. We know this because he wrote of it in his diary; and because he spoke of it to others

2. Bill Lancaster was jealous; it is a certainty he was because we have his own words to this confided to his diary, as well as to others, and his letters reveal this too – he was distraught at the thought of losing Chubbie. He said he would lay down his life for her. There is no doubt he would have.

3. Tancrel and Russell both said Lancaster had said he would 'get rid of Clarke' and that 'One more dead man would not make any difference.' These were not reliable characters, but their accounts were corroborated by that of Lancaster's friend, Gentry Shelton, who told the authorities Lancaster had said he would 'kill Clarke rather than let him marry Chubbie.' Lancaster himself had admitted on the witness stand that he may have issued threats after drinking a pint of whisky. This concurs so closely with the words Tancrel and Russell claim he uttered, that it suggests they were telling the truth in this regard. Unfortunately – curiously, even – Gentry Shelton could not be found by the prosecution at trial, and so could not be called to give his testimony. That Joseph Ince, a fellow WW1 pilot, denied Lancaster had said the words Tancrel attributed to Lancaster, is not

sufficient: why would Tancrel suggest this of a man who could so easily deny it? Words which allegedly were confirmed by Shelton also? It is surely because on this occasion Tancrel spoke the truth. So did Jack Russell. All of the circumstances suggest it. The prosecution was unfortunate in having to rely on such men to prove their case. Then there was Vladimir Virrick, an architect friend of Clarke's, who together with another man had played bridge with Clarke and Miller, a few days before the shooting: he said the phone rang and Clarke returned from speaking to Bill, to say: 'Damn it! He is coming back. I think there will be trouble.' The other man present at the cards table confirmed this account even more robustly. Their testimony suggests a congruency to the claims made by Tancrel and Russell: there were indeed threats. Lancaster claimed he would not use the phrase 'son of a bitch,' as it was not a phrase used in England. That is quite true, but Lancaster had been in the US for four years; his diary and letters reveal a great usage of American turns of phrase – there are numerous exclamations of 'Gee!' and 'plumb crazy!' peppered throughout his diary: some American phrases, by virtue of the informality of English American, are extremely susceptible to adoption by English people. Furthermore, even if Lancaster did not use the exact phrase 'son of a bitch,' British English has its equivalent which would convey the same meaning and which Tancrel might easily translate into an American phrase more familiar to him.

4. Bill Lancaster was responsible for delaying the marriage of the couple – he did so by affecting acceptance and offering his congratulations; even

offering to act as best man at their wedding. This was a brilliant move: he had taken the only step that would ensure the wedding's delay - by his apparent acquiescence to it, he bought himself time to prevent the marriage. It matters not that Clarke's divorce might prove problematic in this respect – Lancaster had no knowledge of this: he believed the divorce could be effected with characteristic American efficiency, in a few days and for a few dollars. It gave him the necessary urgency during his stay at St Louis: he needed delay – and he secured it. In fact, his motive in sending his congratulatory telegram, which was entirely at odds with his true feelings, was solely to delay the marriage.

5. The purchase of the gun on the eve of his return from St Louis – he borrowed $100 for this, presenting a cheque which could never be honoured and which ultimately bounced – was a move of desperation. His claim that he bought the Colt .38 revolver to replace one his attorney Huston had lent him, and which he had subsequently sold, is incredible. He owed many people money; by Chubbie's account they were starving; they struggled to pay the bills for electricity, phone or food; the car needed work, the battery was 'on the fritz,' and there was no money for fuel: would he really spend the little money he had managed to beg from an acquaintance against a bad cheque, to buy a gun and ammunition? And would he do so the day before he returned to Miami? What possible innocent prompt could give it such priority amongst all the other competing claims upon him? Nor does the claim that Huston valued the gun for sentimental reasons ameliorate

this – because the revolver was lost and replaced by a different one. Any personal attachment was thus lost, because sentimental value is obviously not a transferable commodity. Huston's subsequent recollection that Lancaster had said if he lost the gun he would replace it, is nonsensical: he had just informed Lancaster it had personal sentimental value. It would hardly inspire him with confidence for the borrower to offer to replace it if he lost it – nor would it sensibly be proffered. It is an inadequate untruth.

6. Lancaster said he and Clarke chatted and joked that night. All was affable between them. But this is not reasonable: nothing in his character, in his conduct, or that of anyone else's for that matter, suggests he would meekly accept being turned over by a man like Haden Clarke. A man who had probably – in his view - infected the woman he loved with a serious sexual disease. Nothing in Clarke's expectations of 'trouble,' as evidenced by his words to Virrick and Prufert, nor Shelton's as evidenced in his warning cable to Chubbie, suggested there would be rapprochement. Bill Lancaster was angry – he was entitled to be. 'Haden, old man, you have not behaved like a gentleman,' really wouldn't cut it.

7. The defence claimed that Lancaster had written the suicide notes simply for Chubbie's benefit - to prevent suspicions she might entertain that he was responsible for Haden's death - but this was untrue. In the first place he showed these notes to Ditsler and Huston when they arrived, and this, together with the fact that the couple's first thought had been to call an attorney rather than a doctor or

ambulance, indicates clearly their intention was to provide cover for themselves. Lancaster wrote in his letter to Kiki in July that the suicide notes were written in panic and not for Chubbie's benefit at all. This may be a weaker proof of intention - as he would presumably be disinclined to admit to Kiki that he was concerned purely with Chubbie – but it does reveal Lancaster's constant changes in his account, to suit the occasion.

These circumstances, taken in sum, make a formidable case against Lancaster. And yet for all this, there are undeniable problems with Bill Lancaster having committed the murder. They cannot be ignored:

1. Lancaster was a jealous and wronged man; he undoubtedly could kill Haden Clarke, whom he regarded as a cad; he probably said to Russell and Tancrel, as he must surely have said to his friend Shelton and to Ince, that he would kill Clarke. But saying such a thing in anger is quite a different thing from doing it. Would Lancaster have shot Clarke while he was lying asleep in bed – for that is the situation we are faced with? It seems almost incredible that he would do so. Lancaster was not a man without faults – he had deserted his wife and daughters, had not seen or provided for them for much of the five years of his absence, and he rarely thought of them - but he was not a coward. He was a deluded man, a man with an obsession. He took – and was yet to take - enormous risks with his own personal safety. Perhaps the shining jewel of humanity which Carson characterised him as being was too much – but if it was, then it fooled a lot of people. Even Hawthorne seemed conflicted at times as he pressed his case against Lancaster.

There is, in his prosecutor's zeal, a sense of equivocation – and at the end a sense that he had done his best to secure a conviction but was not dissatisfied by the result, because he had a niggle deep within clamouring for his attention: had he made a mistake? Was it possible – as he had certainly thought early on in the investigation back in April – that Lancaster was innocent, and Haden Clarke had committed suicide?

2. There is the purchase of the gun, which was sure to be discovered; no attempt was made at concealment of this by Lancaster: why, if murder was his intention? He registered the gun quite openly with the sheriff in St Louis. It was all perfectly legal. The loading of the gun the night before – information he volunteered to detectives – was surely a dangerous piece of information for a guilty man to give them…

3. Then openly speaking of killing Haden Clarke to men who would obviously testify to that intention if he acted on his words. How utterly foolish it was for Lancaster to have declared such an intention before so many people if he was resolved upon this course! If murder was pre-meditated, then it was poorly pre-meditated. Intelligent people do all kinds of foolish things, labouring under the influence of excited emotions, but after Haden's death Lancaster looked Mrs Ida Clarke in the eyes and swore he had nothing to do with Haden's death. And in such a candid moment, he was able to convince her of his innocence to the extent that she sent James Lathero to act as his defence attorney, when he was arrested for her son's murder. Could Lancaster have been so callous?

Whatever his failings, it doesn't seem to be in character. Mrs Ida Clarke may have felt this too – she was not content that her son had committed suicide, but she seemed not to believe that Lancaster could have done it either. It may well be why she failed to testify at trial.

4. The typing of the suicide letters was hardly one of careful pre-meditation, but one of reaction to an event; it was so profoundly dangerous to his claims of innocence, that it was almost enough to send him to the electric chair in itself. Can he possibly have conceived of this in the days prior to the act? And to have typed them on LAA paper nevertheless? The letters are clearly a hasty and ill-conceived afterthought. It suggests that if murder was done then it was impetuous, in a fit of sudden anger – not qualities Lancaster was known for. Did he commit the murder of a man as he lay asleep, and then seek to conceal it with hastily forged suicide notes?

5. He claims to have been in the bedroom with Clarke, three feet from where the gun was fired – yet the best he could do was to claim he thought the window had banged. Why did he not claim he had slept in another room to Clarke? And wasn't this far more likely anyway in the circumstances? Some witnesses at the scene claimed his bed had not been slept in – it was surely to his advantage to make what he could of this... Yet he was adamant he was in the room at the time Haden shot himself and had slept in the bed. He was adamant too that the gun had been lying between the two men, loaded and ready for use, within easy grasp of them both. Why did he not claim Haden

Clarke had taken the gun and loaded it without his knowledge while he himself slept downstairs? Lancaster was not, reading his diaries or his answers in court, an unintelligent man: he could have done better than this.

Bill Lancaster exaggerated, and he was quite prepared to lie, but he was not despicable – far from it. He had lied for Chubbie, he passed bad cheques, and purloined chickens from dire necessity; he was an adulterer who had deserted his wife and children. But these offences, for the most part, all resolved in his obsession with Chubbie – not laudable by any means, but not sufficiently damning to destroy every vestige of human decency in him – and certainly not indicative of a cold-blooded murderer.

The murder of Haden Clarke was a crime both intemperate and cowardly – qualities Bill did not possess. It was intemperate because no thought was given to its commission; cowardly because Haden Clarke was asleep in bed or at repose when it was done. Bill was reckless, but he was without fear; and he was not a mean man – he was calm in all situations, and he was not cowardly. If he were to shoot Haden Clarke – and he was certainly capable of this and angry enough to do it – then he would have shot him to his face. For all his faults, of which he had many, Bill Lancaster would not kill a man silently in his sleep. A naïve man, rather than a calculating one, he was never a hot head. Nor was he a murderer.

There is only one circumstance that explains all of these anomalies, the missteps and apparent oversights, and the hasty corrections; the improbable statements; Bill's failure to exonerate himself when he could clearly have done so: that is that Haden Clarke was not fatally shot that night by Captain Bill Lancaster: *he was shot by Chubbie Miller.*

20. The Murder of Haden Clarke.

'When you have eliminated the impossible, whatever remains, however improbable, must be the truth.' The Sign of Four, Sir Arthur Conan Doyle

That Mrs Miller killed her lover is the only possible solution to this case; the only one which can make sense of the inexplicable behaviour and acts of Lancaster, and of the circumstances of that night. It seems a remarkable claim to make – and yet it is only so by virtue of the fact that the case was conceived of, as being an unavoidable choice between two alternatives: either Haden Clarke had committed suicide or Bill Lancaster had murdered him. This was how Bill Lancaster framed it in the early hours of 21st April 1932 – of course, he hoped that it would be assumed that Haden Clarke had committed suicide, but the circumstances were described in such a way as to ensure that if this was not accepted, then only Bill Lancaster could have killed Clarke. This was firmly laid down from the outset by Lancaster's invention that he had shared a room with Haden. This established that the only possible alternative to Haden Clarke's suicide, was that Lancaster had killed him. And yet it was a highly improbable circumstance that these two men shared a room that night. It is equally improbable – but most necessary - that the gun should be on the table between the two men, and fully accessible to Clarke. It was also necessary –

and quite implausible - that Mrs Miller should have her bedroom door locked that night, and heard nothing until Lancaster woke her by banging on her door.

It is not surprising that the case against Chubbie Miller was never given the consideration it deserved – but this was an error. The error was Hawthorne's: he accepted not the story Lancaster presented him with, but *the dichotomy he presented him with* – in fact on 23rd April, just two days after the killing, he announced to the press that it was either *suicide or murder*. He also said he believed Mrs Miller's account: it is thus abundantly clear that from the earliest stage of the inquiry he had established the lines on which the case would be argued: either as the suicide of Haden Clarke, or the murder of him by Bill Lancaster. That decision put in place the parameters by which the case has been argued ever since: it remains the way in which it is considered today. And yet it is quite mistaken.

The position is stated with unwitting accuracy by Ralph Barker:

'But if Lancaster was innocent, the necessary corollary was that Clarke committed suicide; no-one else could have killed him.' (Ralph Barker, *Verdict on a Lost Flyer*, 1969)

That was indeed the proposition facing the jury, based on the circumstances suggested by Lancaster's account and on the case laid out by the State Attorney: but the truth is there was neither an implication nor a necessary corollary of Bill's innocence. It was a false dichotomy.

It is necessary to return to first principles; to start with the crime without the artificial presumptions placed on the case by Hawthorne. As soon as we do this, the case against Chubbie Miller presents itself with great clarity. And it is a substantial case, one to which all the evidence and circumstances subtend:

1. The two men were at loggerheads; Haden Clarke had all but challenged Lancaster that evening: there was trouble at hand and trouble to come. Did Chubbie really retire to bed, content to leave the two men alone in a mutually hostile stand-off with a loaded revolver between them? Why did they share a room at all, when there was a bedroom below, which had its own facilities? It was unnecessary and undesirable from all angles.

2. She repeatedly tripped herself up in making claims that she did not know of the revolver's existence until after Haden had been shot. She gave at least three different accounts: I) that Bill told her of it when she opened the door of her room to him that night; II) that he told her of it in the porch room; III) that she had known of it because he had phoned her and told her of it from St Louis. But we know from Bill's evidence in cross-examination, when under considerable pressure, that he had discussed his proposed trip to Huston to return the gun to him, earlier that evening. And Chubbie herself alludes to this conversation – though omitting any mention of the gun, speaking only of Huston in her evidence. There are other suggestive pointers in this respect: could Chubbie have failed to see the gun when she went into the room to say goodnight, and collect and wind up the

alarm clock, if it was (as Lancaster claimed) lying either in its box, or else lying openly on the bedside table loaded? Taken together, it becomes an inescapable conclusion that Mrs Miller had full knowledge of the gun. And it is equally certain she would be deeply unhappy with its presence in the house.

3. It is far more probable that she would demand of Lancaster that he hand over the gun – she would wish to secure it from the reach of either man in this tense and fraught stand-off. She would thus have had the gun in her possession. There is a further probable indication of this. Lancaster's reason for its purchase, quite openly, was not that of killing Haden Clarke; that was an entirely mistaken supposition by the State Attorney's Office: its purpose was for Lancaster to commit suicide. His diary entries are moving irrevocably in this direction. His despair is palpable at the contemplation of a future without Chubbie: 'I will end it all,' 'I will not live without her,' he writes. It is entirely consistent with this that Lancaster threatened suicide that evening; in fact, he admitted he had done so, although it became by means of an aeroplane accident, to secure the insurance money. He had probably threatened to crash the plane previously – possibly in the phone call from St Louis. This was when he spoke to Chubbie in one of two emotional phone calls he made to her, which we know took place, and in which Lancaster first mentioned the gun to her. He might well speak of his desire to end it all and crash his plane on the final leg of his journey. It fits well with the occasion and his admission that he asked her if she wanted him to return or not – she

told him she did. It was natural to move this threat to the night of the tragedy itself, to supplant the real suicide threat, which involved a gun. Because although the threat of an aeroplane crash might be natural in an emotional phone call before he was about to set out on the final leg of his journey, it is not congruent with standing in the living room of the Miami bungalow and discussing it. It is only half believable; faintly ridiculous. The way in which the threat of suicide is brought to its natural crisis point is by uniting the threat and the act to give it immediacy: this is done by placing a loaded revolver against one's head. It brings the matter to crisis. It is accepted that Lancaster threatened suicide that night – whether he meant it or not is a different matter, but if we accept that he did this, then it is highly probable that the gun was employed for this purpose. But if Lancaster produced the gun, Chubbie insisted he hand it over to her – she would not leave this in his possession. She may have become upset, and he found himself unable to carry out his intention. If she knew of the gun, it seems unlikely she would have left it unguarded. If it had been produced in any context that evening, she certainly would have taken it.

4. Chubbie had tried to moderate the situation that evening; she was not at all a meek and mild woman who would be told by Haden he was in charge and order her *not to speak with Lancaster*, an order which she claimed she had obeyed; nor that he had told her to lock her bedroom door, and she did. This was a 30-year-old woman of considerable spirit and determination – a woman who flew planes, had crash-landed, been lost and

survived; had killed a deadly krait in her cockpit with her flying stick; had crash-landed and broken her nose; insisted on continuing when a co-competitor had died in the *Powder Puff Derby* of 1929; who had travelled half-way around the world from her native Australia to London to start a new life in 1927 without her husband; and returned there in a canvas and stick biplane 13,000 miles; had travelled over continents and stretches of shark-infested sea without fear. She was a woman who had looked out of her cockpit and seen hundreds of dead bodies floating in the Ganges below. She had once stood guard resolutely over their aeroplane in the east, with a loaded gun in her hand, surrounded by hostile natives. She was not a woman to be ordered about by 26-year-old Haden Clarke, or anyone else. In fact Lancaster's own testimony contradicts Chubbie's in respect of why she would not speak to him alone: it was her choice, not Haden's, he said. That is surely correct. We know she dominated Lancaster to an extraordinary degree – she told him not to fly immigrants over from Mexico and he obeyed. She told him frankly of his failures, that he had 'cleaned her out'; gave her caustic opinion of his 'passing bum cheques'; of Haden Clarke she was similarly forthright – 'the laziest writer I have ever known', she called him. She was not a woman who would be told to 'go to her room.' She would demand the gun from Lancaster – and he would obey her.

5. Then there is the matter of the gunshot. Her room was 18 feet (5.4m) from where the shot was fired:[52] the sound of a discharged firearm averages

[52] In his signed statement of 2nd May, Lancaster estimated Chubbie's

approximately 160 decibels. To put this in perspective, a motorcycle engine is 95 dB, an ambulance siren is over 100 dB, a Boeing 757 taking off is 140 dB, and a military fighter jet is a colossal 150 dB at take-off. But the sound of a gunshot is 10 dB clear above that – a staggering 160 dB. Its volume is made up of the ignition of gunpowder, and the expulsion of gases; and also from the speed at which the bullet leaves the barrel, which exceeds 1,088ft per second at sea level, *as it momentarily breaks the sound barrier*. In open conditions the shot will be heard 2 miles away. There is not the slightest possibility that Chubbie Miller would not be awoken by that sound. Her claims that she was awoken by Lancaster banging on her door were completely untrue.

6. Mrs Miller claimed she did not inquire as to why Haden Clarke had shot himself – she simply accepted it as a statement of fact. That too is hard to believe. Such an event would elicit the immediate responses of – why? How? Where? A litany of questions, demands for information – and a suspicion of Lancaster. That would be natural and immediate. The two men were sleeping three feet apart, by Lancaster and Miller's accounts – how could she not immediately be drawn to certain conclusions, and to arrive at certain unavoidable suppositions? But she did not have any such

---

room was 35 feet (11m) away. That was a guess, of course, but the disparity between the police measurement and his guess is such that it was probably an exaggeration made with the intention of placing her room at the greatest distance possible from the scene of the crime.

queries or any such suspicions – *because she was in possession of the answers already.*

7. When Mrs Miller learned, as she said she did on 23rd April, that Lancaster had penned the two suicide notes, is it conceivable that she would, with all the other circumstances factored in, have believed Lancaster was innocent? It is not possible – her discovery of the forgery of the notes by Lancaster, whatever her opinion of him, would have led to a conviction that he had killed Haden Clarke. But she did believe him, she said, and the only sensible reason for doing so is that she already knew of the notes - and also knew that Lancaster had not killed Haden Clarke.

8. Chubbie Miller's declaration that she would give her life if it would save Captain Lancaster's indicates a degree of responsibility, even of culpability, on her part. It has such weight behind it. She went further, too: *she said she would admit to the murder to save Lancaster.* It is a telling remark. The implication here is that she cannot allow Lancaster to take the blame and die for her offence. This is quite beyond any guilt she might feel for having precipitated the crisis, by her betrayal of Lancaster with Haden Clarke: such a condition would almost certainly be resolved by an intensification of her anger against Lancaster: only something far weightier upon her conscience could cause such a complete subordination to Lancaster, and a corresponding collapse of any duty or love she felt towards Haden Clarke.

9. And there is one further extraordinary fact that seems to confirm the extent of her debt to

Lancaster: just one month after his acquittal for the murder of her lover, after she had informed the court of what was surely true – that she did not love Lancaster, and had not done so for two years - the couple announced they would marry. Her guilt was palpable; so was her gratitude: she owed him - owed him in direct proportion to her culpability.

The narrative suggested by these points is irresistible. This is why Captain Lancaster claimed to be in the room with Clarke, when all circumstances pointed to the contrary – he would have slept on the sofa if no other bed was available, rather than in the room with his rival; but a superior guest room was available which would have suited all of them better. Why would Haden advise Chubbie to lock herself in her room if he was sleeping in company with Lancaster? It is because he was not. This was, in any case, probably an invention designed to ensure Lancaster must knock on her door, and she must open it in a state of complete ignorance of what had occurred. It is why Lancaster claimed the loaded gun was between himself and Haden Clarke, which is quite incomprehensible - but he could only deny it by telling the police where in fact it was: in Chubbie Miller's possession because she had confiscated it earlier in the evening during a fraught exchange, in which Lancaster offered to kill himself. He could easily have told police it was in his bag and Haden Clarke must have removed it – but that would have admitted the possibility that Chubbie could have had access to it: the gun had to be easily and visibly available only to Haden and himself. It is why he had to type up two letters to himself and Chubbie, because he realised that

Clarke would not kill himself without explaining why or making some farewell to the woman he was going to marry. It was why he invented an unlikely story that he thought it was a window banging – it might well sound like one if he was lying in the room downstairs – but not if he was three feet (90 cms) from an explosion of 160 dB magnitude. As Hawthorne observed: 'It would burst your eardrums.' Lancaster could have rebutted these points on which his life depended, to save himself, but it would be at the cost of making it apparent that Chubbie was Haden's killer. That he patently would not do. He had said he would give his life for Chubbie, and wrote this in his diary – now he had the opportunity of proving it, and his resolve and courage were not found wanting.

Lancaster was, in concocting the story of the bedtime chat with Clarke - about his malady, his despair concerning money, his inability to write, or help his mother, and his remorse etc – intent on creating the *motive* for Haden Clarke's suicide. Every circumstance of this talk was extremely improbable, even down to the notion the two were sharing a room. The presence of the gun on the table between the two men and the contrived explanation of its presence there – Haden Clarke playing with it ('careful, it's loaded!') - had no other purpose than supplying the *means*. And the presence of Lancaster in the same room, three feet from Haden Clarke, while Mrs Miller was '35 feet away' in a locked room, was to ensure that Haden Clarke had *opportunity* and Mrs Miller had none.

Lancaster's anxiety as to whether Clarke would speak again may or may not have alluded to 'so he can tell us why he did it' – it hardly matters, because the motive in its effect remains the same. That is, an anxiety as to whether or not Haden Clarke would speak again – the motive for this may be taken either way, although it seems rather peculiar and improbable to be hoping Haden Clarke would emerge from his wounded state and say, 'sorry old man, I couldn't make the grade – I thought it best to shoot myself, and leave the field clear for the whitest man I ever knew.' Lancaster may have feared that a revived Haden Clarke would have denied the notes – yet that is a strange fear in the circumstances, if he had indeed shot himself! What would Lancaster's offence be in forging the notes in such a case? The overwhelming probability – whatever form of words Lancaster may have used to various people – is that he was greatly concerned Clarke would live to tell what had happened that evening – and this would have led to the sudden, inevitable realization, that Lancaster was lying: he had not chatted with Haden Clarke amicably, the two men were not sleeping in beds three feet apart or even in the same room; they did not part on good terms, still less with Lancaster yawning wearily and saying 'let's talk it all over with Chubbie in the morning.' There were terrible scenes, wrought with emotion; threats and imprecations; Chubbie had taken the gun from Lancaster after his threat of suicide; there was alcohol, too – Chubbie was an alcoholic; so was Haden. Even if he had given it up, which is doubtful, it is unlikely she would – or could – have done so. And in the storm and stress of the occasion there was a revelation... Chubbie, was drunk and dangerous. Chubbie had the gun in her possession. Had a recovered Haden Clarke been able to intimate some or all of this - even if he did not know who had shot him - it would have led to the realization by the police, that Chubbie Miller had shot Haden Clarke.

21. The Other Chubbie Miller

I

Much has been written about the life of the extraordinary Chubbie Miller; there is no shortage of facts, figures and details to pore over - but very little has been done to probe her character, her motivations, the strengths and vicissitudes which mould her actions. She is presented uniformly as a plucky, feisty little woman with sack-loads of determination to succeed in a man's world. This view is not wrong, but it is quite inadequate. It presents us with a two-dimensional cardboard cut-out of the woman, who was at once more complex and difficult than she is portrayed. It is important in the present context because Chubbie Miller is the key element in this story: it is her temperament, her propensity for drink, and her personality which lie behind the tragedy at the Coral Gables bungalow. It seems strange that Chubbie Miller was never properly considered as a suspect for the murder; that she was not, was partially down to the same prejudices which have caused her to be regarded as a feisty little woman struggling to succeed in a man's world: we like to shoe-horn people into neat boxes; into good and bad, strong and weak, clever and stupid. 'Feisty' is almost inevitably linked to a description of a woman; so is 'plucky' – and when we supply the reference 'a man's world', we have a full suite. It removes the need to think; and it deprives us of a meaningful assessment of a person. Human beings strive for order where there is none, or little, and have a desire to see the world in such terms. In 1932 the State Attorney's office could not conceive of a woman of good family and of a certain status, committing the murder of her fiancé – however remiss her personal life might be. A great many women got away with murder during this period due to this prejudice.[53] And added to this prejudice is the part Bill Lancaster played in protecting Mrs Miller.

Chubbie Miller was a deeply conflicted character; there were two distinctive sides to her personality. A strictly religious upbringing was assured – both her maternal and paternal grandfathers were religious ministers – and moral and religious principles were drilled into her from the earliest age. Such principles are the foundations of society: religion provides the oldest form of government and law. Chubbie's family life was steeped in this powerful impetus for conformity, yet she was also, by nature, wilful, curious, strong-willed, adventurous and boisterous. These qualities found resolute employment in athletic and physical pursuits; her activities provided a relief valve for such instincts. In her early years she learned to play piano proficiently, but otherwise chiefly indulged in the active pursuits of athletics and physical games. Not an obviously academic or cerebral girl, she took the route most women did in those years, and married as soon as she turned 18. Her marriage to Keith Miller, a

---

[53] In 1935 the *Chicago Sunday Tribune* led with the alarming statistic that 7 out of every 9 women tried since 1906 had been acquitted of the crime of murder in Cook County. Statistics are often deceptive, or incomplete indicators of a phenomenon, but such figures would give concern to any public prosecutor.

journalist, might have diverted Chubbie's energies into a world of church fetes and bazaars, women's committees; and to the kinds of occupation women of her background and disposition would devote themselves to, after they had established families, in those days. But Chubbie had no children. She miscarried three times, we are told, and she later claimed she was advised by doctors she was not of suitable physique for childbearing. Whatever its cause, the absence of children in the marriage left Chubbie with a void. She had a restless energy in want of employment, and she decided to travel to Britain. From the moment of her departure, Chubbie was freed from many of the constraints placed upon her by her situation in Australia. Marriage, family, her social circle and friends, no longer exerted that subtle pressure which tethers normal human beings to a social framework of values and expectations.

She never lost those religious strictures, drilled into her from her first moments, though – they ran too deep. However much her own nature received licence to draw away from them, they could never be extinguished. This conflict runs like a fault-line through Chubbie's character, and is evident throughout her life:

She was married to Keith Miller yet she cheated on him at almost the first opportunity; and while she was cheating on him she was taking £3 a week subsistence from him. When she ran into financial difficulties during the flight to Australia in 1927, she wired him for money. It shows an astonishing capacity for deceit.

She says she hates liars, yet she knows Bill is one, and she is a teller of tall tales herself.

Throughout the trial she dissembles constantly – from the big meaningful lies – 'I didn't know there was a gun,' 'I knew Haden Clarke had a sexual malady,' to the trivial, somewhat pointless lies, 'we didn't have a duck.' At some level she must know this, suffer certain pangs of guilt for it: but she must also rationalize it by building Chinese walls within, to separate and justify her antagonistic behaviours.

She rebukes Lancaster for his dishonesty, yet readily accepts the fruits of it: she is happy to receive the stolen chickens, rabbits and ducks for their table at the Coral Gables bungalow. If this troubles her, it doesn't show: she is able to function by separating her righteous side, from that which is involved in theft.

She prizes Bill's honour, she tells the press, and the court ('he is the finest man I have ever known'): but she exhibits little or nothing of such a quality herself. Her deception of Keith is only a part of it: she is the married lover of a married man with two children (one only a few months old at the time their affair commences); she conducts a new affair with another married man (Haden Clarke) behind the back of the other married lover, while still professing her love for the first. The degree of overlap she permits in the spheres of her personal relations is extraordinary! How does she justify this to her conscience? She does. She has this capacity.

Her dishonesty has a deeply hypocritical character, too: she exhorts Bill to be honest when he is out west on LAA business. He is tempted to duck under the wire of legality to bring some aliens into the US, as a one-off measure to relieve financial pressures on Chubbie – and she rebukes him for this and forbids it. But she has no qualms about allowing Bill to take the rap for her, after she crashes the Lincoln when she is drunk; and is unconcerned, apparently, that Bill spends an hour in jail, pays a $50 fine and has his licence suspended. Bill expresses the hope in his diary that it will curtail her drinking. It doesn't. She is happy to break the law in obtaining illegal alcohol in Bill's absence out west, constantly badgering him for money so that he sends her even a single $1 bill, he is so broke. She continues to upbraid him while he sends her his last cent, anything he can 'beg, steal or borrow' for her; he sells Huston's gun so that he can send her money even, goes hungry for two days on one occasion – and she is drunk and sleeping with his friend Haden Clarke. However much this inconsistency preys on her mind, she is able to subdue her misgivings by indulging in excessive endearments to Bill and exhorting him to stay the course with the LAA, even though it is clear by now it has criminal intentions.

This aspect of Chubbie Miller's character reveals a prodigious ability to separate herself from two realities: her wants and her obligations. It is a construct in us all, but in Chubbie Miller it finds resolution in her ability to maintain both to a higher degree of tolerance. If it seems like a wholly negative characteristic, it isn't: it enables her to brush aside the inconsequential, the 'should nots' of restraint, to pursue her dreams; and it fuelled her success as a pioneering female aviator.

The second notable aspect of Chubbie Miller's character is that of her temperament. It is both wayward and unpredictable. We see it when she gets frustrated – she calls America 'this bloody country' during a petulant outburst which causes much offence to American reporters. She is a guest in their country, they reasonably point out to her. 'Hinkler butted in' she tells an astonished Australian press in 1928; then when she is criticized for this, she claims she did not say it. It surprised people, when her witty, ebullient personality suddenly altered abruptly and showed a vituperative side. We see it in her letters to Bill also:

'You cleaned me out!' she tells him angrily.

'I don't know why you...bum cheques.' She admonishes him.

'You messed things up as usual.'

'For once in your life...' etc.

Chubbie's temper frayed easily, and when it did, everyone knew it.

She spoke of Haden Clarke having 'a violent temper' to police and in court – but there is no person other than Bill Lancaster who supported this claim. Haden Clarke is, to the witnesses called, laid back; infuriatingly so – 'God will provide' he says smilingly of their hardships in the bungalow. 'I usually did' Chubbie says, tight lipped. It is a loose moment because it gives the lie to a violent-tempered Haden. When the landlady and Chubbie are at loggerheads over the non-payment of rent, Haden is the peacemaker: he uses his charm to placate her. We have Haden's character in his letters: he is calm and measured, logical in his thinking and approach to problems – somewhat like Bill in this respect. He reassures Bill cheerfully in one letter, that they will not starve 'as long as the neighbours raise chickens and rabbits!' It is disgracefully amusing – but it is quite apparent that Haden is indolent, come-day-go-day, living for today if not for the moment; impecunious, lazy, and good-humoured. All the witnesses who knew him testified to this effect. He prevented the disturbed WW1 veteran Dick Lavender from committing suicide on one occasion. He refused to see the gun collection of some friends he visited because of his abhorrence of guns. He sat in New Orleans speakeasies drinking cheap illegal hooch, smoking marijuana torpedoes and indulging himself with the wrong kind of women. He had a 'vile disease', but it never inhibited his pursuit of women. Jumping freight trains back to Miami he is broke and borrowing a dime from the café owner Mrs Throup, whom he never paid back. This is Haden Clarke: a lover and a loser - a clever man who was incapable of giving his intelligence employment.

The important thing here is that the qualities attributed to Haden Clarke of anger and temper, of nervous intemperance, by Chubbie Miller, are her own: she is unwittingly projecting upon him her own character. It is a common human trait to do so. And in doing so she is oblivious to the tell-tale insight she gives into her own personality. We see it in the letters and telegrams she writes, in her newspaper asides and interviews – and even in court. Chubbie Miller is a woman with a temper. And when she was drunk, that temper became violent.

It is the third defining aspect of Mrs Miller's character: the impact alcohol had upon her. Cheerful and ebullient when she was in a good mood, she turned sullen and nasty when she came back down. Lancaster knew it: after they moved into the Coral Gables bungalow he records in his diary his pleasure at Chubbie's improved mood. But a few days later he is alarmed by her drinking, and an accident with a Buick forces him to step in to take the rap for Chubbie, when there is some unpleasantness with the driver. When Haden Clarke arrives she is in a delightful mood – Lancaster notes it in his diary, that Chubbie becomes drunk – '*but not unpleasantly so*.' He knows that is a possible outcome in her, especially when her mood is bad. Psychologically she is nesting – Haden is already (though she does not know it), a potential mate: her mood is good. But her good mood seldom lasted and when the well of her sudden fury broke she directed her ire at anyone in the vicinity. She once hit Lancaster over the head with a spanner when he annoyed her, she later said!

And when she was drunk, Chubbie's temper became highly unpredictable: she was one of those drunks who could be charming one moment and throw a punch the next. Shelton knew it and referred to 'the two Chubbies – Chubbie drunk and Chubbie sober.' It was an insightful remark: the cheerful ebullience could vanish abruptly and be replaced by a vicious, resentful Chubbie. It was this conjunction of wilful character, temper, and drunkenness, which I believe brought about the debacle at the bungalow in Coral Gables, on the evening of 20th April 1932.

When Chubbie declared 'My drinking days are over' in her article published 3rd August 1932, and repeated this to the press during the trial, it suggests a subliminal acceptance of her guilt. She plainly admits that drink is responsible for Haden Clarke's death. It may be argued that she is referring to her succumbing to Haden Clarke's charms under the influence of drink - and that may have been her conscious intention – but it is much more than this. The process of Haden's seduction of Chubbie had begun long before she was drunk; it had involved a courtship dance between them in which Haden Clarke flattered her by degrees and she acquiesced. She responded favourably to his subtle solicitations...the ensuing encounter on the lawn and drunken sex which followed was simply the consummation of nuanced agreements made between them. What she refers to, in her recognition that alcohol is behind Haden Clarke's death, is an unwitting truth: that she shot Haden Clarke while she was drunk.

II

But why would Chubbie kill the man she loved and was planning to marry? It can never be known with certainty; but we have a good indication of it. Chubbie Miller discovered something that night - something that tipped her into a fury: the other Chubbie, the one who was probably drunk that night, who became unpredictable with drink and expressed her anger with violence, took over. It is speculation, of course, but there are strong indications of it.

There are two resolute facts of such moment in this story that they cannot be overlooked because the motive they supply is too urgent to ignore:

1) Is that Haden Clarke was a serial womaniser, and that he became habitually engaged to other women.
2) Is that Haden Clarke suffered with a serious sexual malady and yet told none of his women about it.

'Bigamous' suggested Carson. It is an exaggeration. He may well have had every intention of marrying his women – but if he did it was only a transient intention. He would tire of them soon enough, and move on to a fresh infatuation which would follow the same course. Engagement, for Haden Clarke, was undertaken largely for the same reason he pursued married, divorced, or widowed women in preference to single ones: it was the surest way to sexual conquest in 1932.

Chubbie had known Peggy Brown was Haden Clarke's lover – Peggy had told Lancaster she and Haden were to be married. She certainly believed this. And Chubbie knew Peggy Brown had spent several nights with Haden – Lancaster had even remonstrated with Chubbie over this. Presumably she must have believed Clarke had ended things with Peggy. But Haden Clarke was not in the habit of taking on such unpleasant tasks as breaking engagements, when his passion for a woman had subsided – he simply let them peter out as he moved on to a new conquest and a new engagement. He was still seeing Peggy Brown during the weeks in which he was engaged to Mrs Miller, and she clearly had no idea whatsoever of his proposal to Chubbie. How do we know this? Because Peggy marched indignantly into

Hawthorne's office on 23rd April and informed him that she, not Chubbie Miller, was Haden Clarke's fiancé! She was – but then so was Virginia Van Wert, Eleanor Griffin and Chubbie Miller: and Haden Clarke was actually still married, of course. He had other women in New Orleans, too.

It seems almost certain, far beyond a mere probability, that Lancaster returned to derail the marriage plan – and after other efforts had failed, he informed Chubbie of the fact she surely did not know; that Haden Clarke suffered from a serious sexual disease. Lancaster probably knew of this from Shelton, who had spent much time throughout February with Clarke, as the two drank deep together. It is possible it was the subject of rumours told him by Jack Russell via his well-informed wife, also. He probably had no certainty of it, but intended to confront him with his suspicions: Haden Clarke was suffering with a 'vile disease,' and this did not appear to constrain him in any way in his sexual pursuit of women – 'Someone gave it to me' was his casual rationalization.

How do we know Chubbie did not know of Haden Clarke's condition? It is there in many inferences in the conversations she reports of that night, and in the statements she makes:

- She states that she insisted Haden Clarke would have to be cured of his disease before they married. Yet, Lancaster said in his bedtime chat with Clarke that he vigorously objected to the marriage until Haden Clarke was cured. This seems to deny Chubbie's stated earlier objection because it infers that Chubbie had made no such insistence.

- Chubbie said Haden's last injunction to her was to lock her door so that that 'son of a bitch can't talk you out of marriage.' Again, there seems to be no change of plan at this point, if she is to be believed.
- Chubbie says she told Clarke she wanted the marriage to be delayed until his divorce was sorted out. It is a different version; one that does not admit to any knowledge of his malady.
- She also claims they have both given up drink on account of Haden Clarke's illness. But that is shown not to be the case because she is drunk on 7th April and probably on 14th-16th April.[54] In fact the obvious reason for the purchase of cigarettes on no less than three occasions on the evening of 20th April, is that at least one of these trips was to buy alcohol. Chubbie Miller had not given up alcohol, because she had no reason to do so: she knew nothing of Haden Clarke's malady.
- The story that Clarke had told Lancaster of his malady in the car from Viking Airport was introduced by the device of Bill apparently having suggested a trip to the bootlegger's. The chances of Bill suggesting this when he

[54] On this occasion, Vladimir Virrick said Chubbie was 'not sober,' but Haden was. This may indicate that Haden was indeed refraining from alcohol, but that Chubbie was not. Haden's abstinence might lead to a suspicion by Lancaster, that he was suffering from a particular ailment.

was not a drinker himself, and knew of the deleterious effects on Chubbie, are remote indeed. It is plainly an invention to assert the notion that Chubbie was already aware of Haden's sexual malady. The booze was the objective of one of the three trips made from the bungalow that evening – surely at the behest of the two alcoholics (Haden and Chubbie), and accounts for why the two men might venture out together 'for cigarettes' when they were at such enmity: Haden would know the bootleggers, and Lancaster had the money to pay for liquor.

- Hawthorne pointed out that Lancaster had sought to delay the marriage – even though it was apparently impossible because Clarke's wife had informed him by telegram that he was still legally married. Not only does this cast doubt on his and Chubbie's claim to know of the telegram, it also suggests that Lancaster was not certain at this point of any other impediment to the marriage (i.e. Haden's having a sexually transmitted disease) .
- Why was Haden Clarke sleeping in the porch room on that evening? There can be little doubt he had been ensconced in Mrs Miller's room since the affair began – was it a matter of delicacy on their part taking account of Lancaster's presence? Neither Haden nor Chubbie seem to exhibit much delicacy in such matters; both canoodled on the sofa in front of Lancaster that evening, apparently. It is astonishing that no-one asked this question, yet understandable that

they did not: to ordinary people in 1932, the idea that two unmarried people should be living as man and wife was shocking. This was, therefore, along with many other such embarrassments, not properly explored in court. That Haden Clarke was sleeping alone in the porch room is a clear indication of a row: he had been banished from Mrs Miller's bedroom, probably by the revelation of his disease – or by an accusation of it.

- But more than any of these inferential contraindications, there is a direct and overwhelming one: the notion that Haden Clarke had informed Chubbie that he was suffering with a serious malady – whether it was syphilis or gonorrhoea – and that she wished to marry him in spite of this is bizarre. Syphilis and gonorrhoea were both serious and dangerous diseases in the 1930s. Until the 18th century they were regarded as one disease. It would not be until penicillin was widely introduced in 1943 that there was a medicine capable of curing 98% of cases. The heavy metal and arsenic derivatives used in treatments before then, and their uncertain effects on the disease, ensured that there was not only a stigma, but a terror associated with both diseases.[55] The horror of venereal diseases cast a long shadow over the human psyche. Yet Chubbie had been sleeping with Haden Clarke, had no apparent concerns that she

[55] Syphilis and the Use of Mercury, *Pharmaceutical Journal*, Szu Shen Wong, Thibaut Deviese, John Betts, and Matthew Johnson, 2016.

> might have contracted the disease from him. Nor was there any anger at his having exposed her to it. She still wished to marry him. None of this is at all believable.

These things would be enough to horrify and enrage Chubbie and provide her with a motive to kill the man. She was an excitable woman, quick to anger, who was known to lose her temper, to show violence when she did so – the very qualities she projected onto Haden Clarke, which were in fact quite alien to his character. Clarke was logical, measured and calm; those who knew him spoke of it. There is even an appalling logic in his retort to Dick Lavender concerning his sleeping with women while he had a disease: 'Well, someone gave it to me.'

That Haden's disease was unknown to Chubbie, and provided the motive for his death, is unavoidable – not only because it is the most serious feature in the case, but because its revelation offers the most compelling motive.

In fact, Chubbie stops just short of admitting in court that her falling out of love with Haden was because he 'told her he had not had that malady before.' She had no apparent proof that he did at this time, other than the dubious testimony of the troubled Dick Lavender, which presumably she would have learned of only recently. She dissembles on this by saying it is 'because he was a liar,' and yet, as Hawthorne pointed out, Lancaster was a liar too, when it suited him. He might also have pointed out she was a good deal less than truthful herself: it made it quite obvious that amongst the catalogue of Haden Clarke's misdemeanours, it was not that he hadn't been to Colombia University, nor that he was 26 rather than 31 years old, nor that his experience as a writer was not quite as extensive as he had claimed: it was because he had a 'vile disease.' An admission that this was the cause of her sudden revulsion of him would have altered the consideration of the case dramatically: it would have supplied the motive. Yet it is there and it is plain that this was why she had fallen out of love with Haden Clarke – she clearly had not known it two weeks before, as she claimed: there is nothing in her letters or behaviour to suggest that she has learned of it around 6th April. When Lancaster spoke with Chubbie on 7th April she was drunk. She was still seeking to delay his return. Such a discovery around that time would surely have caused a breach with Haden, at the very least a horror of what she had been exposed to. But nothing in her letters or conduct exhibits anything other than a desire to keep Lancaster away on LAA business, so that she can continue her 'violent love-making,' as it was referred to, with Haden Clarke. Nor is it likely in the least degree that Lancaster was told of it so casually in the car, without there being any reaction:

'I looked upon it as something beautiful,' he said. (2nd May Statement to State Attorney's Office, *Miami Daily News*, 5th August 1932)

Lancaster would have been horrified as a matter of course, and doubly so that this man with so serious and reviled a malady should have been sleeping with the woman whom he professed to love above anything else in the world. Their determination to promote the notion that they were both fully aware of Haden Clarke's illness, and gave it little thought, had a single purpose: to exclude any possibility that it might be considered as a motive for killing Clarke – which it was.

This is what Chubbie Miller learned that night with shock and anger: Haden Clarke had a trail of women in many places, engagement was a well-practised routine for him, and he had a terrifying and shaming physical disease. It was quite enough to enrage her: and to this was added her frustrations, her financial worries, her grounded flying career; her frustrations with Bill, at being reduced to the theft of chickens, of having no fuel in the car, of the battery being 'on the fritz;' and of lazy men who wiled away their time fishing and smoking marijuana torpedoes. And to this cocktail of anger was also added the fact that she had betrayed Bill Lancaster for a man whose interest in her was probably transient. A man who thought 'God will provide' because he did not think of yesterday or tomorrow: his needs were now, and he supplied them now without a thought for anyone else.

How Haden's condition became known to Lancaster is unknown. It may have been no more than a reasonable suspicion on his part – a rumour, based on his nocturnal habits, the discovery of his tell-tale medicine Salvarsan, or a Sulfamide preparation in the bathroom or amongst his belongings. A soldier would know instantly what these concoctions meant.[56] It may be that Haden

---

[56] WW1 had provided an epidemic of venereal diseases and almost half a million British soldiers were treated for these during the war, where it was known as the 'Great Scourge.' In London in 1916, *The Royal Commission of Venereal Diseases* estimated that up to 12% of

was confronted with rumours or evidence about this that evening and confessed. Certain elements of the 'friendly bedtime chat' Haden had with Lancaster that final evening were characterised as 'confessional.' This could well have been as a result of Haden's exposure. We do not know. But all the indications are that Haden's disease was learned of by Lancaster and subsequently relayed to Mrs Miller for the first time that evening.

Along with this there was Chubbie's conflicting character. She was easily excited, easily brought down; quick to act and quick to sink into depression. Above all she had a fierce temper, and when moved by it she exhibited a loss of self-control that was worrying. Drunk she was a danger to herself and everyone else. Lancaster's concerns are apparent when he was out west: he spoke to Haden Clarke to warn him of the dangers; he doubtless spoke to Chubbie about it; he wrote to her the day after he left in early March. It was a running theme throughout his letters. Chubbie was two different people – drunk and sober, and a drunk Chubbie was dangerous. All these things came together on the night of 20th April 1932.

---

the working-class male population had syphilis. (Evans, David, Tackling the 'Hideous Scourge'*: Social History of Medicine*, 1992)

22. What Happened

Bill Lancaster saw the scales of Chubbie Miller's love for him weigh against him in the two years before the tragedy. As her star ascended and his waned, she cooled. It caused him anxiety even though he blocked it from his conscious thoughts. It governed every aspect of his behaviour and drew him ever closer to obsession; the least independence of him she displayed, manifested itself in his ever-increasing subservience. There was a servility in his behaviour towards Chubbie which, though it did nothing to increase her love for him, was intended to prove his unconditional love for her. And when a handsome and charming young man arrived to enjoy her confidence, to listen to the story of her life and transcribe it for her, to laugh and thrill to it in her company; he was worried. If he did not acknowledge it to himself, it fed his anxiety.

He saw Haden Clarke and Chubbie become closer, spending hours talking about her favourite subjects, flying and herself; her loves and dreams - they got drunk together and he would see the uninhibited Chubbie emerge on such occasions – dangerous, unpredictable. He saw their laughter, the light in her eyes which he no longer saw for him, dancing for Haden Clarke. A jealous lover does not miss the candour of these things. His love of Chubbie was no longer love, it was obsession; obsession borne of the fear of loss. His letters, his conversations, his diary all speak of nothing else.

In 1932 he had not seen his two young daughters for five years – and yet he never spoke of them in his diary. He didn't worry how they were managing financially, or wonder what his daughters were doing, even while he apologetically sent single dollar bills to Chubbie, or $5 ones if he had them, to win her favour. Chubbie had thoroughly eclipsed everything else for him.

When he left for Arizona and LA, he left with the best of intentions, and Chubbie wrote to him unwillingly, sparing in her words; sometimes resentfully, her letters filled with admonishments, or else complaining of her woes, her lack of booze. And then they changed: now she supported him; endearments in her letters increased, enough to keep him away, to prevent any just fears prompting his return. He fretted and she allayed his fears, while she made love to his rival with all the abandon of a new love – 'hysterically,' as she put it herself. She seems to have been drunk a great deal of the time – 'ginned up' – to use the words of Mrs Russell, or else 'on a bender.'

Lancaster's fears, a subliminal warning perhaps, can be sensed in his pleas to Clarke on his departure: he asks him to take care of Chubbie, to stop her from drinking. It is a plea to his decency, not to take advantage of his absence; not to steal the woman he loves and not to allow Chubbie to do anything dangerous. It is a forlorn plea. Haden Clarke is not such a man. He lacks self-control. He is lazy, self-indulgent - Chubbie claimed in court she had known of Haden's physical condition – if so it is extraordinary that this impediment did not appear to dampen her ardour for him. Haden Clarke had no qualms about sleeping with a woman, even though he had a serious long-term condition. Chubbie knew nothing of it.

They embarked on an affair soon after Lancaster had left – the long-suppressed attraction was released. The sudden torrent of emotion released led to the sudden decision to marry – a ridiculous, impetuous desire, borne of a surge of passion rather than of sense. And, of course, they both understood that Lancaster would be devastated – he was – but any trouble it gave their consciences was easy enough for them to control - and because all is fair in love and war. Whatever guilt it wrought upon Chubbie, it was unequal to her desires, because she was writing Lancaster love letters at this time, signing herself, 'All my love, Chubbie,' and, 'Don't hurry back.' She certainly meant one of these.

Lancaster was devastated when he found out about the affair at St Louis – his worst fears were confirmed. And he acted with haste to delay the finality of marriage. It was the best he could do. He thought carefully about his predicament: he would do all he could to prevent the marriage – and if he could not prevent it, then he would shoot himself. He said as much in his diary – without Chubbie life would have no meaning for him. There can be no doubt he meant this.

When he returned to Miami that Wednesday evening of 20th April, how he greeted them was disputed. Bill and Chubbie claimed it was cordial. But the aircraft worker who witnessed it said it was not; the men did not shake hands; it was hostile. The two men were competing stags circling tentatively, watchful. He had accomplished his objective – that of delay – and could afford to be candid with them now: he had every right to be aggrieved at how they had behaved towards him. He had had time to think too. He certainly had a plan – there was too much time for him to think one out for there not to be. But that plan did not include murder; it was fashioned around a last fling of the die.

He would try to dissuade Clarke by some means, and by entreaties to Chubbie, devout imprecations, he might regain her. They were forlorn hopes, and he cannot have depended on their success: Clarke was in possession of Chubbie; he would not relinquish her without a fight. He had said as much in his letter to Bill: he would meet him half-way. He spoke of violence even – his position is clear. There may have been a physical altercation of some kind between the two men: bruising was observed on Clarke's head and right shoulder post-mortem. In any case, whether there was a fight or not - and if there was whether it was physical or merely verbal - Clarke had emerged the clear victor: Lancaster was leaving in the morning; the old stag had withdrawn; he threatened to commit suicide. This is alluded to. It is a subcurrent in their conversation and it is also implicit throughout. He spoke of an aircraft accident and life insurance claim, said Chubbie. Perhaps he did, but it is more likely that he mentioned this in his phone call from St Louis: now he had need of something far more dramatic and immediate. The gun was surely a more dramatic and immediate manifestation of his threat. He bought the gun quite openly with this purpose in mind. A dead man has no need of an explanation for the possession of a gun. The threat to blow his brains out with a revolver in his hand was an expression of his angst, his final, desperate, theatrical gambit in the game. He intended suicide if he could not halt the marriage. But Chubbie forestalled him: she demanded the gun and took it from him as from a child. He could never refuse her. But at some point in that fraught, alcohol-fuelled evening of rows and misjudgements of word and action, Lancaster told Chubbie the devastating news about Clarke's women, his multiple engagements, and surely the horrifying news that Clarke had either syphilis or gonorrhoea. Appeals to Clarke's decency had failed; those to Chubbie failed too; when his threat of suicide had been frustrated, he played that final card.

Of course, she didn't know. The claim that she did was absurd. Nor did Lancaster – at least not with certainty - or his diary would have recorded greater anxiety on Chubbie's account, even horror, and a duty to inform her of it. In court Hawthorne tried his best to hold this up to the cold light of probability by asking if he thought the relationship was 'beautiful,' nonetheless? In truth Lancaster, like Chubbie, would have been horrified by the knowledge of Haden Clarke's disease and its implications for Chubbie. He had learned of Haden's disease previously by some unknown means, but quite probably from Shelton. He had doubted it; that was his nature. Perhaps there were no more than suspicions, which led to a direct accusation of Clarke. The conversation Lancaster refers to between the two men that night has a certain candour, but not of a spontaneous kind – it was a 'confession' in Lancaster's words, but it has something of a response to being exposed. It is at this point, in their claimed convivial chat – which was the exposure point of all Clarke's lies – where such revelations were drawn from him or realized: this was the moment of truth, as it had been when Dick Lavender had made the sordid discovery and Clarke had retorted 'well, someone gave it to me.' Lancaster told Chubbie that night, possibly after Haden had retired. Lancaster did not sleep in the same room as his adversary; nor was there a revolver between the two men. If Chubbie's door was locked, then it was to keep Clarke out, in the fury of her discovery. Certain witnesses claimed Lancaster's bed had not been slept in. The condition of the bed was irrelevant: *Lancaster was not there*.

Chubbie Miller would not believe Lancaster at first; but it would gain in credibility as she dwelt upon hints she may have received, but not acknowledged. And as they grew to a congruency, she would be aghast at what she learned – the man she had been sleeping with, who professed to love her, had a serious sexual disease; he was also casually engaged to other women. Both she and Lancaster were aghast – angry. Chubbie would naturally arrive at the fearful conclusion that she would have it too, because that is the way human minds work, and in any case, it would not be an illogical train of thought to follow. Her thoughts would go through a quick process of denial; Lancaster was making it up to 'break down Clarke's wagon'; then rationalisation; followed by acceptance: an immense shock, as the horror of this and its implications struck her. Then rage – a rage fuelled by alcohol. A somewhat quick succession of emotions would follow in Mrs Miller.

She took the gun, which she had earlier sequestered, and went to Clarke's room, perhaps to threaten him or demand the truth of him. He was asleep. But in the moment of blinding intuition, taken by her alcoholic fury, her anger fuelled by the knowledge of his deceit, and of her own deceit in consequence - the wrongs she had done Lancaster no longer capable of separation from her righteous indignation - she shot Haden Clarke in the head as he slept. It was, of course, the 'other Chubbie' who did it. The one who became dangerously - furiously - unpredictable, with alcohol.

Lancaster – wherever he slept that night, but probably downstairs in the third bedroom, and if not, on the sofa – was on the scene in seconds; the sound of that gunshot would wake the dead. Perhaps he did think a window had been slammed, from the depths of his slumber, in the room downstairs, but it was sufficiently loud and alarming on such a fraught night to warrant hurried investigation. He ran up the stairs - and there he discovered Chubbie, gun in hand and Haden Clarke dying. Chubbie was in shock. Murder has such a sobering effect.

He lost no time. He took the gun from her. Now all his actions were directed to protecting Chubbie from arrest for murder. He suspected Haden Clarke would die: the hole in his head would lead to such a conclusion. He saw all the dangers immediately – the importance of removing Chubbie's fingerprints from the gun, and then of tucking it beneath Haden Clarke, using the barrel end to hold it by. It was a position which would present a strong psychological impression that the gun was in the possession of the victim. As Haden was still alive and moving, it would not be advisable to place the loaded gun in his hand - which would obviously be the first choice. He saw too the deficiency of the absence of a suicide note. It was absurd to imagine that a man of Haden Clarke's literary pretensions, who knew how to express himself in writing with great facility, should shoot himself without providing an explanation for his fiancé and his mother, or simply for those who would find him: Lancaster therefore sat down to write two notes, and carefully forged Haden's signature. He never asked Haden Clarke to sign these notes because Haden Clarke was obviously incapable of doing so. Lancaster probably did use words and phrases Haden Clarke had used previously – but not ones made that night; that is not credible. They were probably made on some other occasion, when the men were filching chickens from neighbours, or contemplating some other misdemeanour, or fleecing some pigeon at bridge: 'Bill, you're the whitest man I ever met.' But he didn't say it that night. That night Haden Clarke regarded Bill Lancaster as a son of a bitch.

They called the attorney Huston in preference to a doctor – surely an odd choice when a man who had attempted suicide lay injured on his bed with a serious head wound – but they realised how imperative it was to ensure that the best legal advice was secured to protect Chubbie as soon as possible. Huston said it was Chubbie who called him. Lancaster in his several statements said it was he. It may be that both spoke to Huston that night, because Huston's account is deficient in too many respects to be accepted at face value, and it is certainly much abridged. Ernest Huston called an ambulance. A little later Chubbie called Dr Deederer. It was the ambulance service, Philbrick's, who informed the police – Bill Lancaster, Chubbie and Huston signally failed to do so. It clearly couldn't be avoided and yet in some self-deluding way Chubbie hoped it could. A curious action for Chubbie, if she had found her fiancé shot and dying in his bed, 3 feet from his rival. She should, of course, have been desperate for him to receive the best medical attention: but she wasn't. They delayed all they could – the shot was said to have been fired at 2 a.m. It may have been much earlier than this – Chubbie said she went to bed at 12.45 a.m. and was tired, but that she read for one hour. They rang Huston at 2 a.m. In any case it may be assumed some conversation was had, some urgent discussion about the matter before they took even this step. They would want to get their stories straight – as much as they possibly could. There must have been a great deal of setting of the scene, too, a tidy up: the removal of certain pieces of evidence – including the letters. And Huston himself may have delayed his journey to the house – perhaps he was being told more than he wished to know – he certainly knew a great deal more, and his story is unquestionably filled with half-truths and even falsehoods. It took him 75 minutes from the time of Chubbie or Lancaster's phone call to arrive at the bungalow. We will probably never know why. It was Chubbie who did all she could to prevent the ambulance man Ditsler from taking Haden Clarke to hospital. Ditsler stood there for 45 minutes, informing her it was unlikely Haden Clarke would survive but his only chance was to be taken to hospital immediately. Her delay wants explanation. It is a mark of her guilt. She was desperate to avoid the police inquiries which must follow a hospital admittance. Both Lancaster and Huston knew it could not be avoided. Haden Clarke was beyond doctors.

Chubbie would be now in the stage of acute remorse: Lancaster took charge in a way he had not since they had first flown to Australia together in 1927. The scales were now in his favour: he was the only person who could save her. He did.

But the matter of his open purchase of the .38 revolver for his own suicide now looked damning. He realised it. It had been used to kill Haden Clarke. He tried to persuade Huston to say the revolver was his, but naturally Huston refused this – it was an unsustainable lie. The best Lancaster could do was to claim he had been sleeping in the room with Haden, had placed the gun on the bedside table between them, that a bang had awoken him, and he had discovered Haden had shot himself. It certainly exonerated Chubbie, and whatever risks it presented to himself, he was prepared to shoulder them. There was a certain fear of Haden surviving and being able to talk – Lancaster inquired of several people anxiously concerning this: what tales might Haden Clarke tell of the events of that final evening? It seems likely that he did add the rider 'so he could tell us why he did it.' It would be crass not to try to cover such a damning inquiry as 'do you think he will ever talk again?' And adding the important qualifier 'so he can tell us why he did it' has a more important purpose: it suggests to others that Clarke did it. It moves them beyond the 'who did it' to the 'why did he do it.'

In any case, Clarke died just hours later having never regained consciousness. But Lancaster's story, hurriedly conceived, did not make sense; it was the result not of careful premeditation, but of thinking in the moment; and it was quickly apparent that he was lying; and that placed him under the gravest suspicion. He had the keenest motive for wishing his rival dead. It was also clear that Chubbie Miller's account was not the whole truth either. The conclusion formed by the authorities, was that Chubbie was lying to protect Lancaster: in fact, it was quite the opposite. When she said if Lancaster was arrested she would confess to the crime herself she meant it quite literally: she meant she would admit that she had done it, and it would be the truth. But it was taken as being an expression of her devotion to Lancaster. It was not. The Chinese walls could no longer sustain her two sides. Her guilt had caught up with her.

Lancaster was clearly worried about the letters: they may have been intended to be seen only by those first on the scene, to lend credibility to the story of suicide. But he was prevented from destroying them by Huston, who would have been mindful also that Ditsler had seen them, and possibly by the turmoil into which they were plunged by the night's events. In any case, Lancaster was a man quite prepared to take a risk even when the odds were poor. He always was. It was his character. The documentary evidence was preserved, and the police were suspicious of the unusual strength of motive on Lancaster's part. He was the jilted lover and therefore the chief suspect. The coincidence of Bill's return, just hours before a man who was about to marry his lover was found dead, was hugely incriminating. So was the recently purchased gun. It raised suspicions that warranted investigation – the suicide letters, almost destroyed, were found to have been written by his rival. The case was undeniable. Lancaster's only means of dispelling the case against him, involved implicating Chubbie Miller – something he would not do. He had to tread a perilous tightrope to save himself. He was, unquestionably, as he had confided to his diary, willing to die for Chubbie.

That the investigators, the police and State Attorney's office were suspicious of Lancaster was held in a degree of balance by the difficulties proceeding from the notion that he had shot Haden Clarke. That fine balance between suicide by Clarke and murder by Lancaster has been the subject of debate ever since. They hold each other in perfect check – but there is a third option that is surely the truth.

This is speculation, of course, quite beyond the standard of proof required by any court of law, but one to which a historical judgement may be made, which depends only on likelihood and probability. I believe it likely that something of this kind occurred on that night in Miami in April 1932.

His appearance before the court was Bill Lancaster's finest hour - one in which he lied and did so with stunning conviction. He rarely faltered in giving his testimony; nor did he waver under cross-examination – for three gruelling days he remained calm, and utterly focused, because his purpose was to save the woman he loved. In this circumstance, lying and perjury became a virtue.

It was almost impossible, while Bill Lancaster maintained his story, for any case against Chubbie Miller to be made for the murder of Haden Clarke. In fact, she was never even suspected.

23. Aftermath

After the trial, Chubbie Miller and Bill Lancaster met at James Carson's house, but any hopes they had of continuing their lives in the US were soon dashed: on 22nd August illegal entry charges were proffered against the two, and Lancaster's diaries were confiscated. They were considered scandalous material. Other charges were considered, including conspiracy to smuggle Chinese people across the Mexican border – the existence of contracts drawn up by Huston in both Chubbie's and Bill's names made them subject to immigration offences. This was surely a technicality, though, the chief animus against the pair being that of suspicion of the murder of Haden Clarke. That case was now officially closed, of course, but the suspicions of the authorities in the matter were intact. Moreover, the question of moral turpitude, by now exerting a profound influence on middle America, had to be considered: the lifestyles and morals of the two aviators were considered scandalous. Lancaster's insistence, according to James Forrester of the Federal Labor Department, at an immigration hearing on 20th September, that Lancaster had said he would marry Chubbie 'whether she liked it or not' hardly improved their situation. Lancaster claimed that Kiki had applied for a divorce and said in fact this might already have been granted – both claims were untrue. The fact he insisted on marriage or believed he could is consistent with Chubbie's being guilty of killing Clarke, and him helping to cover it up: it was his right. It was a clear expression of confidence on his part, that he had earned his right to her: she owed him, and they both knew it.

Lancaster sought the British Ambassador's intercession in the matter of their deportation but was refused – there could be no question of Her Majesty's Government making representations to the US on behalf of the pair, whose scandalous mode of living and trial in Miami was regarded with disdainful embarrassment from across the pond. It was also the case that press and public opinion in Britain were not as benign towards them as they had been in the US. There was a suspicion that Lancaster had got away with murder.

On 7th October the deportation orders were held in abeyance on condition of Lancaster and Miller's voluntary departure from the US. Accordingly, Chubbie, dressed in black and white check suit and a black hat sailed seven days later on the *American Banker* out of New York Harbour, and a few hours later, Lancaster sailed for England on the Cunard Liner *Scythia.* It was the 14th October, 1932 - five years to the day, since they had left Britain on their epic journey to Australia in high hopes; now they were returning in disgrace. They returned to England separately to avoid further attention. Bill's ship docked in Liverpool several hours before Chubbie's, on 24th October, and he made post-haste for London where he met her at East London docks shortly before her ship docked. Chubbie was permitted to disembark privately by means of a ladder hung over the side, while the *American Banker* was negotiating a lock. Captain

Lancaster was waiting with a car on the bridge above. It was reported that he wasn't wearing a hat, and that the couple walked off hand in hand to the waiting car.

A month later they formally announced they would marry. Lancaster lived with his parents, who still hoped for reconciliation between Kiki and their son – that was natural. They did not regard Chubbie as a suitable woman for Bill – that was natural too. There is a clear sense in this period that Chubbie did not love Bill Lancaster, but she felt guilt, and gratitude towards him; and she certainly owed him. Chubbie sold her story to the *Daily Express* in late October, days after her arrival back in Britain; it was serialised through to November. Her account sheds little light on the matter, but it does on her character. Perhaps with an eye to the rehabilitation of her reputation, she claimed everything was lies, leaks and worse. She claimed that 'Bill's marriage was on the rocks long before I even met him.' It was untrue – when she met Bill he had a three-month-old daughter, and she knew this. If there were rocks they were cast in shallow waters. She also claimed she had remained in the US after Haden Clarke's death to support Bill. In fact, she had no choice in the matter as a material witness. She said that Haden Clarke had probably been 'drugging her drinks.' This was her first mention of this and must be regarded with scepticism. Chubbie needed no encouragement to partake of alcohol, and its effect on her was quite sufficient without the addition of drugs. She also said she and Bill had been waiting five years to be married. She was an adaptable woman.

If she hoped her account would recover her reputation she was to be disappointed. Her love of the limelight had brought her fame, now it saddled her with the indelible reproof of notoriety. But it made her some money – and she had to live. Lancaster forbore publishing his own account. The *Empire News* would dearly have loved to serialise his story, but he knew his rehabilitation would not be aided by this. He needed a job - preferably a flying one.

Chubbie moved into a small apartment in Oxford Terrace, London, intending to write the autobiography she had hired Haden Clarke for a year earlier. She hired a new ghost writer, a *Daily Herald* journalist called Walker, to take up where Haden Clarke had left off some months before. Nothing came of this collaboration. Perhaps his muse was absent too.

She saw Bill only occasionally while she lived in London – Bill was in Croydon at his parents' house a few miles away, and the journey was just 25 minutes by a direct train line into Victoria, but her love for him had gone, and whatever gratitude she felt towards him over the Haden Clarke business had been spent; perhaps overshadowed by the notoriety which dogged her like a black shadow:

'I didn't have the same feeling for him at all... There was no question of partnering up... He would still have liked to, but I was through. There was no future for us,' she told Ralph Barker in an interview in the late 1960s.

She claimed also that Kiki turned up at Oxford Terrace, leaping improbably from the shadows when Bill was visiting to go dancing with her, and slapped her face. Certainly, her relationship with

Bill remained ambiguous: they saw each other but she undoubtedly wanted to make a clean break. Their continued association merely doubled their disgrace.

The winter and New Year of 1933 was a difficult one for them – they could only read of the Miami Air Races that January, or look longingly skywards at some aeroplane droning across the clouds. Their wings were clipped. The general belief that Lancaster had got away with murder was a cross he had to bear, and both were tainted by the trial and the scandal.

Chubbie continued to write her autobiography, and Lancaster, unable to find work for himself, and generally shunned in flying circles, grew increasingly despondent. He didn't get the jobs he applied for. His half-brother Gilbert Lancaster (1886-1964), who lived in South Africa, invited him to make a new life for himself there. But Lancaster would not consider this unless Chubbie was to accompany him. She was not interested. Lancaster was unhappy, he brooded, and the trial had taken its toll on his health. He looked much older than his 34 years.

Some months before, in July 1932, while Lancaster was languishing in his 22nd-floor cell on Flagler Street awaiting trial, the indomitable Amy Johnson (1903-1941) had set a solo record for the flight from London to Cape Town, South Africa, of 4 days 6 hours and 54 minutes in a Puss Moth monoplane. Lancaster had heard of it in his cell while pacing up and down listening endlessly to his radio – one of the few luxuries he was afforded. It now returned to his mind as the New Year ushered in 1933, when Lady Mary Bailey (1890-1960) attempted to take the record herself, but had to be rescued 1,400 miles south of Oran: it was a record there for the taking...

He decided to try to rehabilitate himself with the world by setting a new flying record for this route. Amy Johnson's record was a soft one, he knew. There was plenty of slack in the record. He inveigled his long-suffering parents to fork out £700 (£50,000 in 2022) for Sir Charles Kingsford Smith's blue Avro Avian V *Southern Cross Minor*, fitted with a Gypsy Moth II 100 hp engine, capable of 95 mph cruising speed. It was overhauled at the Woodford, Cheshire works, and its range was extended to 1,600 miles by the fitting of larger fuel tanks. His cruising speed would be 20 mph slower than Amy Johnson's, but Lancaster calculated he could make up the difference by taking fewer breaks. This time the visas and permits and insurance, the bureaucracy of flying across Europe and Africa, he handled alone. Chubbie took no part in this. He was disappointed that they could not do this together; he believed it might reforge their alliance, bring back something of the old days – but she was attempting to distance herself from Lancaster. Their future was now the past for her. She would not go to see him off from the airfield at Lympne, either, although this was probably to avoid Lancaster's parents. Lancaster planned to spend a few weeks with his brother Gilbert in South Africa, before returning to Britain.

In early April Bill Lancaster took his wife and two daughters to a restaurant. He visited Chubbie one last time to say goodbye, and asked her if he could borrow her watch for the journey, but she refused him saying it was too small to read. It was, but he sought it more as a keepsake, his Lady's Favour, like a knight of old before battle. It was to be her last refusal to him.

On 9th April Lancaster flew the Avro Avian from Croydon, to Lympne in Kent, the last stop before the channel. The previous day he had visited his solicitor and made a will in case he didn't make it. On Monday 10th April he held a press conference at the Grand Hotel, Folkestone, where his parents were staying. He said he wanted to make the world forget the trial which dogged him still. He surely hoped too – and it was a forlorn hope – to recover the love of Chubbie. She longed to extricate herself from him: to start again.

11th April was Tuesday; Lancaster arrived at the Lympne airfield before dawn, with the barest of essentials for the flight: he had 100 gallons of fuel on board, and two gallons of drinking water. It was a 900-mile flight across France and the south-east corner of Spain; from here he would fly across the western Mediterranean, the vast arid space of Algeria, and south by Gao in Mali, across Nigeria to Cape Lopez; then along the coast of West Africa to Cape Town. It was 6,000 miles south as the crow flies – 64 hours at his 95-mph cruising speed. He had stops to factor in, fatigue, refuelling and weather conditions, the vagaries and whims of nature and fortune to contend with. But he had 4 and a half days to beat – a total envelope of 110 hours in which to shoehorn his 64 hours potential. It was a soft record: there was, he thought, plenty of slack to be taken up. All he needed was a little luck.

His departure was hardly remarked – his mother and father and a handful of airfield personnel accompanied him to his plane in the early hours as he awaited dawn. No Chubbie, no Kiki, no daughters to scrawl on the side of the plane – and no dignitaries: just a few curious onlookers, and reporters. It was a journey for one. He was impatient to be off. His mother gave him a thermos flask of coffee; chicken sandwiches and a bar of chocolate: it was school lunch. He had £25 in his wallet all in £1 and 10-shilling notes, and two photos of Chubbie, which 12 months earlier had adorned his prison cell wall.

'My son has promised that he will not take any undue risks, and I have every confidence in him,' his mother told reporters. 'But it must be remembered that he has not done any flying now for a year and during that time he has gone through terrible mental strains.' (*Yorkshire Evening Post*, 11th April 1933)

At 5.35 a.m. the propeller was spun, the engine spluttered and then roared into life. He ran it for a few minutes until the oil temperature was up; the choke was released by degrees. He went back to his parents and said goodbye and his mother gave him some cotton wool which he pressed into his ears to deaden the roar of the aeroplane engine. He quickly returned to the *Southern Cross Minor* and climbed into the cockpit. He made a few final checks and then moved out to the end of the grass runway at the north-western point of the airfield, using the rudder and a light touch on the throttle. Here he positioned himself and reduced the throttle to idling speed, as he performed his pre-flight checks from the open cockpit: the rudder response from the pedals, the ailerons, the elevator from the stick. The throttle was now pushed forward to its limit, the engine note rose steeply, and the plane lurched forward, breaking momentum, and accelerated down the runway, gathering pace slowly, inhibited by its heavy cargo of fuel. The tail eventually lifted, and the nose levelled, giving him a sudden sight of the field ahead until, with a slight pull back on the stick at the judicious moment, the plane lifted from the field. It was 5.38 a.m. He ascended in the circuit and circled the airfield twice, and waved goodbye before turning south. As his plane rose in the dawn sky, those in the field had their last sight of Bill Lancaster.

Edward Lancaster meets his son on his arrival back in Britain. (*Daily Herald*)

Maud Lancaster gives her son some chicken sandwiches for his journey at Lympne in Kent on 11th April 1933. (*Daily Herald*)

A new aeroplane and a new hope: Lancaster's parents paid £700 for Charles Kingsford Smith's Avian V. (*Daily Express*)

Final checks and a quick smile for the camera. (*Daily Express*)

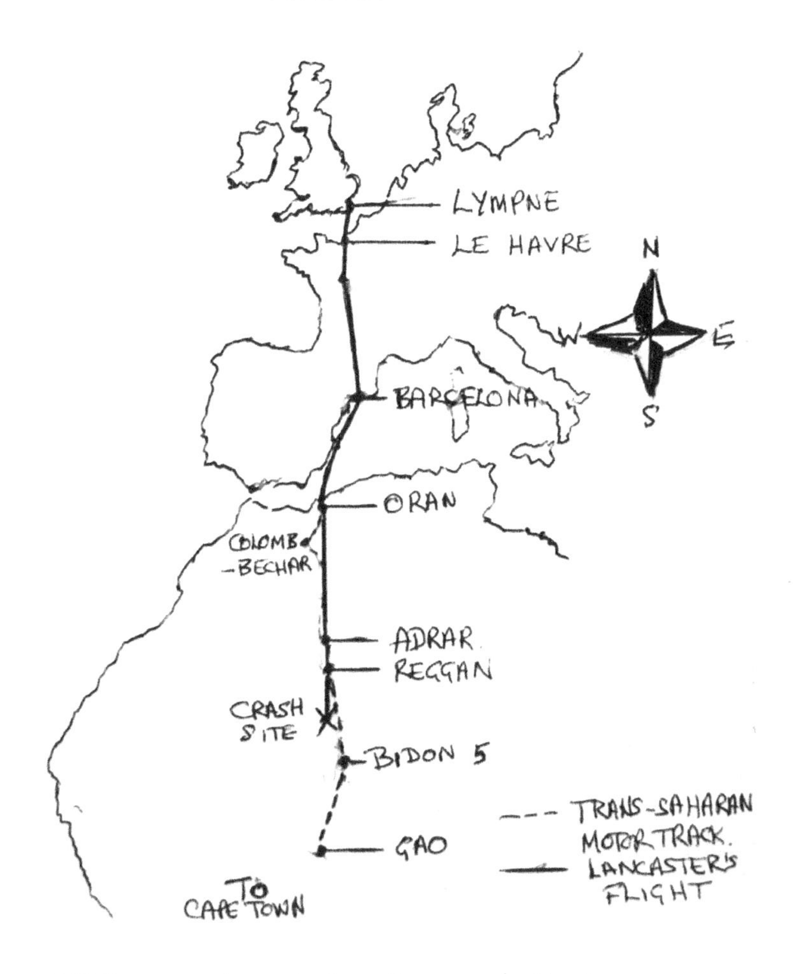

Bill Lancaster's route from Lympne in Kent across France and south across the great Trans-Saharan Motor Track to Gao. From here he would follow the coast of West Africa down to Cape Town.

24. The Last Journey

The little blue Avro Avian aeroplane, the *Southern Cross Minor,* crossed the channel and made a brief stop at Le Havre for registration and customs reasons. Lancaster hoped to make Oran in North Algeria by the evening. It was 1,150 miles away, and would require a good day - but he soon hit problems. He found he was flying into the teeth of the west wind which blew in off the Atlantic; south-west he flew, constantly correcting against the drift of the plane, across France towards the Pyrenees, the natural border with Spain. Here he landed at Barcelona to refuel. He was already behind on his schedule: a 20-mph headwind had eroded his precious advantage; the slack in Amy Johnson's record was becoming precarious. He would make it up on the long haul south across the Sahara. He made the short hop across the Mediterranean, south-west, and landed at Oran, on the north-west coast of Algeria at 9 p.m. He was late but still in touch. Here he had to sign a statement that he was flying at his own risk across the desert before being allowed to take off.

It was 3 a.m. when he took off on Wednesday, 12th April: he was now six and a half hours adrift of his schedule and the circumstances were against him. His preparation was wanting too: without lights or a lit dash panel in the open cockpit, he had to light matches to see his map and instruments in the brief initial flare of sulphur, before the howling wind and propwash extinguished them.

He crossed the Atlas Mountains, blind in the darkness. At dawn he saw the Trans-Saharan Motor Track below, the great rough unmade track south across the desert, marked out by day beacons along its way. White enamelled sheet metal structures every 10 kilometres, littered the desert, signing the way to Mali. He put down at Adrar, another unscheduled stop at 8.30 a.m. and refuelled. Time was running through his fingers like sand. He was tired. At 9.15 a.m. he took off from Adrar, heading for Gao in Mali, 800 miles away: 9 hours. A good day's flying would make up some of the lost hours, he thought. He followed the Great Motor Track south across the Sahara.

But a sandstorm blew up and although he could fly above this, such conditions being typically low altitude events, he would lose the silk thread of the motor route in the drift of the plane; visibility was already poor. His face was caked with the fine white desert dust as he persisted doggedly against the conditions. He landed briefly at Aoulef at 11 a.m. to check his bearings and took off again 10 minutes later. Still the sandstorm raged, a furious nemesis at his tail. He flew low and made Reggan at 1 o'clock that afternoon. He was now adrift of his schedule by a considerable margin. His slack was almost gone.

Monsieur Borel, Chief of Post at Reggan Trans-Saharan Company, told Lancaster to sleep while the plane was refuelled. He could sit out the sandstorm. Lancaster was upset, frustrated, and completely exhausted. He refused food but slept for three hours. When he awoke the sandstorm still raged, intense in its ferocity. The gods were against him. He had little choice but to sit it out. Finally, as darkness descended, the sandstorm blew itself out, its low moan subsided into silence: he had lost more time. He was overdrawn again on his account.

Borel argued with Lancaster that he could not fly in the early blackness of the night, which engulfed the desert; he should wait for the moon to rise at around 10 p.m., then he could follow the track south until dawn. Lancaster was in arrears; he was desperate and in denial. It was a familiar condition to him – an untempered optimism and a certain desperation fixated him on his object, drove him on: the record attempt was receding. In the conditions prevailing it was now over. Only he could not have known this. Or known it but no longer cared.

He was blind to failure and blind he took off, haggard, into the night at 6.30 p.m. Monsieur Borel watched him go: he said he seemed very tired. He gave him an electric torch and some matches to help:

'We'll give you 24 hours. If we don't hear anything of you from Gao by then, we'll send a convoy along the track,' he said.

Lancaster's plane tottered along the rough desert runway, wobbled uncertainly into the sky, its wings see-sawing as it rose: he seemed to Monsieur Borel to be disorientated and moved off in the wrong direction before correcting his flight. And then he was lost in the dark sky. Just the faint sound of the engine was heard, attenuating in the night, before he vanished.

Bill Lancaster was never seen again.

*

By 6 a.m. Lancaster should have arrived at Gao, but he hadn't. He was more than three hours late. French military stations along the route were alerted by radio: none had seen him. By 6 a.m., 24 hours to a promise, Monsieur Borel ordered a search out of Reggan. It was believed that north-west winds that night might have blown Lancaster off course, so the area to be searched was broadened from 50 km west of the motor track, to 100 km east of it. Searches further south were undertaken also: all proved fruitless. In the afternoon, radio chatter had been picked up in Britain and the *Daily Express* informed Chubbie of the news: Captain Lancaster was missing.

Two more days passed; Chubbie rallied the press and began to campaign to raise funds for her to pilot a search and rescue flight – and for someone to lend her a plane for this enterprise. She tried to borrow Dame Mary Russell's plane, but nothing came of this. It was an extravagant gesture; perhaps driven by guilt; and she had made him a promise. At any rate, it was unwanted. Lancaster's father was emphatic in his reply to this:

'It is not our wish that anyone who doesn't know the terrible flying conditions of the Sahara Desert should go out to try to find our son. It would be a futile attempt and very much against our wishes. Everything that can possibly be done is being done.'

The Trans-Saharan Company and the French authorities were indeed making heroic efforts to find Bill Lancaster. Chubbie's search could have no practical value.

On 23rd April, 11 days after his disappearance, the search was over. A French search pilot, M Minguet, made a statement:

'When Captain Lancaster was ready to resume his flight there was no moon and a strong northwest wind was blowing. M Borel, the head of the Trans-Saharan Company at Reggan, told him it was madness to take off when he would not be able to see the day beacons on the motor track, and when he had no lighting on his instrument board for steering a compass course. Captain Lancaster made a very bad take-off, and that was the last seen of him.'

In May, Lancaster Snr told the press that messages had been received from his son, from 'the other side.'

'He did not suffer; that is a great relief to his mother and me,' he said. It was not the first time the spirits had steered the Lancasters wrong.

If the Lancasters – father, Mother and Kiki - were infuriated by Chubbie's grandstanding, then they were even more angry when Bill Lancaster's will was read in late November 1933: Chubbie was his sole beneficiary – his wife and children, his parents who had bought the plane and funded his adventure, received no mention. They contested the will in court on behalf of Bill's children, Pat and Nina, but it was settled out of court. There was little money involved – a sum of £170 (£13,000 in 2022) - but it was a matter of principle for them. They knew he had no money. The Lancasters abandoned their action; the will remained in Chubbie's favour. She argued that she had paid for his trial, but this was not so – his parents, as ever, funded the lion's share of this, but she probably felt she had paid out such a sum for Lancaster many times over the years.

*

Lancaster was lost and no-one knew what had happened to him. Rumours of lone white men in West African villages inevitably surfaced from time to time, but nothing came of these. Chubbie Miller obtained her Private Pilot Licence in England later in 1933 and went to work at Hanworth, which was involved in a project of mapping Africa. She met Flight Lieutenant John Pugh (1908-1981) an Irish ex-RAF pilot here in late 1934 and they became lovers. Chubbie subsequently attempted to fly the London – Cape Town route herself, the same one Lancaster had attempted, setting out on 4th

January 1935. Her progress was reported haphazardly over the next two months, flying a small 'Redwing' aeroplane. She was reported three weeks later to be 'halfway across the desert,' and then at Gao in late January. In late February the *Cheshire Observer* reported her flight was still in progress. And there it ended. She crash-landed soon after making it as far as the Niger River. It was her last flying adventure.

Chubbie Miller finally moved on; she married John Pugh at Epsom Registry Office on 16th May 1936. Three weeks later it was reported that the *Red Rose*, the plane that had started Lancaster and Miller in their association, and on their flight to Australia, and which Lancaster had sold in Sydney in 1928, had taken off from Singleton in New South Wales, where it crashed, caught fire and was destroyed. (*Bradford Observer*, 8th June 1936)

She gave up flying after her marriage to Pugh. The couple moved to Singapore in the late 1930s and were there during the war, and afterwards moved to Santiago de la Ribera in Murcia, Spain. She became ill in the early 1970s and returned to Britain where she was treated for stomach cancer in West London hospital. She died in 1972 at the age of 71 and was cremated at Kensington and Chelsea. There were few obituaries. Apart from a brief period in early 1962, when interest unexpectedly flared up in her again due to a strange occurrence in the Algerian desert, and she was returned once more to the spotlight, Mrs Pugh or Mrs Keith Miller as she was known to the world, or 'Chubbie' as Bill Lancaster knew her, was forgotten.

By this time, James Carson was dead, so was Vernon Hawthorne; Kiki had died in 1953; and both Bill's parents had passed the way that everyone who has ever lived has passed. Very few people who knew of the trial or remembered the two pioneering aviators who flew to Australia in 1927, and who had shocked the world in Miami in 1932, remained. Haden Clarke's grave was lost. But sometimes the dead still speak.

12th April 1933, Bill (second from left) watches as his plane is refueled. He is no more than a silhouette. (*Alain Brouchard*)

Last photo of Bill Lancaster taken at Reggan. Face caked with sand and the desert dust; he is exhausted. (*Alain Brouchard*)

Mr and Mrs Pugh: John Pugh and Chubbie (*The Bystander*).

Epilogue

It was late in the morning of 12th February 1962, when Titus Polidori leading a motorized patrol two days out and 170 miles south of the French military outpost of Reggan, spotted what he described as an 'anomaly on the horizon' in the flat wastes of the Tanezrouft desert. The sun was climbing in the sky, the heat of the southern Sahara held the image fixed and quivering in the distance. It was enough to cause him to change direction to investigate the anomaly further. As he drew near it took on a definite form, and it was soon apparent that it was an aeroplane wreckage.

Upon reaching the wreckage Adjutant Polidori ordered the patrol to halt. He got out and walked alone to inspect the plane: it was clear that this was not a recent mishap - the plane was an old biplane of 1920s construction. It was stripped clean of its canvas covering, its rubber tyres long perished, but its bare ribbed aluminium bones were remarkably preserved, polished bright by the desert wind and sand. The desert does this – imbues something of its own unchanging stillness to those objects it captures and holds prisononer. It lay broken, a long-lost plane, its nose pointed east, mysterious as a sphinx. A thrilled surmise ran through the patrol.

Only a haunting low moan of the scorching wind disturbed the scene; a ghost stirred.

Polidori walked to the upturned cockpit. It was empty, but beneath the fragile denuded wing, which once would have offered shade from the searing sun, partly concealed by the sand, there lay a mummified body. Dried like a fig in the desert sun, its skin was tanned and taut, fragile parchment on the bleached bones. Hanging from the starboard lower wing was a bag: in it Polidori found a British passport. He opened it – the name inside was Captain William Newton Lancaster. There was also a logbook which had been turned into a kind of diary by the airman.

Polidori radioed Adrar to inform them of his find. The bones of William Lancaster were taken to the outpost of Reggan, where he was given a funeral with full military honours.

2,000 miles to the north, a few days later, on the morning of 19th February 1962, a neighbour rang Chubbie Pugh nee Miller in London, and told her that the *Daily Express* carried the story of the discovery of Captain Lancaster and the *Southern Cross Minor*. Her name was mentioned in the report. She was stunned. Now the memories flooded back to her. And she was apprehensive too, to learn that Lancaster had left a diary: while he awaited rescue or death in the Tanezrouft desert waste, he had kept a diary... What might it say? Her thoughts raced. Lancaster's now middle-aged daughters flew to Algiers to attempt to get hold of their father's diary and documents, but failed. It was passed by the French authorities at Reggan to the British Consulate. Jessie put in a counterclaim via her solicitor. The Consul-General determined that she was his sole beneficiary. She had an anxious period until April when the diary was finally passed to her by her solicitor. She read the stained pages, written almost exclusively for her benefit decades before, with great emotion. She published Lancaster's diary in the *Daily Express* in October 1962, adding a foreword of her own:

'I had never forgotten Bill Lancaster,' she wrote, 'The world we had known together, the roaring twenties, the death-or-glory flights in tiny biplanes, the Depression, when there wasn't much in the way of picking for pilots like us, then drama, headlines, and Bill's tragic exit from it all; it was half a lifetime away.

'The passing years had taken the sharp edges off the memories. Sometimes it seemed like a different world. But it hadn't been another world. The headlines that said that his body had been found told me that. I have been happily married for 26 years. Then suddenly the past reaches out and takes hold of the present.' (*Daily Express*, 1962)

Amongst the possessions recovered were a wallet with two photos of Chubbie Miller in it, the torch Monsieur Borel had given Lancaster, and the pilot's log, which told of the plane's final flight and the last days of its pilot.

Its final entry, made on 13th April 1932, was written at 5 a.m. It read:

'I have just escaped a most unpleasant death. Why? My first act was to go down on my knees and thank God for it and implore his help in my dire need. It happened like this – I was flying a due compass course for Gao when something went wrong. The engine spluttered and she died. It was pitch dark, no moon being up (about 8.15 pm). I tried to feel her down but crashed heavily and the machine turned over.'

He had been unconscious but on coming to he scrambled from the upturned cockpit of his craft with a bad cut to his head and was blinded by dried blood in his eyes.

The remaining pages of the logbook he turned into a diary – his obsession throughout was with Chubbie Miller – what she was doing, what she was thinking; conversations and advice to her which would not be requited; also, thoughts of his mother and father.

'If I die I hope it will be fairly quickly,' he wrote later on that first day. 'Feel low.'

He had 2 gallons of water with him, a flask of coffee, a bar of chocolate and the chicken sandwiches his mother had made him. For the next 8 days he eked these supplies out, drinking 2 pints of water per day in half-hourly sips to slake his thirst in the terrible desert heat. At night he endured freezing temperatures, and lit strips of canvas torn from the *Southern Cross Minor's* fuselage, doused with aeroplane fuel and wrapped and tied with wing wire and held them aloft every 20 minutes in the hope that searching aircraft might see him. None did.

He continued to hope:

'I must conserve every bit of energy to keep me alive for about three or four days in the hope that I will be rescued... Mind you, I do not unduly complain of my plight. After all, I brought it on myself and must call it the luck of the game and play it out to the end.'

He never mentioned Haden Clarke or the incident of just 12 months earlier; no expiation, no exculpation; no regrets, no final confession; he had none to make: his silence as steadfast on

Chubbie's behalf as it had been throughout the court case. He must surely have contemplated the irony of the timing and the cruel whims of fate, the strange parallel he bore with Haden Clarke. He said nothing.

He suffered terribly as the sun and heat exhausted him.

'The hours from 11 a.m. to 4.30 p.m. are the dreaded ones. The heat of the sun is appalling... But I don't mind as long as I can get water. That is my constant craving. WATER.'

On Sunday 16th April, the fourth day, he wrote:

'The most tantalising thing happened last night. It commenced to RAIN. Yes, it really did. Cold icy raindrops. Alas it was only for a few brief moments and I was unable to gather even a teaspoonful.'

On 17th April, his fifth day, with his supplies running out, he thought he saw a light in the sky, signalling a search aeroplane – he lit his makeshift flares and held them aloft frantically, but by evening his hopes had gone:

'I am resigned to my fate. I can see I shall not be rescued unless a miracle happens. Chubbie sweetheart, remember I kept my word. I 'stuck to the ship.'

As he sat beneath the broken wing of the plane day by day and hoped, and watched his supplies run out, he sometimes saw a bird pass over or hop nearby – he envied its gift of flight. Perhaps it was one, like him, who could not make the great trans-Saharan migratory crossing that April. He wondered if an oasis might be close. Perhaps the bird thought the same on seeing him.

He saw a butterfly too and marvelled at its beauty. How precious and fragile, and conscious, all living beings seem in isolation. Gradually, his hopes of rescue declined as his water supply diminished. He suffered.

He bore it all with remarkable courage and fortitude, as slowly, painfully, and racked by fever, his water ran out.

On Wednesday 19th April it was the seventh day; he wrote:

'The last day of a week in the middle of the Sahara Desert with a crashed light plane and a can of water.

'Chubbie darling I have stuck to my guns...and I have stayed the course for a week anyway... my water will give out today. It cannot be made to last longer. It is then just a matter of a few hours and please God a quick end.'

He also wrote:

'If there is another world, if there is something hereafter (and I feel there is) I shall be waiting. Bill.'

Fearing he would no longer be able to write, he decided to tie his logbook and passport to the wing above him:

'The chin is up right to the last, I hope. Am now tying this up in fabric. Will write anything else on strips and push inside...'

Eight days had passed. On 20th April 1933, he wrote for the last time on a Shell fuel card and pushed it inside the logbook:

'I have no water...no wind...Goodbye. Bill.'

He must have been able to reach up that day because he put his note into the bag secured to the lower wing, knowing it was now all over. By this time, he would have been weak, as the sun climbed inexorably in the desert sky. He will have become delirious that day and then lost consciousness, probably before nightfall; then organ failure will have followed and, it is unlikely that he saw the sun rise on 21st April 1933 - which – as a matter of entire coincidence, was the one-year anniversary of the day on which Haden Clarke had died.

Clothes tattered to strips still clinging to the body, his bony leather hand clutching his throat, Bill Lancaster had kept faith with Chubbie Miller to the end.

The remains of the Southern Cross Minor, 1962. (*Daily Express)*

French motorized patrol at the scene of the wreckage. The mummified body of Bill Lancaster is in the foreground. (Picture by Soldat Humbert)

The mummified body of Bill Lancaster, 1962

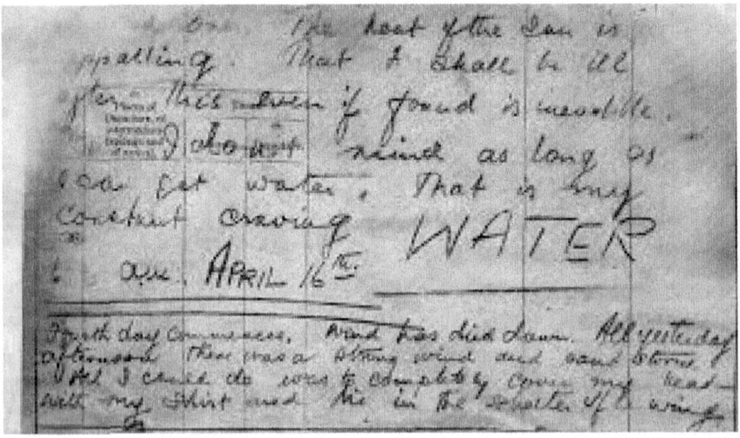

An entry from Bill's diary for 16th April 1933. 'The heat of the sun is appalling,' he writes, and of his craving WATER.' (*Daily Express*).

Chubbie Miller in 1962, reading Lancaster's diary/logbook. (*Daily Express.*)

Lancaster's wallet, found tied to the wing of the Southern Cross Minor, with photos of Chubbie Miller in it. (*Daily Express)*